RESEARCH METHODS FOR UNDERSTANDING PROFESSIONAL LEARNING

BLOOMSBURY RESEARCH METHODS FOR
EDUCATION SERIES

Edited by Melanie Nind, University of Southampton, UK

The *Bloomsbury Research Methods for Education* series provides overviews of the range of sometimes interconnected and diverse methodological possibilities for researching aspects of education such as education contexts, sectors, problems or phenomena. Each volume discusses prevailing, less obvious and more innovative methods and approaches for the particular area of educational research.

More targeted than general methods textbooks, these authoritative yet accessible books are invaluable resources for students and researchers planning their research design and wanting to explore methodological possibilities to make well-informed decisions regarding their choice of methods.

Also available in the series

Research Methods for Pedagogy,
Melanie Nind, Alicia Curtin and Kathy Hall
Place-Based Methods for Researching Schools,
Pat Thomson and Christine Hall
Research Methods for Education in the Digital Age,
Maggi Savin-Baden and Gemma Tombs

Forthcoming

Research Methods for Classroom Discourse,
Jenni Ingram and Victoria Elliott
Research Methods for Early Childhood Education,
Rosie Flewitt and Lynn Ang
Research Methods for Educational Dialogue,
Ruth Kershner, Rupert Wegerif, Ayesha Ahmed and Sara Hennessy
Research Methods for Social Justice and Equity in Education,
Liz Atkins and Vicky Duckworth

RESEARCH METHODS FOR UNDERSTANDING PROFESSIONAL LEARNING

Elaine Hall and
Kate Wall

BLOOMSBURY ACADEMIC
LONDON • NEW YORK • OXFORD • NEW DELHI • SYDNEY

BLOOMSBURY ACADEMIC
Bloomsbury Publishing Plc
50 Bedford Square, London, WC1B 3DP, UK
1385 Broadway, New York, NY 10018, USA

BLOOMSBURY, BLOOMSBURY ACADEMIC and the
Diana logo are trademarks of Bloomsbury Publishing Plc

First published in Great Britain 2019
Reprinted 2019 (twice), 2020 (twice)

Series design by Clare Turner

A catalogue record for this book is available from the British Library.

A catalog record for this book is available from the Library of Congress.

ISBN: HB: 978-1-4742-7461-6
         PB: 978-1-4742-7460-9
       ePDF: 978-1-4742-7463-0
      eBook: 978-1-4742-7462-3

Series: Bloomsbury Research Methods for Education

Typeset by Integra Software Services Pvt. Ltd.
Printed and bound in Great Britain

To find out more about our authors and books visit www.bloomsbury.com
and sign up for our newsletters.

CONTENTS

LIST OF ILLUSTRATIONS

Figures

Tables

SERIES EDITOR'S PREFACE

The idea of the *Bloomsbury Research Methods for Education* series is to provide books that are useful to researchers wanting to think about research methods in the context of their research area, research problem or research aims. While researchers may use any methods textbook for ideas and inspiration, the onus falls on them to apply something from social science research methods to education in particular, or from education to a particular dimension of education (pedagogy, the digital dimension, equity, to name some examples). This application of ideas is not beyond us and has led to some great research and also to methodological development. In this series though, the books are more targeted, making them a good place to start for the student, researcher or person wanting to craft a research proposal. Each book brings together in one place the range of sometimes interconnected and often diverse methodological possibilities for researching one educational context, research problem or phenomenon. You can expect a discussion of pertinent methods that is critical, authoritative *and* situated. In each text the authors use powerful examples of the methods in use in the arena with which you are concerned.

There are other features that make this series distinctive. In each of the books the authors draw on their own research and on the research of others making alternative methodological choices. In this way they address the affordances of the methods in terms of real studies; they illustrate the potential with real data. The authors also discuss the rationale behind the choice of methods and behind how researchers put them together in research designs. As readers you will get behind the scenes of published research and into the kind of methodological decision-making that you are grappling with. In each of the books you will find yourself moving between methods, theory and data; you will find theoretical concepts to think with and with which you might be able to enhance your methods. You will find that the authors develop arguments about methods rather than just describing them.

In *Research Methods for Understanding Professional Learning*, Elaine Hall and Kate Wall address teachers' learning, primarily in the UK school context, exploring ways of researching not just the what and how of this, but also the why. They interweave philosophical underpinnings with practical guidance in ways that readers familiar with their body of work will have come to expect. There is no downplaying or over-simplification of the messiness of professional learning here, and no research recipes or toolkit to be found. There is, however, a series of research tools – 'socially constructed artefacts that allow teachers to engage with their practice at a number of levels' – which are highly practical. In the various examples showing the use of these tools, the interwoven nature of the challenge of understanding teacher learning and understanding the learning of those they teach is explored. The authors are highly committed to educational research for practitioners and appreciate what it can do to support and enhance professional practice. In this sense this is as much a companion text for inquiring teachers as it is a research methods book.

This book cannot be the only book you need to read to formulate, justify and implement your research methods. Other books will cover a broader range of methods or more operational detail. The aim for this series, though, is to provide books that take you to the heart of the methods thinking you will want and need to do. They are books by authors who are equally passionate about their substantive topic and about research methods, and they are books that will be invaluable for inspiring deep and informed methods thinking.

Melanie Nind
Series Editor

1 DEFINING

What do professionals do all day? How we answer this question has implications for what they need to know, how this can be learned and consequently the provision made for their initial and continuing education (Zeichner et al., 2015). While the nature of professionalism is contested and subject to change, the capacity to make judgements about what to do in complex, uncertain situations and the assumption of collective responsibility are the moral and practical basis. Professionals, therefore, have a dual responsibility for their own ongoing learning as well as for the induction and development of others within the profession. The added jeopardy of professionals in education is the fact that their professional learning is for the majority inextricably linked to the learning of their students. In this book we explore *what* professionals know and *how* they learn. The perspectives and tools we share can be used to gain insight into professional learning and will be of value to researchers, policymakers and practitioners with an interest in improving professional education.

Thinking through practice

It is critical to acknowledge that professionals engage in practice; indeed, many adopt the identity of practitioners. It is perhaps this relationship with practice and practical contexts that leads to definitions of what it means to be a professional and which occupations can claim the status of being a profession changing over time. It is also what makes some traditional approaches to research challenging to apply. Practice is complex and messy; therefore, any associated enquiry needs to either attempt to assert control, which arguably leads to criticisms around the creation of artificial simplicity (a lack of connectedness to real life), or 'embrace the chaos' leading to claims of bias, lack of rigour and difficulty in generalising claims. However, this all depends on what we believe practice to be.

Lampert (2010) outlines four typical conceptions of practice, all connected by its focus on what people 'do'. She outlines how it

1   is contrasted with theory,

2   is used to describe a collection of habitual or routine actions,

3   as a verb speaks to the discipline of working on something to improve future performance, and

4   is in global terms used as a short-hand to indicate the way that professionals conduct themselves in their role.

To understand practice then we have to address the contrast with theory by exploring conceptions of practice through concepts offered by number of theorists. However, this is not 'the theory part' of the book, divorced from the goal of finding useful ways to describe, improve and identify what practitioners and professionals do in a grounded illustration. We have chosen therefore to use extracts from an example of practitioner enquiry (Lofthouse, 2015) in which a conscious attempt to bring theory and practice alongside one another leads not necessarily to tidy resolution but rather a picture of the difficulties and dissonance. In this way we will, without delving too deeply into Aristotle, be directing attention to the working together of theory (episteme) and products (poesis) in the crucible of practice or phronesis which is sometimes translated as practical wisdom wisely used in context, 'the ability to see the right thing to do in the circumstances' (Thomas, 2011, p. 23).

It seems important to ask: What are the circumstances? Contemporary views of practice and professionalism are not rosy: Sachs (2001), for example, contrasts managerial professionalism with democratic professionalism. The former prioritises accountability and thus encourages efficiency and compliance, while the latter promotes teachers as agents of change. Democratic professionalism creates opportunities for more nuanced development of practices, with the implication that in that democratic space both 'reflection in action' and 'reflection on action' (Schön, 1987) can and will take place.

The rise of managerialism, however, is arguably in response to the 'normal chaos' of modernity (Lash, 2003), in which the choices and risks of each individual as part of a pattern of interactions which shapes all our lives, through a globalised economy, a dissociated state and new configurations of family and community. Lash argues, 'This choice must be *fast*, we must – as in a reflex – make *quick* decisions' (2003, p. 51, original emphasis):

> Thus certain aspects of practice and research feature strongly ... because of my working relationship with my professional and academic role and the policies that influence it. At times I have been less reflective or deliberative in my actions than I would choose to be because measured judgements have been replaced by reflexes, and this has led not to certainty in the knowledge I have created but to what Lash describes as precarious knowledge. I state below my ontology and epistemology as part of my self-narrative, which as Sachs proposes relates to my 'social, political and professional agendas' (2001, p. 159) and which have created, through reflexivity, iteration and reciprocity of practice and research, my professional identity. (Lofthouse, 2015, p. 14)

Thus, when we engage with Schön's (1987, 1991) description of reflexive practice, this is arguably a counsel of perfection. The chaos and structural constraints of practice suggest that for 'in action' reflection, practitioners are unlikely to be able to habitually perform this at the speed required. Reflection 'on action' can lead to a shift of attention in practice however, creating slightly longer 'moments of opportunity'.

There is another important critique from Eraut (1994), who focuses on skilled behaviour and deliberative processes in 'hot action' situations to unravel the dilemma of practice that characterises the competition between efficiency and transformative quality in professional life. Eraut argues that these skills and deliberations are resting upon but also sometimes muffled by routines and taken-for-granted aspects of context, with the result that the idealised reflexive practice seems further out of reach.

There is help from an unlikely pairing to make this both more concrete and more hopeful of finding the 'democratic space'. We need a frame for understanding (to borrow from Richard Scarry) – *what people do all day*. In his beloved, richly illustrated children's books, Scarry invited readers to consider the activities engaged in by different (but all 'busy') people and proposed simple comparisons (inside/outside) and points of debate (hard?/easy?) that are arguably the bedrock of the philosophical inquiry we undertake here. We want to think about what it is that practitioners are up to all day, why they concentrate their busy-ness on particular activities and how much agency and intent are involved in that balance of concentration.

Arendt's typology of 'labour', 'work' and 'action' serves to illuminate the realities of the classroom. Arendt distinguishes in a clear hierarchy between labour, which serves an immediate and life-sustaining purpose but leaves no lasting trace of itself (e.g. cooking, washing up, laundry), work, which produces lasting artefacts that shape how we live in the world (e.g. a table that we then sit around to eat), and action, which gives meaning to the individual within the society (e.g. singular, unusual, theatrical and problematic deeds that do not fit a pattern and provoke 'histories and essays ... conversations and arguments') (Higgins, 2010, p. 285). It is worth emphasising that the majority of human activity is labour and work, while action – almost by definition – happens rarely. As practitioners, we can instinctively judge for ourselves which aspects of the day are labour and work and which might have the potential for action.

Arendt's position is a strong riposte to managerialism and its normative discourse of standardised best practice, since what counts as work and action has both objective and self-determined aspects: *the table is there, the people around it are arguing, I made both of those things happen.* Unfortunately for this chapter and our argument, Arendt didn't think education practitioners had much capacity for action as they were too highly constrained by the routines and structures of the system. We would, returning to Eraut, suggest that everyone is to a certain extent constrained in this way and that awareness of the constraints might be a way to move from moaning about them to deliberative practice and learning from/through experience (Ericsson et al., 1993).

There is a remaining problem for us with Arendt's framing: the motivation appears to be highly moral and individualistic, whereas our understanding is rooted more in ideas of participation in communities of practice (Lampert, 2010) with strong ties to our colleagues and students, so we find the transactional and democratic ethics of Dewey (1916; Baumfield, 2016) to be helpful in explaining why certain problems draw education practitioners' attention, driven by immediacy and the practical problems of the learning community. Practitioners are by very nature of their practice problem-solvers, with Dewey reminding us that experience is *experimental inquiry*: he challenges the idealist representation of experience as confined by its particularity and contingency through a recognition of our purposeful encounter with the world and the goal of learning.

Lofthouse (2015) suggests that the process of practitioner enquiry is a key component of reflecting on and improving practice: practitioners actively asking questions of their practice and using the process of engaging in and with (Cordingley, 2015a and b; Hall, 2009) research as a 'pragmatic, but scholarly approach' (Lofthouse, 2015, p. 12). She offers three ethical principles on which practitioner enquiry should facilitate:

> Firstly I have an allegiance with my successive cohorts of learners. Secondly I believe that my practice can always be improved and that reflection on my own practice is the focus for improvement, and I promote reflection on practice for my cohorts of learners. Finally I recognise the strategic priorities of the institutions for which I work, which in effect are both the university, the schools and colleges in which my students and research participants practice, as well as the institution of education more generally. Thus I believe that my episodes of practitioner research are grounded in the ethics of the improvability of practice, the desire to meet the needs of the professional communities, and my deep understanding of the demands and cultures of their workplaces. (Lofthouse, 2015, p. 12)

If that is what practice can be, we must not avoid discussion of what it is *for*: Billet (2011) describes practice-based learning as having three broad purposes. In professional contexts it should enable leaners to develop an informed desire to enter the profession (or not) and ensure that they have the opportunity to demonstrate the necessary capacities required for entry, while also facilitating the development of occupational competencies for future professional learning. Billet also articulates the significance of three dimensions of practice-based learning. These are the practice curriculum (how the learning experiences are organised), the practice pedagogies (how the learning experiences are augmented) and the personal epistemologies of the participants (the means by which the individuals come to engage). Again, we want to nest this within the understanding of managerial and democratic professionalism. Performative cultures such as those experienced across many publically funded services (Ball, 2003) may open up limited spaces for democratic professionalism, instead heightening the role of managers to direct and validate the work of those they manage, leaving less room for professional discretion and perhaps creating an argument for training rather than learning. Managerial professionalism relies on routines and procedures.

What is practitioner enquiry?

In 1904, Dewey first discussed the importance of teachers engaging in pedagogic enquiry to fully engage with processes and outcomes in their classrooms. Since then the concept has been in and out of fashion and more or less tied up with the concept of the research-engaged practitioner. Underpinning these debates has often been an assumption that practitioner enquiry will lead to an engagement with research as a means to generate answers to pertinent questions of practice (Nias and Groundwater-Smith, 1988). This could be research-informed and/or involve research processes on the part of the practitioner (Cordingley, 2015b; Hall, 2009). For many this position naturally involves the participation of university academics to facilitate this engagement (Baumfield and Butterworth, 2007; McLaughlin and Black-Hawkins, 2004), and Timpereley (2008) states an important role for the expert (although not necessarily university based) in facilitating professional learning and providing critical support.

The current models of teacher-practitioner research can be largely traced back to the work of Stenhouse (1983), and as a result, over recent years, there has been more or less sustained interest in the process and impact of developing a research-engaged teaching profession. Completing a systematic review on the topic, Dagenais et al. (2012) found that practitioners with an inquiry standpoint were more likely to have positive views of research and therefore were more likely to use it to inform their practice. However, this link with research as a given of practitioner enquiry is a significant turn-off for some, and so how we manage this aspect of practitioner enquiry as professional learning is an important issue. There is something significant about the way that experts, whether colleagues in school, in local authorities, in specialist organisations or in universities, portray the accessibility and manageability of research in relation to everyday practice.

There are two dominant standpoints on practitioner enquiry with a potential lack of transfer between the two. On the one hand we have the likes of Cochran-Smith and Lytle (2009) who suggest practitioner enquiry is an epistemological stance, a way of understanding the world and how it is made up – a way of being that is tied up with views of democratic purpose and social justice. As such it is about giving informed voice to teachers in such a way that supports them in improving outcomes for students. By engaging teachers in better understanding the teaching and learning interplay in their context, and enacting and evaluating change as part of communities of practice, then practice will be improved (Baumfield et al., 2012). This process of engagement is likely to involve a research process, but it is primarily about questioning and looking for answers as part of a general professional commitment to keeping up to date with new developments.

On the other hand, we have a standpoint much more directly associated with research. Menter et al. (2011) defined enquiry as a strategic finding out, a shared process of investigation that can be explained or defended. This can often manifest as a more project-based approach to practitioner enquiry and as such could be perceived as more doable in its increased tangibility. One of the challenges here, though, is that the popular language of research is dominated by evaluation and as such a scientific understanding of process. As such, it is tied up with conceptions of expertise and academia and can seem a long way off from the remit of a practitioner in regards to knowledge and skill. It can often be seen as something that is finite and therefore not cumulative as would connect more easily to career-long professional learning (Reeves and Drew, 2013). This increases the likelihood of an individual feeling like they have *done* practitioner enquiry once a piece of research or a project has been completed. For this approach to work then a more practice-friendly understanding of research has to be promoted (see Figure 1.1).

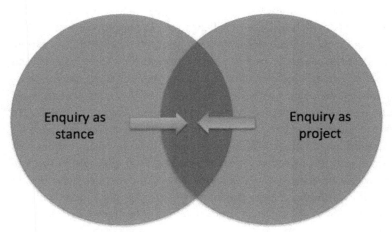

FIGURE 1.1 Bringing the two predominant practitioner enquiry stances together.

The two standpoints are not and should not be put in opposition. That is not the intention here. Rather it should be a meeting of two minds as for the experienced practitioner-enquirer they merge forming a dynamic interaction between a desire to question practice and a systematic approach to finding out the answers. It becomes a synergetic process of engagement in and with research (Cordingley, 2013; Hall, 2009) that sustains and informs a world view where the practitioner has agency (individually and as embedded in the professional community: Priestley et al., 2015) with an informed voice on education within and beyond their context (Wall et al., 2017a). How we facilitate an individual in getting to this point and how we encourage the two aspects as complementary rather than oppositional, to access the implied understandings and processes, are something that need work. In practice, we see both sides being used as a way-in, but somehow we don't get the connection right and the power of the concept is lost to whole groups in the profession.

We have seen individual practitioners access an enquiry approach from both a questioning orientation and a research one. The former tends to be characterised by individuals naturally disposed to ask questions, to want to know and understand more about the world around them. They have a learning trajectory characterised by a constant striving to improve individually and for those living and working around them. It can be quite a solitary endeavour as they are driven by a personal ideology to improve outcomes for children and are fascinated by this process, implicitly seeing that greater understanding will bring positives for themselves as a professional but also for the students that they teach. For this group, the daily grind of practice can be a challenge and can mean that it is difficult to prioritise their own enquiry against the deluge of other stuff. In addition, there can be a significant issue of fit between their own interests and wider school agendas. This can often drive the individual to experience significant dissonance with the system in which they work, as their ideal and real-life experience becomes oppositional (Leat et al., 2015). To ensure that this mindset is facilitated, then looking for access to supportive communities of like-minded practitioners to share their enquiries is paramount; this provides a means towards greater codification through sharing of experience (practice and research) and enquiry questions. In turn this promotes a more collaborative and strategic enquiry process, embedded by a co-constructed understanding of the knowledge, skills and permissions to be able to effectively find out answers that the individual can be confident in (Baumfield et al., 2012). The community could be within school or via an outside agency (although the latter is problematic if and when that agency moves on), however ensuring that enquiry is not a solitary endeavour and is supported ensuring motivation and increased warrant. It also prevents isolated disaffection.

On the other side, we see practitioners roped, sometimes literally, into undertaking a piece of enquiry-based research through involvement in a project – via a school research group, university course, a bit of Continuing Professional Development (CPD) or via a colleague or group membership. The individual might be reluctant at first, but as long as they have ownership of their own enquiry and see the connections to their students' learning (Timperley, 2008), they often become enthused by the way research provides new and improved 'goggles' with which to view their practice. Key here is ensuring that it is not an isolated one-off project which stops once the course or group finishes. Practitioner enquiry should be iterative and has more of a cumulative process than a single-project approach might encourage. Also the type of research promoted should not feel so removed from practice as to be unachievable or unmanageable within the constraints of a normal working day. Thinking is needed around sustainability, how engagement is maintained once the project finishes, what research support looks like with more limited contact with the 'experts' and manageability within the wider challenges of school life. Generally, there needs to be greater consideration of the question: what does research look like when it is maintained alongside practice?

Regardless of the way in, if issues of ownership, manageability and sustainability are tackled at both an individual and group level, then over time there can be a move towards a more integrated and pragmatic standpoint where useful knowledge is prioritised. It is important to recognise that either way in is perfectly acceptable, and neither is better nor worse than the other; however, what is important is that we reach a pragmatic balance between the two: research is not something that is constantly engaged with, but neither is it switched on or off. Similarly, a questioning standpoint is not something that should be allowed to drive an individual to distraction but rather used to contribute to a wider codified dialogue around improvement. Both contribute to a professionalism that combines a striving for better outcomes for children and young people with a set of tools that can be supportive of strategic and reflective thinking around what works and why in any specific context.

Practitioner enquiry's greatest strength is also its greatest weakness: its fit with normal practice and being a professional. There are two key commitments that I think mark the practitioner enquiry process as something different and that add value. These were highlighted by Stenhouse (1983):

1   The commitment to engage with the enquiry process systematically including a clear rationalisation of what is 'good' evidence (recognising the need for understandings of evidence that emphasise fit for purpose and practice links); and

2   The commitment to share the process and findings with a wider community (with flexibility around whom this community might comprise).

To ensure that a practitioner enquiry approach is appropriated, then we need to ensure that practitioners are engaging with these two commitments and their productive overlap. There needs to be a variety of overlapping networks for professional learning operating at different levels of the education community and for different purposes. To enable these communities to run successfully alone and in combination, then we need clearer communication of the diversity of research traditions available in education and how they link to practice and being research-engaged. We need to value this difference and celebrate it, rather than seeing oppositional models. A bridge is needed between the research, policy and practice notions of evidence and tools for enquiry, with greater thinking around commonality rather than difference: a productive question being, 'What is enough evidence to warrant action and how does this vary across contexts?'

Developing a model of research for engaging with practice

Practitioner enquiry becomes more doable when we see the productive connections it has with normal practice (Wall and Hall, 2017), when it is not something else to fit onto the long list of things to do and the outcomes feel useful in helping to progress practice. Fundamentally we see the enquiry cycle as having good fit onto the plan-do-review cycle that is core to how we teach and how we implement our practice (Baumfield et al., 2012). The only additions, as indicated in Figure 1.2, are the conscious elaboration of each step: as we Plan, it is important to reflexively explore the nature of the Question (as discussed in detail

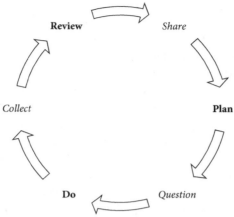

FIGURE 1.2 Practitioner enquiry as building on the process of plan-do-review.

in Chapters 2 and 3); as we Do, we ensure that we strategically Collect evidence (by making informed choices as described in Chapter 4), and when that is processed in Review, we have a commitment to Share the outcomes and the thinking underpinning the enquiry (the discussion of which takes place in Chapters 5 and 6).

In this way we are fulfilling Stenhouse's (1983) blueprint of systematic enquiry made public. We are not recommending research on every lesson or all the time. Indeed one of the critiques we would level at the project stance on practitioner enquiry approach is that it seems to imply an on/off model of enquiry: rather it would seem more pragmatic to think about a dialling up and down of the research element depending on the motivation of the enquirer and the qualities required of an answer to any particular enquiry question.

The model of research that underpins this turning up and down needs to be flexible depending on the nature of the enquiry question, and the answer required, and on the context in which it is being undertaken. To help make this doable, then it is helpful to look for bridges and associations that enable a more pragmatic, manageable outlook for the research process. This is difficult in a system dominated by the language of evaluation, measurement and intervention (Hargreaves et al., 2001). The move towards standardised testing and the what-works agenda (Biesta, 2010; Katsipataki and Higgins, 2016) in many systems around the world means that the common discourse of research most practitioners are familiar with is not sensible or even possible within a practitioner enquiry frame. These are research terms that are more positivist in their epistemology and as such imply a position of distance between the researcher and the researched to avoid bias, increase reliability and encourage generalisability. If you are researching your own practice as we have defined earlier in this chapter, then you are immersed in the context and integral to the very thing that you are exploring: to try and be true to a viewpoint that fundamentally requires something alternative can lead to an unsatisfying and uneasy marriage. Rather we would suggest a position that say recognises the usefulness of the meta-analyses of, for example, Hattie (2008), the Education Endowment Foundation (Higgins et al., 2013, 2016), and the positivist tradition in education (Morrison, 2001; Spybrook et al., 2016) but politely suggests that practitioner enquiry is about doing something different, but complementary, to this. Practitioner enquiry is not about undertaking large-scale experiments to explore high-level trends in education, but rather it is about exploring these ideas in detail in the real-life context of practice. We believe that when you have a systematic review saying, for example, that self-regulation and metacognition have a range of effect sizes from 0.44 to 0.71 (Higgins et al., 2016), then it is a good bet to focus on in your practitioner enquiry. However, the extent to which it works in your context will depend on multiple things worthy of examination in detail. It is only when the lenses provided by different types of research are taken together then the two perspectives provide a more convincing and useful way forwards (Thomas, 2016).

This book therefore intends to act somewhat as a bridge between methodology and pedagogy. For the majority of busy practitioners then the techniques of research need to be translated somewhat to be manageable in the complexity of normal practice. Indeed, we believe that greater connections between the understandings of evidence that we use in teaching and learning with those that we see in research will be supportive of a dialogue that will be supportive of education research generally. However, first and foremost this is a pragmatic stance that encourages practitioners to see research as something that is doable, as integral to their normal practice and useful for their own and students' learning. As such, it builds on core skills that they already have and supports an understanding that will facilitate greater understanding in the long run.

First and foremost, we need to open our eyes to the fact that practice sites are data-rich, and as practitioners we use a wide range of evidence all the time to assess progress and outcomes. Why isn't this evidence good enough to be used in your practitioner enquiry? A key stumbling block to be got over is the idea of 'proper', which has got tied up in traditional research techniques, and of a fairly uncompromising stance. The first thing to recognise is that there are many researchers in universities doing other types of research, for example, case studies and ethnographies, that are exploratory in intent and usually have relatively small sample sizes. There is no agreement that research has to be experimental and, on a large scale, to involve statistical analysis and be generalisable. There is a good basis in the research literature for other types of design that are much more sensitive to context and make an advantage of the fact that they are generating insight about the nuance of individual real life.

Even in this more interpretivist field, the practitioner-researcher might find that the researcher is still predominantly removed from the practice. The research textbooks and the published articles are predominantly written by university researchers doing research on practice and to participants, whereas in practitioner enquiry we are talking much more about research 'into' and 'with'. With this level of embeddedness, there comes another level of consideration about research techniques, process and judgements that need to be qualified and adapted for this standpoint. This is not well-recognised and developed in the research text books and can lead to an unease that the research is not feasible or needs something extra to achieve the criteria set out: not proper enough. We will talk about this in relation to Heikkinen et al.'s (2012) criteria for assessing action research in Chapter 4.

As a group of researchers, practitioner-enquirers generally, and we include ourselves in this statement, need to be more confident in translating how we think about the effective practice and pedagogic tools that we know work (in capturing children and young peoples' learning and perspectives, for example) to thinking about tools for engaging in research (Baumfield et al., 2012). Teachers set themselves high standards of 'warrant' (Dewey, 1938/1991) – they know what evidence is good enough to support next steps for themselves and their students – but we are shy at translating this thinking about what works and why to the world of research. Yet from our perspective it is too similar not to be a productive synergy. Connections can be seen between how teachers learn and how students learn (it is not coincidence that enquiry-based approaches are also useful in classrooms), how we support student voice and teacher voice (the spaces, tools, dispositions and cultures), and how we support teachers' and students' metacognition. These different aspects should be interconnected and complementary. A practitioner enquiry frame not only can help bring them together (Wall and Hall, 2016) but also, by seeing them as connected, can make a practitioner enquiry feel more doable.

Metacognition for practitioners

This section will re-frame the ideas introduced so far, about practice, enquiry and research, in terms of strategic and reflective thinking – metacognition for practitioners (Moseley et al., 2005a and b). For us the enquiry process and its link to plan-do-review encourage the reflective practitioner, the dispositions and skills to look back on practice and thinking about what worked or not in a systematic way and crucially to think forwards about what would be different next time (Wall and Hall, 2016) – therefore to be metacognitive about practice (Portilho and Medina, 2016). This will include a discussion of how to go about exploring metacognition and the tools that support a move to this kind of thinking (Baumfield et al., 2009). It will draw on the idea that learning, in its broadest sense, is a productive topic for authentic and inclusive enquiry and discuss how teachers engaged in such enquiry are more likely to see themselves as metacognitive. The end result is a mirroring of the values and beliefs about student learning to the professional domain. We will explain how we believe catalytic tools tighten the feedback loops between students' and teachers' learning trajectories reinforcing effective behaviours and dispositions for both. A typology of tools will be exemplified and the different categories we see used within practitioners' real-life enquiries outlined: frames, lenses, scaffolds and measures (Lofthouse and Hall, 2014). This will then feed into our use of (research) tools for the enquiry process later in the book.

Learning as a focus for professional enquiry

In our work we have found that an enquiry focus on improving learning has significant potential for productive practice. Learning is at the heart of what we, as education professionals, do, and as such it is difficult for a community member, whether adult or child, to not admit some vested interest. Of course to facilitate reflection on learning, participants need to be asked in the right way and be given appropriate language with which to express themselves (two factors obviously more pertinent when including children but relevant for all age ranges (Wall, 2012)). However, if this is done appropriately then because participants are being asked to engage with the learning process, to think about thinking, they will move into the metacognitive realm: thinking about (their) thinking (Flavell, 1977, 1979).

If we look at the practices used to promote metacognition then we can see a drive towards making the process of learning explicit, with a range of synonymous pedagogies, for example, Thinking Skills (for example, Higgins et al., 2001), Learning to Learn (Higgins et al., 2007; Wall et al., 2010), Building Learning Power (Claxton, 2002) and Assessment for Learning (Black and Wiliam, 1990). Across these approaches a practice emerges that taps into values and beliefs that target learning as learnable focusing on the process, knowledge and skills it encompasses. The resulting classroom environments privilege conversations about learning and allow students time to talk through how they have achieved their learning successes and failures (Wall, 2012).

Developing metacognition and twenty-first-century learning skills, competencies and dispositions is important (for example, Ananiadou and Claro, 2009). Raising children's metacognitive awareness has been shown, alongside feedback, to be one of the most impactful and cost-effective ways of raising attainment (Higgins et al., 2013; Hattie, 2008). These same researchers have consistently found across meta-analyses of empirical studies that children who experience pedagogies to promote metacognitive awareness are on average likely to do eight months better in standardised assessments than their peers who have not been given the same opportunity: so there is warrant to spend some time and energy on metacognition. This is challenging to implement however within the neo-conservative agendas of many current education systems, and it means there is great diversity in regards to how and why these techniques are implemented and the impact they have.

One of the reasons for this inconsistency in practice is the slipperiness of the term 'metacognition' within the theoretical and empirical literature (Gascoine et al., 2016; Williamson, 2005). The concept is vague. and beyond Flavell's (1977) original definition, there is little agreement with increasingly complex theoretical nuances emerging (for example, Efklides, 2008). There is no doubt metacognition has a close relationship with concepts such as self-regulation, learning dispositions, literature and motivation, but what the connection is and how it works are still debated and in some cases are deeply divisive.

This vagueness and the complexity, however, in both theory and practice, can be seen as an advantage rather than a disadvantage when viewed under an enquiry lens. The doubt arguably results in a creative space around which authentic enquiry can be undertaken. It means that questions can be asked where even the 'experts' are not yet convinced of answers, therefore, opening up meaningful dialogue for all. It means, as a focus for professional enquiry, learning is a productive and influential topic that facilitates practitioners' questioning of theory and practice but in such a way as to keep relevant to their professional commitments. Indeed in Timperley's review of professional learning literature, this closeness of professional learning cycles to the (learning) needs of their students is essential for it to be effective (Timperley, 2008).

Developing teachers' metacognitive awareness

The literature and practices around metacognition so far discussed are firmly student orientated. The idea of taking such an approach with teachers is under-explored despite the small literature base stating the importance of teachers' knowledge of metacognition (Wilson and Bai, 2010; Wittrock, 1987; Zohar, 1999) and the potential for teachers to act as metacognitive role models (Wall and Hall, 2016). In general these literatures on student and teacher learning remain separate, developing in parallel (Vermunt, 2014; Vermunt and Endedijk, 2011). Teachers who learn through professional enquiry are being shown to have positive impact on student outcomes (Timperely et al., 2009), but the ways in which the gap between the two learning trajectories, students and teachers, can be narrowed and can become mutually reinforcing are less (Wall and Hall, 2017).

In an enquiry scenario that focuses on learning for the student, this is a relatively simple thing as learning is a fundamental preoccupation, successful or not, of the school-aged years. For teachers it is more complex and has multiple strands. They have their view of the students' learning progression and the influence that teaching and learning practice have on this. This is the everyday business of the classroom. But they also have their own learning, whether as part of professional development or in their personal lives, to reflect on. We have noticed that, for the teachers, an enquiry that focuses on student learning tends to draw together these elements producing a mirroring affect between their classroom practice and their own learning trajectories, both professional and personal supporting this idea of metacognitive role model (Wall and Hall, 2016).

With an intent to narrow the gap between teachers' and students' learning, the communities with which we have worked have been drawn to the definition of metacognition or metacognitive thinking derived from Moseley et al.'s (2005a) substantial review of learning theory and practice. Within their overarching framework a meta-level is indicated, called reflective and strategic thinking (Figure 1.3). It could be considered that this term has been chosen for accessibility in practice, especially its use with younger children, but we would argue against that (anyone who has talked to a three-year-old with a fascination for dinosaurs knows they can get their tongue around technical vocabulary such as stegosaurus and so metacognition should not be considered a particular problem). Rather the term was chosen not only because of the link to the learning theory and pedagogy that is the basis of the *Frameworks for Thinking* book (Moseley et al., 2005a), to the potential answers to questions about learning raised in the classroom, but also because of the familiarity of the language to key education 'buzzwords'.

STRATEGIC AND REFLECTIVE THINKING
Engagement with and management of thinking/learning, supported by value grounded thinking (including critically reflective thinking)

COGNITIVE SKILLS		
Information Gathering	Building Understanding	Productive Thinking
Experiencing recognising and recalling Comprehending messages and recorded information	Development of meaning (e.g. by elaborating, representing or sharing ideas) Working with patterns and rules Concept formation Organising ideas	Reasoning Understanding causal relationships Systematic enquiry Problem solving Creative thinking

FIGURE 1.3 An integrated model for understanding thinking and learning (Moseley et al., 2005a, p. 378).

By linking explicitly to the term 'reflective' then we are intending to make productive associations to the idea of reflective learners and importantly reflective practitioners (Schön, 1987; 1991). It is a language and concept that most practising teachers are familiar with and confident in its attribution to professional dispositions. It is also a term that teachers are likely to apply to students. The desire for students to be reflective on their own learning is central to such approaches as Assessment for Learning (Black and Wiliam, 1990) and DIRT (dedicated improvement and reflection time (Beere, 2013)), as well as being an idea integral to many national curriculums, thanks to Bruner's spiral curriculum (Bruner, 1960).

The fact that reflective thinking is not alone in Moseley et al.'s (2005b) meta-level and is teamed up with strategic thinking is important for us. It adds an important dimension to the theory of metacognition that we see developing in classrooms undertaking enquiry into learning. The strategic encourages action on reflection therefore emphasising an active process (Wall and Hall, 2016). Reflective practice on its own, indeed being solely a reflective learner, could be considered to be quite passive and introverted, whereas to be strategic with that reflection, to do something with it, drives a prerogative to move forwards in an attempt to improve and to share that thinking and experience. This helps to give a creative and productive purpose to the reflection and is more fitting with what we believe are effective learning dispositions and characteristics for both learners and teachers. The fact that this cycle of action and reflection is also mirrored within an action research cycle is also not lost on us.

Tools for professional metacognition

In this final section we want to explore the nature of these parallel metacognitive processes and the way in which some tools within the practitioner enquiry frame can be catalytic to the process of closing down the gap between students and teachers metacognition. We conceptualise tools as Deweyan (Dewey, 1938) 'technologies', socially constructed artefacts that allow teachers to engage with their practice at a number of levels, and crucially, at the level which has the most immediate use to the individual and their enquiry. In this we make a critical distinction between tools and 'toolkits', in which the formulation of the question and the solution is preset. In contrast:

A tool is also a mode of language ... so intimately bound up with intentions, occupations and purposes that they have an eloquent voice. (Dewey, 1938, p. 46)

Tools have the epistemic quality of revealing their properties under the questioning gaze of the user. Some of these properties have been described in earlier work (Hall, 2011, see Figure 1.4).

An effective tool for professional learning is characterised by the tight feedback loops it supports between the practitioners' enquiry questions and teaching and learning practice (see Figure 1.5). They are flexible enough to allow for iterative development moment to moment, as well as providing robust enough evidence to fulfil judgements of quality and to give warrant for change (Baumfield et al., 2009). Within the context of learning-focused enquiry then, a tool should enable insight into the process, knowledge and skills of learning and facilitate the development of language and opportunity to talk about metacognition.

To exemplify this interaction then, we will give two examples from partner schools. In each we include a brief description of the tool and how it was used. The latter is important because effective tools can be used in more than one way and have increased pedagogic value due to this versatility; however, care should be taken not to overuse them as the value is likely to diminish with each use. We will also suggest the nature of the students' and teachers' learning as a result of the tools use, and how this relates to our typology, and explore how the two were supported in mutual development. A graphic is used to show how the teachers and students might be using the tools differently and gaining different feedback to support learning as a consequence, but that this adds to the power of the tool.

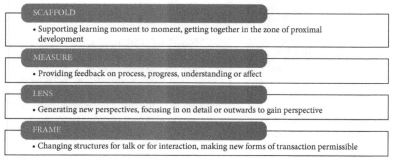

SCAFFOLD
- Supporting learning moment to moment, getting together in the zone of proximal development

MEASURE
- Providing feedback on process, progress, understanding or affect

LENS
- Generating new perspectives, focusing in on detail or outwards to gain perspective

FRAME
- Changing structures for talk or for interaction, making new forms of transaction permissible

FIGURE 1.4 Descriptors of purposes to which tools are put (Hall, 2011).

Example 1

At Hipsburn First School, Dot Charlton and her staff team wanted children across the school (four to nine years) to interact beyond their friendship groups (Charlton et al., 2008). They used a jar of lollipop sticks in each class, one for each child, and each morning the children would pick out their lollipop partner for the day. This created quite a bit of friction that had to be negotiated, but the children, over time, became able to see that different children made different types of lollipop partner, which might be appropriate or not for different types of learning task and therefore impact on the way they interacted with each other inside and outside of their friendship groups. The reflection also allowed them to think about themselves as a partner and the skills they brought to a pairing (generating new perspectives of themselves as learners and as facilitators of others' learning). For the teachers, the tool enabled them to look critically at grouping strategies used across age ranges, curriculum and different types and styles of pedagogy. It was a scaffold that increased depth of understanding about which groups should be used, while also acting as a lens for staff to understand, and sometimes reassess, the capabilities of the individuals in their class.

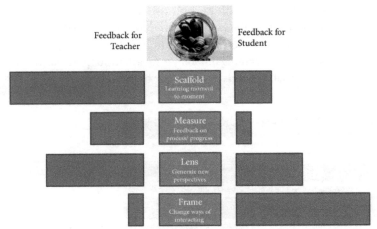

FIGURE 1.5 Hipsburn First School, Lollipop Partners, exemplifying feedback for students' and teachers' learning.

Example 2

Vicki and Helen (High Street Primary) used pupil views templates (Wall and Higgins, 2006) with Years 1 and 2 (aged five to seven years) as a lens to facilitate self-assessment and reflection on learning (Lewis and Barwick, 2006) (see Figure 1.6). Each week children would choose a template and fill in the speech and thought bubble to reflect on the key learning they had achieved. These templates were often shared as part of circle time so they could see different people learned different things in the same way and the same things in different ways (framing the interaction). The templates were logged in a 'thoughts and feeling book' owned by each child allowing reflection on how their learning might differ (or be the same) across the curriculum. They kept the book throughout their time in school, and this scaffold enabled them to reflect on how learning changed (or not) over time. For Vicki and Helen the templates enabled them to have greater insight of their pupils' learning capabilities, attitudes and beliefs about learning. On many occasions this meant they needed to reassess their expectations because of the insight provided.

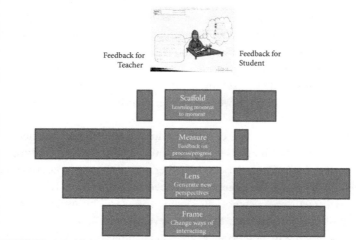

FIGURE 1.6 High Street Primary School, Pupil Views Templates, feedback loops for students' and teachers' learning.

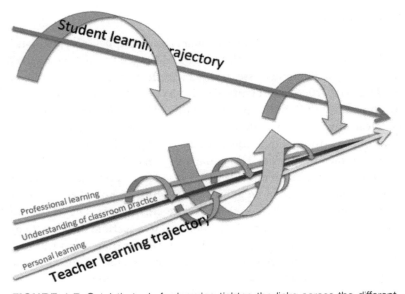

FIGURE 1.7 Catalytic tools for learning tighten the links across the different dimensions of teacher learning and between student and teacher learning trajectories.

Any tool used in the classroom for the purposes of practitioner enquiry should therefore be judged in regards to its usefulness in drawing types of learning into juxtaposition. A tool's usefulness for professional learning in facilitating the teachers' reflective and strategic thinking about practice as well as their own learning (professional and personal) is more potent when placed alongside its usefulness for student learning (in improving student outcomes, although we use this term in its broadest sense) (see Figure 1.7).

Ideally this combination of information facilitates the teacher in engaging critically with practice and obtaining a better understanding of the underpinning learning process, whether originating with the students or teachers, allowing the generation of theories of practice. If it is true that 'it is [practitioners] who will change the world by understanding it' (attributed to Stenhouse), then the development and ownership of theories of practice by practitioners are crucial. It has been the purpose of this chapter to frame this practice-theoretical mission, and the chapters that follow are intended to support the explorer.

2 QUESTIONING

'Oh, just get on with it!' (everyone we've ever met, at some point)

Practitioners often self-identify as both practical and pragmatic, as 'doers'. We privilege activity and engagement in the here and now, with the immediacy of the needs of the person in front of us. This is something that we find satisfying in terms of tangible achievement but also ethically congruent: we are engaged in real and hopefully positive relationships, 'enacting change' (Hall, 2011). This description of practice is familiar and often juxtaposed with a contrast, with a 'but' which separates practice from theory (Hammersley, 2004). Our sense is that, unintentionally, such juxtapositions serve as a cultural meme fencing practitioners off from their own philosophical and speculative thinking, and we will make an argument for what we think *praxis* (Aristotle in Ackrill, 1987; Carr, 2007) is: not something that practitioners have to be taught but implicit processes already in play. Practitioners become conscious of these processes through reflection (Schön, 1987), and we would argue, more conscious and critical through processes of enquiry (Wall and Hall, 2016). This is because the enquiry cycle requires us to keep asking challenging questions at a number of levels: *How is it going? What does this data mean? How does this odd thing relate to my original question? What if it doesn't? What other questions could I ask? What if the thing I think is the problem isn't actually the problem?* The potential to ask questions which are practical, professional and philosophical is a rebuttal to theory/practice and research/practice divides we talked about in the previous chapter and so, in this chapter we seek – as in relational therapy (Rogers, 1961) – to replace the 'or' with 'and'. In this way, practitioners can track their thinking and explore their hunches with a sense of rigour and structure.

Why are we moved to ask questions?

Recent research (Blackmore, 2005) on perception and cognition suggests a growing consensus that human beings are only paying close attention to a fraction of what is going on around us. We imagine our consciousness as some sort of 360-degree, high-definition picture, complete with surround sound and digital recording and playback. In fact, most of what we are half-aware of is 'library footage', replaying from memory, with a degree of storytelling, while our attention is fixed on an immediate stimulus or engaged in 'wistful synaptic surfing' (Miholic, 1994, p. 84). If this is the case, then questions could arise from either of these principal activities, that is to say questions relating to pressing problems – the learner, stuck and frustrated, right in front of you – or from the emergent awareness of a pattern in apparent randomness. These kinds of questions, problem-solving and speculative, do not 'belong' to different professional thinkers, to front-line or ivory tower educators; they are a recognisable part of everyone's innate enquiry process (Peirce, 1878). Furthermore, we are going to argue that consciously moving from problem-solving to speculation and back again also encourages us to catch inconsistencies in the 'library footage' to notice that what we assumed was going on in that corner of the classroom is fractionally (or significantly) different. Our practitioner enquiry partners have long referred to this as 'clean windows syndrome', that moment when you turn, triumphantly, cloth in hand from the window and notice how grubby and untidy the rest of the room looks in full, clear sunshine. This is the health warning: asking questions can come from immediate necessity or inclination but it is by no means painless.

Our understanding of questions is drawn from Peirce and his paper 'The Fixation of Belief' (1877). He describes how a question emerges from a sense of dissatisfaction: an awareness either that we do not know something or that our existing belief about how the world operates is no longer a 'good enough' fit with our experience. This stimulus for discomfort could come from an immediate and novel event – the learner who does not respond to the 'tried and tested' lesson as expected – or from a gradual realisation that the 'tried and tested' has gone stale for learners and teacher alike. Peirce, unlike Descartes, doesn't expect us to be constantly stress-testing all our ideas against experience; instead, he recognises that we naturally wish to hold to our existing and functional beliefs and will only be moved to doubt by genuine discomfort. Moreover, when one of my beliefs becomes unsatisfactory, provoking discomfort and doubt, then I want to return to a state of comfort and certainty as quickly and effortlessly as possible. From this beautiful and humanist perspective on inquiry, in which real, flawed individuals do their best to navigate a complex universe in good faith, Peirce develops a typology of inquiry (in Figure 2.1 and unpacked in Figures 2.2–2.5).

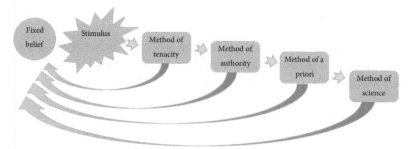

FIGURE 2.1 Fixation of belief and methods of inquiry – overview.

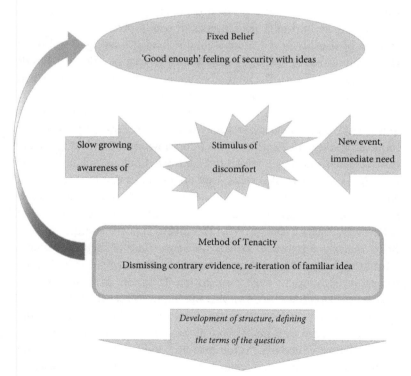

FIGURE 2.2 The process of Fixation of Belief 1 – Methods of Tenacity.

Although Peirce presents each of these methods of inquiry as necessary developmental steps, he does not, as some later commentators do (described by de Waal, 2013), discount the usefulness of what is learned at each stage. Tenacity and authority are not stupid pre-steps to 'proper inquiry' to be skipped over if possible; they are critical indicators of the context in which these questions are being asked, as such they are as worthy of attention as any other stage.

The method of tenacity is particularly vulnerable to being dismissed as a waste of time: the confirmation bias and defensive position it implies are recognisable as part of a topical discourse in which Breitbart and Guardian readers visit one another's websites to comment below the line about the shakiness of their arguments and sources and to accuse one another of living in 'echo chambers' in which only assenting voices are heard. These dissenting voices are particularly ineffective in this phase, as tenacity requires the contrary evidence to be debunked and rejected quickly, not on scientific grounds but as misguided or in bad faith. We want to get back to Fixed Belief as soon as possible, so we're not hanging around to check statistics or read footnotes. However, the method of tenacity is not mere stubbornness: just saying 'I still think what I thunk before' (as one of the fairies in Disney's *Sleeping Beauty* memorably remarked). The method requires the thinker to reiterate their familiar idea, to bring it into conscious awareness and to provide a degree of structure to the argument, to define some of the terms of question. This is vital to the method of tenacity, since this reiteration provides the soothing quality ('this makes sense, I do know what I'm talking about') that facilitates not only a return to Fixed Belief but an enhancement of the original idea. By enhancement we do not mean that the idea itself is any better (or worse) but that our understanding of it and our intellectual relationship with it are changed since the act of examining an idea, even defensively, causes a change. What this means is that the return to Fixed Belief is never a return to exactly the same *place* of security, rather a return to a *feeling* of security, since the original idea will have undergone some level of change through examination. This is one of the reasons why tenacity is helpful and necessary to the inquiry process. If the method of tenacity is not entirely successful and if I am still uncomfortable, this clarification of my ideas helps me to navigate the next stage(s) of inquiry.

The method of authority is the next step, where I make appeals to the trusted institutions in my life: church, state, professional community, family and friends. There are strong links to tenacity, since it is likely that my

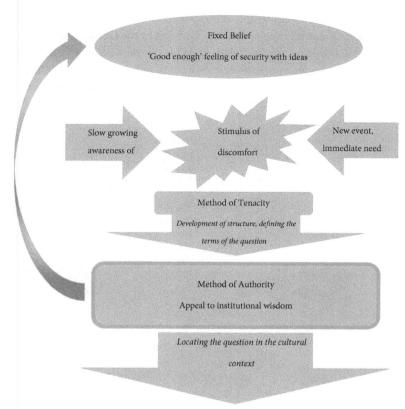

Fixed Belief

'Good enough' feeling of security with ideas

Slow growing awareness of

Stimulus of discomfort

New event, immediate need

Method of Tenacity

Development of structure, defining the terms of the question

Method of Authority

Appeal to institutional wisdom

Locating the question in the cultural context

FIGURE 2.3 The process of Fixation of Belief 2 – Method of Authority.

original idea has been socially constructed from within these relationships with powerful figures. Essentially, still hoping to get back to Fixed Belief *soon*, I am seeking corroboration of belief, rather than corroboration of evidence, so not necessarily asking my authority figures to 'show their working'. I am referring to the guidelines, to the executive summary, and in doing so, hoping to recognise my clarified idea from the method of tenacity in the language used by my authority figures. Again, there is an inevitable confirmation bias but once more we urge you not to reject the method of authority as a waste of time: however much this is an 'echo chamber' dialogue, it is still a dialogue in which the thinker brings her own ideas alongside that of her community. In this dialogue, where the method of authority is successful and there is a return to Fixed Belief, the interaction of language and ideas is soothing, either because the similarity lends weight to the thinker's original idea or because the authority's new ideas or language is understood and incorporated into the Fixed Belief. Where the method of authority is not successful, this may be because the similarity does not address the lingering discomfort or because the new ideas or language causes confusion and an erosion of security in the authority. As institutions, however autocratic, never manage to produce definitive answers to all questions and tend therefore towards uncertainty and contradiction,

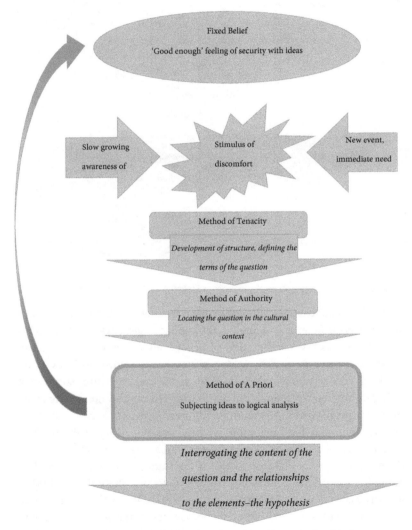

FIGURE 2.4 The process of Fixation of Belief 3 – Method of a priori.

individuals in turn tend to have ambivalent relationships with institutions (Amini et al., 2000), moving along a continuum between total trust to rough dismissal, and in this movement, there is the opportunity to understand more about how each individual fits into the cultural context. The method of authority therefore provides richness of context either for the Fixed Belief or for the next stage of inquiry.

Where institutions fail to soothe, we are forced then to investigate the underlying logic of our ideas. The method of a priori requires quite a lot of initial intellectual effort, since we have to embark on the time-consuming task of taking apart our ideas and examining their constituent elements. We have to ask ourselves what we mean by particular words or phrases and once we have done that, we have to ask ourselves whether the relationships between these phrases are actually what we have assumed them to be. Like the under-resourced and confused recruits, it can be hard to connect this exercise of 'naming of parts' (Reed, 1942) with the reality of our question, and the process of constructing a hypothesis can be alienating at both a practical and a philosophical level.

> Today we have naming of parts. Yesterday,
> We had daily cleaning. And tomorrow morning,
> We shall have what to do after firing. But to-day,
> Today we have naming of parts. Japonica
> Glistens like coral in all of the neighbouring gardens,
> And today we have naming of parts.

> This is the lower sling swivel. And this
> Is the upper sling swivel, whose use you will see,
> When you are given your slings. And this is the piling swivel,
> Which in your case you have not got. The branches
> Hold in the gardens their silent, eloquent gestures,
> Which in our case we have not got.

So tempting therefore to bypass this stage or to consider it somebody else's job, though, this is another barrier erected against the theorisation of practice, the application of theory and the development of practical wisdom (praxis). For this reason, there will be a lot more about logical arguments and hypotheses in this book, since we believe that it is a vital element and one that is not so alien as it may first seem. There is some new language and new application of familiar techniques that take effort to engage with, but mostly it is about confidence. If we 'have not got' the confidence to work with logical tools and arguments, to sort out our ideas and prepare the surfaces, then we are reduced to calling on others to do the job (authority) or fated to botched attempts at our own DIY method of science. The a priori method produces a clear, cogent account of what we think we know and the relationships between them – a hypothesis. It must be sanded down and cleaned before it can be satisfactory either as a 'good enough' explanation to return us to Fixed Belief or as the basis of an exploration through the method of science.

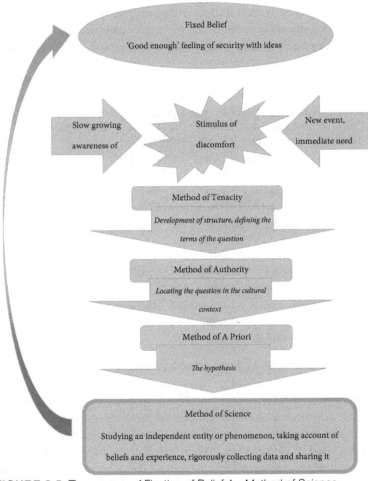

FIGURE 2.5 The process of Fixation of Belief 4 – Method of Science.

The method of science therefore builds upon the crystallisation of ideas in tenacity, the contextualisation of ideas in authority and the development of the hypothesis in the a priori method. It is the moment in the process of inquiry where there is a deliberate attempt to separate the thing being studied from the inquirer and the context, so clearly these aspects have to be considered and it is not advisable to bypass them. It is where Peirce's 'inquiry' starts to look like 'empirical research' and where the big philosophical questions that underpin our doubts have to be sliced into manageable investigations.

Peirce asserted two key things about the method of science: that in the long run it would enable humanity to understand the world (an objective idealism that is still in battle with post-modernist theory, de Waal, 2013) and in the meanwhile, it provides a robust structure in which we can tolerate, examine and manage doubt. The robust structure comes from the clarity of the hypothesis, as one might expect, but also from the connection to the cultural and individual context of the questioner – so this is not a cartoon 'hard science' with only positivist values. Rather, the method of science is integrative, socially constructed and constantly open to challenge. Hypotheses, research methods, data and conclusions are the shared property of the community of inquirers who both set the standards for what counts as rigorous and conduct enquiries into those standards. The rest of this book is intended as a resource for conducting inquiries using the method of science, so we will confine ourselves to some key principles here.

1   The hypothesis and all methods employed to explore it must be capable of producing positive, negative and ambiguous results (*falsifiability*).

2   The underlying ideas, the methods used, participants involved, data collected and the analysis must be clearly articulated (*transparency*) so that other inquirers can follow or repeat the exploration (*replicability*).

3   The connections between the hypothesis and the methods chosen are clear and congruent (*reliability and validity*).

4   The impact of each aspect of the exploration (from forming the question, through design, execution, analysis, dissemination and future use of the inquiry) on each actor (whether directly or indirectly concerned with the inquiry) is considered (*ethics*).

5   Everything that happens (or fails to happen), whether part of the plan or not, is part of the data to be shared (*trustworthiness*).

Putting this into practice – A worked example

It's probably a good idea at this point to see how this is made more complicated by the kind of question being asked and by the nature of the phenomenon under investigation. For example, a problem-solving question focused on why a cohort of students appear to have catastrophically failed a multiple choice test that previously produced a normal distribution curve of results (Figure 2.6) could follow a number of pathways.

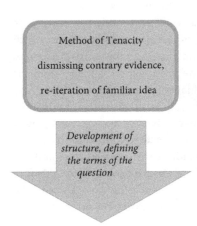

The method of tenacity might look for an external factor, since the teaching, the students and the mode of assessment cannot be active factors. So *'the students all failed because their revision was disrupted by [insert socio-cultural event of choice e.g. Pokémon Go/ US Presidential election/ Cup Final]'.*

The tenacity explanation contains the unspoken ideas:

i *There's nothing wrong with the test*

ii *Or the teaching*

iii *Or the students.*

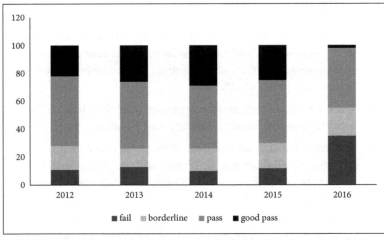

FIGURE 2.6 Exemplar – performance of students on multiple choice test.

However, the 'it was a big dog and then it ran away' explanation has only a moderate success rate – even when sanctioned by the method of authority and even if it was objectively a very big dog. As most education practitioners will recognise, changes in performance tend to attract challenge to Fixed Belief and authority figures tend to get involved, whether the individual inquirer asks them or not.

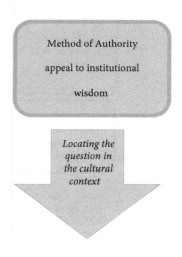

Method of Authority

appeal to institutional

wisdom

Locating the question in the cultural context

The dominating question 'What's wrong with?' will inevitably be applied in turn to students (and their families and communities), individual teachers, departments and schools. Crucially, the question is reliant on established beliefs about each of these individuals or groups, not an investigation of them. The cultural context then shows us the hierarchy of responsibility, which in this hypothetical (but not invariably in reality) is inversely related to power.

i   *It's down to these students ...*

ii   *Well, when you look at their backgrounds ...*

iii *Of course that teacher was new and inexperienced/old and knackered ...*

iv   *That school has been coasting/needs a SuperHead ...*

If these unsupported explanations fail to satisfy, an a priori approach could help us to separate what was *supposed to happen* from what *did happen* and to make explicit the logical links we *think are there* between the elements in the situation and thus develop and interrogate possible hypotheses. This is normally the point where logic demands that we consider all the elements, even the sacred standardised tests (see Figure 2.7).

This has not happened in this instance, so we take each element as potentially faulty in turn (see Figure 2.8) so *either*

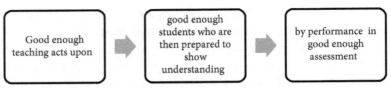

FIGURE 2.7 Base hypothesis (how the world is supposed to work logically).
Note: This excludes hypotheses D, E and F where two or more things go wrong at once.
Note: In this hypothesis, everything is good enough.

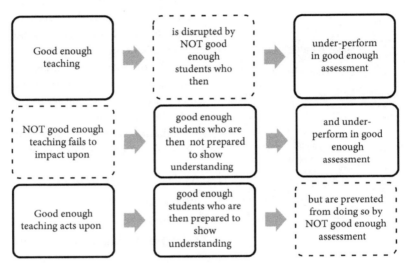

FIGURE 2.8 Alternate hypotheses.

Note: This excludes hypotheses D, E and F where two or more things go wrong at once.

The a priori method prepares the ground for the scientific enquiry, making it clear both what the underlying belief is and the range of possible explanations for the observed phenomenon. A robust enquiry into this cohort's performance would need to investigate

(a) the past performance and qualities of the students,

(b) the curriculum and the learning experience and

(c) the nature of the assessment, its reliability and validity.

If the a priori stage is missed out, it would be possible to inadvertently create a pseudo-enquiry in which some of these alternative logical explanations were not considered. This is not to say that all research has to collect data for all possible hypotheses but good research does have to acknowledge which relevant hypotheses are not being addressed in the current exploration. This is a quality threshold that a lot of published research doesn't meet, which takes us back to why people don't trust authority figures.

Another layer: Naming parts that we can't see

It is possible to add a further level of complexity to this complication, if we consider that many of the questions we are drawn to ask are about less tangible aspects of learning, such as motivation, engagement or quality. Quality is simultaneously an extremely difficult and disputed concept (see Wittek and Kvernbekk, 2011 and our discussion in Chapter 5) and ethically central to most of the questions we want to ask about learning. Hattie's work on measurable outcomes in education and meta-analysis might seem to place him firmly with the hard empiricists and the 'what works' camp of educational researchers (Biesta, 2010). However, he makes the point (Hattie and Yates, 2013) that meta-analysis data tells us (rigorously and reliably) only what we have measured. It does not tell us whether or not those measures are (as we might assume) a direct representation of the phenomenon, such as a record of my height or whether they are 'cognates and signifiers'. Hattie unpacks cognates and signifiers by using the everyday examples of school uniform and after-school activities as indicators of school quality. Parents recognise these indicators and make choices about schools using this evidence, while Hattie notes that there is no correlation between uniform or activities and attainment outcomes. So who is wrong? The method of tenacity suggests that key positive things about a school, such as discipline and variety, are represented by uniform and activities. This might be reinforced by authority, as Ofsted, ministers and newspapers use these signifiers (or lack of them) as ways of judging schools. However, the a priori method requires us to create logical connections that then lead us to ask more searching questions (Figure 2.9).

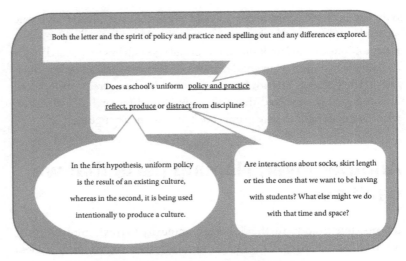

FIGURE 2.9 Unpacking a question about school uniform.

Taking questions out into the field

In Chapter 3, we will focus on the intent and reflexive process of the researcher in framing a question and designing an enquiry. The examples in Chapter 3 are also available as full narratives in the Appendix, so you can choose to read the story and analyse the process in the order that suits you best.

3 DECIDING

We are going to start this chapter with the assertion that there is no perfect research project. Every single one, even by the most eminent professors, will have advantages and disadvantages relating to the decisions made at different points in the research process. A good research project has consistency in the associations made between research questions, research design, data collection and analysis tools, and dissemination. It will also have clear rationales for each element within those stages. For example, within an analysis stage, there is a great range of techniques or tools that could be used to engage with a sample of photographs taken by fifteen–year-olds to show their favourite places to learn. But there will be advantages and disadvantages associated with all these decisions and you as an individual will have professional understandings about which approach will give the best answer. Within the context of this book, the match to the aspect of practice under investigation is also very important; how the tool helps you to get a better insight into what is going on and how this informs your professional understanding will be a marker of quality. To manoeuvre your way through this, you must show that your final choice has been considered in relation to alternatives and in regards to inherent implications for the rest of the research process, particularly the generation of findings.

These decisions become particularly important when the research is completed in a real-life setting and in association with practice. Within an examination of professional learning then the research will often come secondary to practice, your primary role, and as such it will have to be a moveable feast depending on professional demands. As a result, it might therefore be subject to complex forces way beyond your control: you are allocated to a different role, the participants whom you are following leave or fall sick, an inspection is announced or the policy changes. How the research process is set up and managed to deal with these influences and, when something happens to change the process, how you react and make considered research choices to accommodate this change will be paramount. As before the transparency with which this is articulated is a key marker of quality rather than the accuracy with which you stick to a premeditated plan of the research. We see quality therefore centred on the clarity with which each of these dilemmas is articulated, considered and communicated to the audience. Indeed, we would go further and say there should be an ethical prerogative around how we talk about our research and communicate the process and findings to others (Groundwater-Smith and Mockler, 2007).

Distinguishing means and ends: Methodological and practical considerations

The pathway through the research process starts with your research question, an articulation in question form of that thing that is bugging you about practice. The nature of the question and how you word it will set the course for how you proceed in making research design choices, the types of data and analysis tools and techniques you choose, and the way that you will report your findings. Broadly the question might be exploratory or it might seek to test something out; whichever it is, a key decision will be deciding on the nature of the data that will convince you that you have found an answer (Baumfield et al., 2012).

To generate your research question then you need to go through a process of refinement. It is important that your question is not too large or unwieldy; there are no prizes for the largest enquiry project. It is also important that you try to avoid ambiguity, where your meaning is unclear or your interpretation could draw from one of many accepted definitions. You need to ensure that your question is answerable by ensuring the language is as precise as possible as well as keeping the scale manageable within the confounds of your normal practice. In Figure 3.1 we work through this process showing how terminology might be clarified and focus refined. Finally, you need not get caught up on originality. Unless you are using your practitioner enquiry as the basis of a doctorate thesis (and some do), then being different to the wider field should not be an overarching concern. The fact that you are asking a question about your practice that you don't know the answer to is novelty enough.

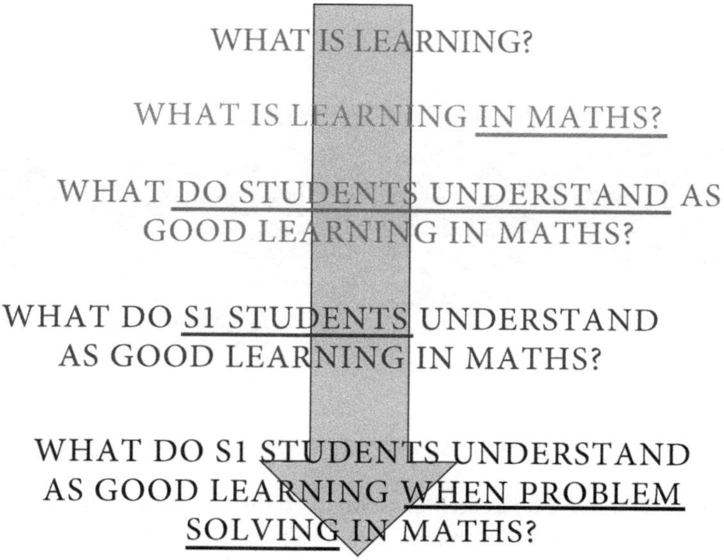

WHAT IS LEARNING?

WHAT IS LEARNING IN MATHS?

WHAT DO STUDENTS UNDERSTAND AS
GOOD LEARNING IN MATHS?

WHAT DO S1 STUDENTS UNDERSTAND
AS GOOD LEARNING IN MATHS?

WHAT DO S1 STUDENTS UNDERSTAND
AS GOOD LEARNING WHEN PROBLEM
SOLVING IN MATHS?

FIGURE 3.1 The process of refining your research question.

Your research question will be the hook on which all the other stages and decisions are hung. Many researchers are very good at articulating the first stages – the nature of the data collected, but the analysis and dissemination methods are seen to follow unquestioned from those tools, when in fact there are just as many decisions to make at these stages. It is important to maintain the narrative and show how you have thought through all elements and the way that you have connected them to answer your question. The cautionary example is the student who was presenting her research about nurture groups; part of the way through her write–up, there was an ambiguous paragraph – ambiguous in that it presented an idea out of kilter to the rest of the argument, a research red herring as it were. This one paragraph meant that two different readers ended up in very different places in understanding the rest of the research process. It wasn't that she was a bad researcher, but rather the way that she had presented her process was not consistent and was disconnected at this one point. A good researcher will take the reader by the hand and lead them through the stages of their research and the decisions made in such a way that these misunderstandings are less likely to happen. They will have a clear pathway from research question through research design, data collection and analysis to findings (Figure 3.2).

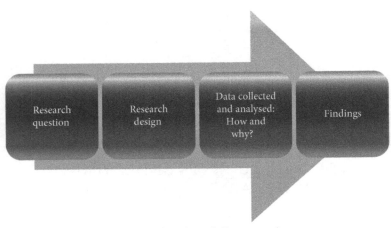

FIGURE 3.2 Making connections through the research process.

From developing a research question, then the first point of decision is the research design. Research designs offer a scaffold that helps to hold the data collection tools and analysis procedures together: to provide a more robust pathway for you to follow. A good research design will provide the structure to facilitate the connectedness between the different elements of your project. In Figure 3.3, a range of different research designs are outlined. This is in no way a definitive list; some of the definitions are arguably influenced by our particular world view and are open to debate and discussion. It is also a very simplistic overview of each, and so if you intend to choose one or other then you will need to delve into the literature to find out more and to get the full detail of what each entails. However, they are included to represent the importance of this stage and what these pre-agreed designs can offer. In this book we have offered the idea that practitioner enquiry is a world view (Cochran-Smith and Lytle, 2009) and that you can choose any of these designs as a blueprint on which to base individual cycles or, in the case of action research, multiple cycles of enquiry on. As Symonds and Gorard (2010) argue, these designs are tools to be used and are not epistemologically predetermined. It is for you to decide if there is one that is useful for you in supporting your enquiry. The strength of these 'designs' is that they more or less provide a recipe which you can follow and be relatively assured of a strong coherence to your study and a shorthand through which you can explain to your audience what you intended. This of course does not stop outside agents acting on your research and changing it, but they do give a sound basis, and for a novice researcher particularly this can be reassuring.

- **Experimental**: impact of a standardised intervention with participants randomly allocated to control and experimental groups
- **Quasi-experimental**: like experimental but no control group, so pre and post test on the same group
- **Survey**: investigation of a population's characteristics, attitude, behaviour
- **Case study**: in-depth study of a clearly defined individual, group, location or 'thing' using one or more types of data
- **Observation**: watching what people/what happens (including ethnography)
- **Longitudinal**: engaging with the same subject multiple times over time
- **Secondary data analysis**: using data that already exists
- **Participatory**: involving your participants in the research
- **Action research**: a cyclical approach to improving practice through a process of research and reflection

FIGURE 3.3 Overview of research design types.

These predetermined research designs are useful, but we would place a health warning on their use. While they do provide a recipe to follow, they should not be considered as infallible or something to follow unquestioningly, particularly when applied to the messiness of real life. We encourage a sceptical standpoint and the courage to make changes to suit the context in which you are researching – just make sure you explain these decisions and their implications. This might mean playing with the ingredients within each recipe, merging recipes to create a hybrid or ad-libbing completely and coming up with your own recipe (Figure 3.4). For example, if you are researching in an early years setting with children with a range of verbal capabilities, then exploring the types of data that are developmentally and pedagogically appropriate will be essential, but that does not stop you, as long as you consider the implications, from doing a survey. Alternatively, if you are asking questions about the implementation of an intervention, but the sample size is small or true randomisation is not possible, an experimental design might still be possible but with some qualification of the impact of the associated decisions. Merging research designs might also be appropriate; for example, tracking a target group of children through their experiences of one aspect of the curriculum might be longitudinal, but the focus on a specific group could also suggest case study would be useful. Again, you would need to be critical about which elements of each design you were taking, engaging with the theoretical standpoint as represented in the research textbooks and explaining what you are leaving behind, articulating how you have combined them as clearly as possible.

The main challenge to these designs comes from the fact they all originate from a traditional research model where the researcher is

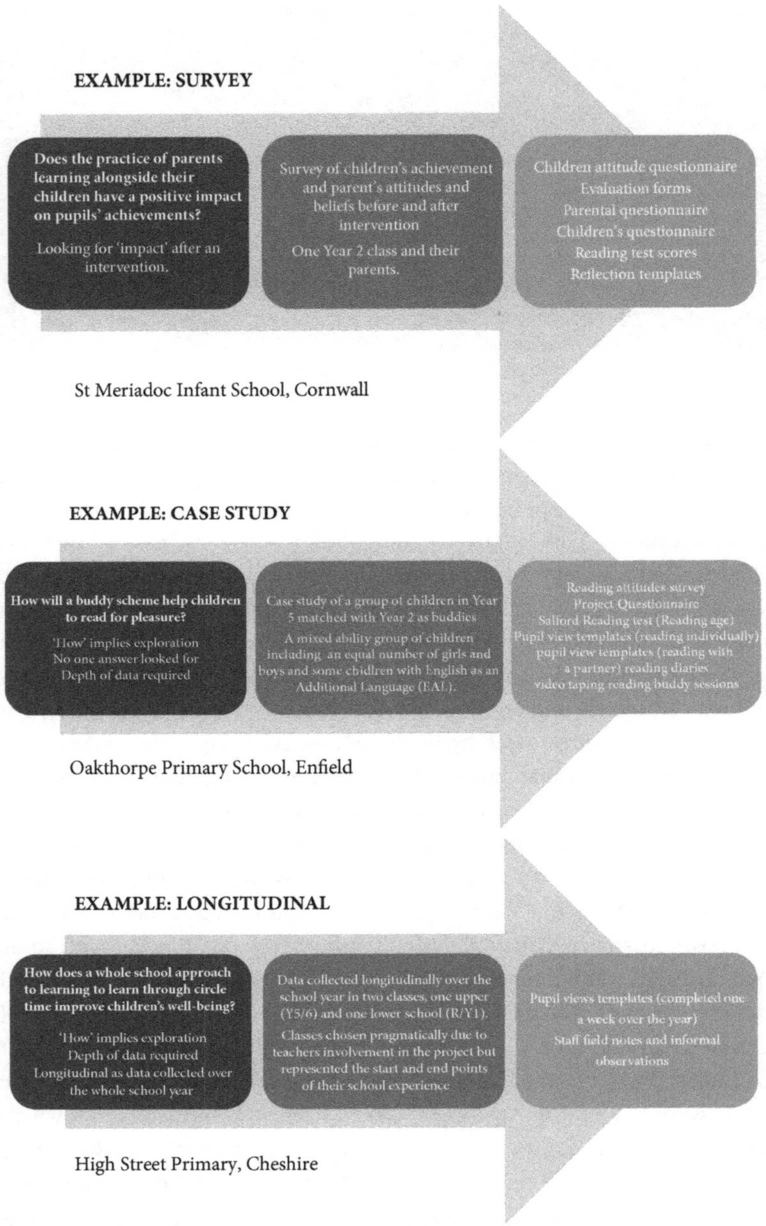

EXAMPLE: SURVEY

| Does the practice of parents learning alongside their children have a positive impact on pupils' achievements? Looking for 'impact' after an intervention. | Survey of children's achievement and parent's attitudes and beliefs before and after intervention One Year 2 class and their parents. | Children attitude questionnaire Evaluation forms Parental questionnaire Children's questionnaire Reading test scores Reflection templates |

St Meriadoc Infant School, Cornwall

EXAMPLE: CASE STUDY

| How will a buddy scheme help children to read for pleasure? 'How' implies exploration No one answer looked for Depth of data required | Case study of a group of children in Year 5 matched with Year 2 as buddies A mixed ability group of children including an equal number of girls and boys and some children with English as an Additional Language (EAL). | Reading attitudes survey Project Questionnaire Salford Reading test (Reading age) Pupil view templates (reading individually) pupil view templates (reading with a partner) reading diaries video taping reading buddy sessions |

Oakthorpe Primary School, Enfield

EXAMPLE: LONGITUDINAL

| How does a whole school approach to learning to learn through circle time improve children's well-being? 'How' implies exploration Depth of data required Longitudinal as data collected over the whole school year | Data collected longitudinally over the school year in two classes, one upper (Y5/6) and one lower school (R/Y1). Classes chosen pragmatically due to teachers involvement in the project but represented the start and end points of their school experience | Pupil views templates (completed one a week over the year) Staff field notes and informal observations |

High Street Primary, Cheshire

FIGURE 3.4 Some real-life examples of enquiry pathways using different research designs.

somewhat removed from practice. Of course, in the kind of research we are talking about this is not the case; the whole point is you are involved in what you are researching so that outcomes will contribute to your own professional learning and lead directly into your day-to-day practice (Hall, 2009). Therefore, for all these designs, there will need to be a certain amount of adaptation and flexibility applied to the advice given in the textbooks to fit the variation of practice. As a practitioner-researcher you will be engaged in both the research and practice; this means a closeness that can be seen as an advantage in regards to access and insight on the topic, but also, particularly in some designs, will mean compromises in regards to the recipe and ingredients used. You can choose to see this as problematic in impacting on the fidelity of implementation, or you can see these designs as tools to be used. This means for the application of these different designs, the role and positioning of the practitioner-researcher will be an important consideration. The extent to which you acknowledge any biases and make visible preconceived conflicts of interest will be essential. The narrative will vary over the process, depending on the research stage and the choices that you are needing to make. This process of reflection and critical engagement with the role that you as researcher play is called reflexivity, and we consider that it is central to research quality. We will come back to this later in this chapter when we look at positionality as well as in our discussions of quality in Chapter 4 and warrant in Chapter 5.

We see a range of dimensions on which flexibility of design could work and how far you are happy to push these dimensions will be up to you and your understanding of good evidence. The continuums presented in Figure 3.5 can be seen in theory as independent, but in the real-life application of research, they are likely to be interlinked. They act as a

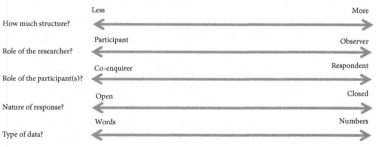

FIGURE 3.5 Research design continuums.

research balancing act impacted upon by your own levels of satisfaction that an effective answer to your question will be generated with particular sensitivity to the fit of your research to the real-life context under examination. For example, if you are going to undertake a survey on a large scale, targeting a large sample size, because you feel that the whole year group should be included, then to keep the data manageable, you will probably need to tighten the structure and close down the response from participants. So if your target was opinions, rather than doing interviews, a questionnaire may be more appropriate. Alternatively, if you are surveying attainment, then tests rather than self- or teacher assessments might be the pragmatic decision. Alternatively, if you are going to focus on a sample of one or two individuals, then the nature of the data set can be more nuanced and complex with participants, maybe, given more space to respond to your prompt over a longer period of time or through a more sustained engagement, or they could have more of a participatory role in exploring the issue.

Of course, each of these decisions has repercussions. You need to question your own beliefs and values regarding these continuums; the extent to which you are happy that closing data down provides an accurate view of the practice you want to explore, or the extent to which examination of detailed complexity facilitates generalisation of findings to wider groups. It depends on what you want to know and how you know when you have found an answer. There will always be compromises and we do not think there will ever be a definitive research method or tool; recognising the affordances and constraints of any design or tool is the first step. Of course, one solution is to collect more than one type of data and therefore to balance the faults of one tool with the advantages of another: a mixed method approach (Johnson and Onwuegbuzie, 2004).

Once you have decided on your design, then there are a wide variety of data collection tools that you can use within its structure. Some will have better fit with your design than others, and the research literature will provide a guide to this; however, be guided by your knowledge of practice and your respondents and argue your decisions clearly. The tools that we provide in Chapter 4 are given as a starting point, but as with design, they are not a definitive list, and so we encourage you to be creative while assessing their affordances and constraints in regards to what you want to know. There is a productive bridge between what is considered methodological and what is pedagogical that is worthy of exploration (Wall 2018). We believe that practice is full of tools that are tailor-made to the contexts in which you work and are therefore enquiring into; the extent to which they can be turned to a research intent is a useful avenue for consideration. A number of the tools we present in this book have their origins in our backgrounds as school and university teachers – we know they are effective at drawing out students' thinking in different ways and so have turned their use to research – we have just started considering the evidence they generate as research evidence rather than, or as well as, pedagogic. Not only does this provide new ways of seeing practice with a research lens, but it also is a pragmatic solution to keeping the workload from doing enquiry more manageable. The greater the overlap between your research and your practice, the more manageable it will be.

In the same way, we have suggested different research designs can be adapted in regards to the six continuums in Figure 3.5, tools and how they are analysed can be treated similarly. For example, a tool such as diamond ranking (Tool 6 in Chapter 4) can be used to elicit detailed thinking around a topic with transcripts of verbal explanation taken forwards to analysis or, if just the ranking is used, they can be considered a relatively closed and quantitative measure that can be used with a larger sample. Similarly, data from social media can be counted (as in how many retweets or likes for a tweet; how many downloads/reads of a blog) or can be analysed as more discursive data (what are people saying about; what is the response to …). A more robust challenge to our assertion might be data such as standardised questionnaires or attainment data analysed to produced effect sizes, and while we would not encourage making changes to the way the data is collected – these tools' reliability and validity is tied up in their design – how you use the data can be played with. There are no rules, for example, that you have to keep the data to yourself, and so what would happen if, at analysis stage, you shared the process or even got the participants involved, and how would this impact on a deeper understanding of practice? As before you need to consider your intent in regards to your research questions and the kind of answer that you will be satisfied with. All the decisions made have advantages and disadvantages that you need to tune in to and discuss, but considering tools in this way does provide you with options that might not be immediately obvious if some of the research theory is to be believed. The detailed exemplification of a range of tools in Chapter 4 will show the range of ways different techniques can be used and the opportunity to adapt each to your own intent.

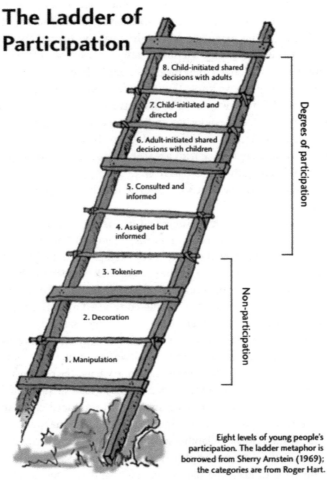

The Ladder of Participation

8. Child-initiated shared decisions with adults

7. Child-initiated and directed

6. Adult-initiated shared decisions with children

5. Consulted and informed

4. Assigned but informed

Degrees of participation

3. Tokenism

2. Decoration

1. Manipulation

Non-participation

Eight levels of young people's participation. The ladder metaphor is borrowed from Sherry Arnstein (1969); the categories are from Roger Hart.

FIGURE 3.6 Hart's ladder of participation (replicated from Hart, 1992).

One of the continuums worthy of spending a bit more time on is the role of the participants. Participatory research is on the increase in social sciences generally (Cook-Sather, 2014). By participation we mean a spectrum of activity, whereby the participants are given an increasingly significant role in making decisions about and generating understandings from the research process. A lot of this work has involved on the participation of children or individuals who are less powerful in society, but the analogy works with all participants in research. Hart's (1992) ladder of participation gives different levels of participation that might be observed in practice, and we can see a use for this in considering involvement in research (see Figure 3.6). We do not think there is a need, if participation is something that you want to engage with, to operate for the whole of the research process at level 8 or indeed in one of the levels attributed a degree of participation. If we consider the four stages of the research process outlined in Figure 3.7, then you may include a degree of participation at any or all of these stages. So, for example, you might ask children who have experienced the care system to decide on the right enquiry questions to improve transitions between care facilities; at data collection stage, you could involve students in interviewing other students as a way of getting around adult–child power dynamics, or at analysis stage you could ask your undergraduate statistics module to engage with your data as a real-life example or share the analysis of test scores across schools with teachers to explore their interpretations. Not all of these examples are manifesting at Hart's level 8, but if done well, they can certainly be located within the upper half of the ladder. We do think, however, that to say your research is participatory, in regards to design, then it is probably necessary to have at least two out of the four stages include a significant level of participation.

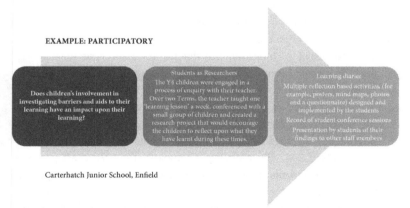

FIGURE 3.7 An example of an enquiry pathway using participatory approaches.

One of the challenges we face is considering what this continuum of participation looks like when the researcher is also an active participant. In Figure 3.8, this can be seen as a convergence between the role of the participant and the role of the researcher, with both moving towards the active end, but in such a way that they are intertwined and mutually responsive. We don't think the explanation above of the potentially active role that the researched can take becomes invalid, but rather it is complicated by the researcher also taking an active position in the context being researched. The movement up and down Hart's ladder might be similar for both the researcher and the researched, but it might also be different. The task is to recognise the differing positions at different times and the relationships that each has to the other and how they are impacting on each other. This is fundamentally about the positioning of the researcher in relation to his participants.

Positioning of the practitioner-researcher

So far in this chapter we have spent a lot of time expanding the limits of research and suggesting that at all stages there are multiple possible options. Before we start to exemplify different design pathways, it is important to focus on the positioning of the practitioner-researcher in research as a practice. We hope it has been clear up to this point that the big caveat around all this choice is the reflective orientation that we encourage around making these decisions and the transparency needed when you talk about the alternatives open to you and the potential impacts of what you choose. This means identifying for yourself what is making some choices more or less likely, from a personal, professional or epistemological perspective, and the influence of the inevitable bias that this might exert on the answers you find. To a large extent, this is your underpinning values and beliefs, your world view. But it could also reflect the nature of the context in which your research is based and your role within that context. How you manage this and make the enquiry process valid and transparent is reflexivity.

The theory of reflexivity combines elements of positionality and subjectivity (Dean, 2017). Positionality encompasses the researchers' position in relation to participants and also to the research setting – issues of power, identity and intent, and unpicking the potential affordances and constraints they have on the research process, at all stages. So, for example, if you are a programme leader exploring the impact of that programme on student outcomes, how does your role impact the nature of students' and colleagues' engagement with research tasks that you set? How would you navigate the process to support a more valid response and how do you understand what is at risk for you and for your participants as a result? Subjectivity focuses on the role of the individual and their interactions with society and the surrounding world, so considering how what you do, whether research or practice, influences and affects the nature of the enquiry. In the example above, this would mean thinking about how you could communicate the nature of the enquiry and organise the process in such a way that it doesn't put undue pressure on those students and colleagues who participate and maybe involves them in such a way that they have a vested interest in the outcomes of the research. Both elements can be seen to be highly significant within a practitioner research frame and both can be considered in relation to your professional practice as well as your research practice.

What we consider good practitioner enquiry practice would be characterised by a critical examination of these dual concepts as transparently as possible, in such a way as to ensure that the reader or consumer of your research (and this could be yourself) has clear understanding of how your own standpoint could influence the research at the start of the project, then, as you make selections on protocol throughout, how you have engaged with the different aspects of the decision–making, and finally how those decisions have knock-on influences to your final conclusions and therefore any resulting understandings about your practice.

Because of its nature, reflexivity is not a simple process to be contained at the start of the research process but rather should be a narrative or monologue of reflective and strategic thinking (metacognitive awareness) that influences the nature of the research undertaken and your resulting interpretations. As such, it is a good practice to incorporate any marker of quality that should be foregrounded in your head as a practitioner-researcher. Questions that prompt a reflexive approach could include:

- Why did I do that?
- How did I understand that?
- How did my role influence … ?
- How did that tool impact on … ?
- What concerns do I have about the way that … ?
- Did I make any assumptions about … ?
- How best should I communicate … ?

One thing you might like to consider when identifying your own biases is to think about how you view data. A scenario we have given previously (Baumfield et al., 2012), and it is worth reiterating here, is considering the type of data that you instinctively privilege. If you have a student entering your class, do you pay most attention to their previous test scores as an indicator of their ability or will you listen to different people's narrative assessments? In reality it is probably a bit of both and you will probably validate or triangulate in some way with your own assessment, however, thinking about what evidence you pay attention to, how you use that data to inform your practice and why, is useful in thinking about your own belief set in regards to research approaches.

Another way-in is to think about how you view your participants and your role in relation to them. It is useful to consider questions such as to what extent do you feel *you* should have a voice, personally and professionally, and how do you feel this voice is best communicated and in what circles? Linked to this, to what extent do you feel your students and colleagues should have a voice and what is your potential role in facilitating that voice? To provide a more concrete example, how do you feel about initiatives that give seven-year-olds active roles in decision-making about their schools? How active have you been in staff–student committees or in similar initiatives throughout your career? This may feel a bit loaded, but we are not advocating a point of view; it is thinking through questions like these that helps to identify your own positioning and the beliefs and values that underpin it. You might be someone who has a political engagement with the concept of voice and as such believe that critical to your role as an educator is giving students the knowledge and understanding to voice their own views; or you might be more aligned with a psychological perspective that believes voice should be developmentally considered and appropriately facilitated with adults having a enabling role; or it might be a view that isolates certain things as no-go areas for students to have a say on: we have met many teachers for whom issues of teaching and curriculum are no-go area for any consultation process as it is outside their remit and understanding. This is not about judging your stance but supporting a reflective process that enables a personal engagement with issues that will be important in any professional enquiry process.

Reflexivity is ultimately about maintaining a standpoint that is slightly off balance and embracing the dissonance that is inherent in doing so. It means accepting there is no perfect answer to your enquiry as a whole, or even to each of the minor decisions that you have needed to consider on the way through the process, and being constantly aware of the dynamic and facilitatory relationship between professional and research practice. The key is about communicating this state of not knowing as an integral part to better understanding your enquiry outcomes, not making too many assumptions and ensuring that you step out of the 'doing' regularly to reflect on what is working and what is not. It should be appropriately challenging of self, of your assumptions, biases and values.

'If ... then': Potential design pathways for questions

At this point, then, you the practitioner-researcher have a 'good enough' sense of your intent in carrying out the inquiry. You enter the research design stage and promptly feel overwhelmed by choice and possibility. We began in our work with teachers to counter this overwhelmed feeling by talking about research methods as a 'sweet shop', encouraging the autonomy of a 'pick and mix' approach while cautioning against making oneself sick. However, this implies that practitioner enquiry is a discrete activity, unconnected with the myriad demands of practice. For many practitioner-researchers, the design phase is like going to a very large and unfamiliar supermarket with no list. There are all sorts of things I know from experience that I need for basic survival in my daily life – loo paper, breakfast cereal, gin – and there are many things that will catch my eye as I wander the aisles, unfamiliar ingredients and new products that seem to promise solutions to intractable problems. It is possible, indeed probable, that I will lose sight of what I came in for – the ingredients for a particular meal – and that I will leave with an incoherent jumble of basics, novelties and only some of my key ingredients.

This section is both a partial solution to this problem and an attempt to reconcile all of us to the inevitable. We will present a number of potential exemplar pathways to a family of questions around a core topic area to demonstrate how important it is to recognise and hold onto intent in order to produce a coherent and effective research design. We will show the potential and limitations of designs that are predominantly qualitative and quantitative as well as those that take a mixed methods approach highlighting the implications for particular assumptions or strategic decisions and demonstrating the range of options available. Nevertheless, these are not fool-proof shopping lists, nor should they be. Practitioner

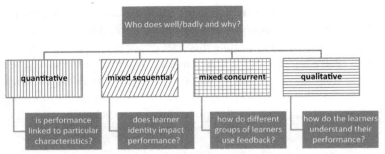

FIGURE 3.8 Family of questions descending from 'who does well/badly and why?'

enquiry takes place in the real world, where the shop has run out of broccoli, where the number and dietary requirements of diners are subject to change and where the right of the cook to alter the recipe as he goes is sometimes the only thing that keeps him in the kitchen (Barnes, 2003).

The scenarios will be presented as full narratives in the Appendix so that you can follow each story; here we will focus on the choices being made and how that is managed reflexively.

The family of questions are descended from that perennial favourite 'Who does well/badly and why?' and the main problem is one of choice. It is not possible to simultaneously address all of the questions offered in this example, not just because of time and resources but also in terms of focus. It is therefore necessary to choose one approach, with the knowledge that, for the moment at least, we are depriving ourselves of the other options. The mixed designs appear to offer more 'having of cake and eating it', but this is not the case – the additional effort of interrelating the different kinds of data, together with the smaller portions of each means that this is not a superior option, just a different one.

An exploratory quantitative approach: Is performance linked to particular characteristics?

We are familiar with discourses about particular characteristics and academic performance, whether driven by a particular set of beliefs or as a response to perceived trends in the data (these are unpicked in a very accessible and rigorous way on the Education Datalab blog https://

educationdatalab.org.uk/). These hypotheses can be tested quantitatively using population studies: large data sets, distributed across a range of contexts subjected to correlational analysis using appropriate statistical tests. A quantitative practitioner inquiry is unlikely to have the data set to establish correlation, and it isn't looking to theoretically engage with causal relationships; it is instead about exploration and accurate mapping of what is going on.

The first stage is collection and cleaning of the data available to address the question: who is in the research population and what do we know about them? Table 3.1 introduces us to class 9G and to a range of things that are known about them. For the purposes of this worked example, we have simplified reality – our genders are limited to male and female, our ethnicity categories to the aggregates used by the UK statistics office rather than more diverse groups, and our indicators of deprivation by free school meals (FSM) and additional needs by school action, school action plus and special education needs (SA/SAP/SEN) are very broad. Even so, we have small numbers in an individual class – only two people with identified additional needs, only four with Asian heritage, six eligible for FSM. This emphasises the underlying problems of apparently simple categorisation. Individuals experience their lives intersectionally; meanings are constructed locally (Jones, 2015). This does not mean that this information is useless but nor is it definitive. We may be able to identify patterns and then try to test them out.

Nevertheless, looking at this group, you might begin to create narratives for particular individuals: Ian is young for the year, from a white working-class background and has some identified support need; Lara has English as an additional language (EAL). Each of us will draw from our own experiences *as a* learner and of working *with* learners, and it is difficult, if not impossible, to approach without some expectations. So we note them alongside the hypotheses generated by other scholars from their experience and remain curious about whether this group of learners will show patterns that conform to these ideas.

In this case, Jo is new to the school and to the class. She scans the class data, prioritises a conversation with the special needs coordinator about what she needs to consider to support Bobby and Ian and wonders how different the dynamics in the class will be from her last post, a small suburban school with a middle-class catchment and mainly white British students.

Although Year 9 might be considered a relatively low-stress cohort to teach as they are still two years away from their public exams, Jo feels that

TABLE 3.1 An overview of Class 9G

Class 9G	Gender	Month born	Ethnicity	FSM	EAL	SEN/SA/ SAP
Adam	M	January	W	yes		
Abby	F	September	W			
Bobby	M	November	M			yes
Bella	F	July	W			
Colin	M	October	W			
Carrie	F	August	W			
Donald	M	March	W			
Debbie	F	December	B	yes		
Euan	M	July	W			
Ellie	F	December	W			
Fred	M	September	A			
Flora	F	May	W			
Grant	M	July	B			
Georgia	F	March	W	yes		
Harry	M	February	W			
Helen	F	November	A			
Ian	M	August	W	yes		yes
India	F	October	W			
Jordan	M	June	B			
Juliet	F	January	W	yes		
Karim	M	June	A			
Kelly	F	April	M			
Louis	M	September	M			
Lara	F	February	W		Polish	
Mohamed	M	October	A			
Maria	F	March	W			
Niall	M	February	W	yes		
Natalie	F	May	W			

Table 3.1: Characteristics of class 9G

Categories for ethnicity
W – White (all groups)
M – Mixed multiple ethnicity (all groups)
A – Asian (all groups)
B – Black (all groups)
O – Other
EAL – English as an additional language
SEN – Statement of special educational needs
SA/SAP – Special needs recognised by plan of school action or school action plus

she has something to prove as a new member of staff. It is important to demonstrate that she is competent, and one of the key indicators of this is her students' performance in assessment. Therefore, although she is also interested in classroom interaction and whether gender and culture have an impact on participation, her focus in this first year is on understanding her students' performance and her own. In other words, she is choosing to engage with two elements – the 'good enough' teacher and students – of the hypothesis explored in Chapter 2, and in order to do this, she needs to engage with the naturally occurring assessment data. Jo has no power over the kind of assessment used to test her students, so whether or not she thinks it is a 'good enough' measure, it doesn't make pragmatic sense to make the assessment itself the focus of the first round of her enquiry. As we'll see in the full narrative (Appendix 1), these two elements contain more than enough complexity to be getting on with.

Class 9G are studying geography and have undertaken a mid-module assessment using a past exam paper with a mixture of multiple choice questions designed to test recall of facts, short answer questions designed to test basic understanding of concepts, and extended answer questions designed to test the ability to link concepts in an argument. This assessment is repeated at the end of the module with another past exam paper. Figures 3.9 and 3.10 reveal that there are relative normal distributions of grades across the class, with some indication of general improvement (ten students' grades improved). Jo now has a number of key reflexive questions to consider:

1　Jo now has a number of key reflexive questions to consider: Does this improvement satisfy her, and does it chime with her sense of 'good enough'?

2　Will it have weight with her head of department and other authority figures?

3　If the answer to both of these questions is yes, is the enquiry complete?

4　If the answer to one or more of these is no (or ambiguous), what *additional* analysis of the *existing* data could be done to remedy this?

The use of italic formatting is our unsubtle signposting of a problem in research: that we are rarely prompted into a more fine-grained analysis of data. This may be because of the fixation of belief from both a positive and a negative perspective: Jo's headline data that she appears to be 'good

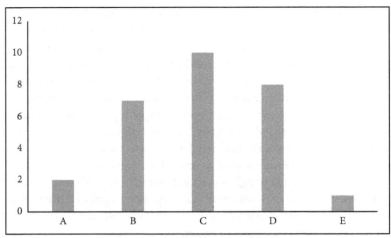

FIGURE 3.9 Class 9G – Geography mid-module grades.

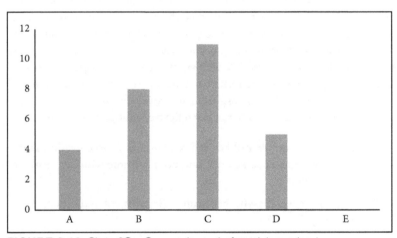

FIGURE 3.10 Class 9G – Geography end-of-module grades.

enough' may be enough to soothe her unease at working in this new school, or her instinctive recoil from negative feedback could lead her to shut down the investigation, at least temporarily. This is a perfectly natural response to negative feedback and data; it is more unusual if it doesn't happen. It's really important to demystify and normalise this reaction (common to all learners of all ages and stages) and to make compassionate space for it, giving permission to everyone to be disappointed and hurt when things are 'wrong'. The idea that we will carry on regardless is the main fallacy, and the only significant problem that arises from 'feedback recoil' is when the shame at having recoiled at all stops us from recommencing learning. That is why there are a lot of papers in file drawers, half completed projects in cupboards and uncomfortable shifts in conversation when we discuss research.

Jo, being fairly typical of teachers in general, is not completely satisfied by the outcome. Her initial broad performance questions about herself and the students become more focused. 'Am I "good enough" for every student?' and 'Is each student performing to their individual potential?' are still addressing the core elements of the hypothesis but with more detail and nuance. She realises that there are a number of things she can do, beginning with a survey of the data to look for patterns: this reveals variations in rate of progress across the class. Again, this might satisfy Jo as fitting in with her view of the world or she might be moved to ask if there are ways to understand the patterns – explanations from authority (more experienced teachers, policy or research literature) or from a priori reasoning – and then to test these explanations for fit on her class. At this stage Jo is still assessing the data by eye. Technological advances mean that it is possible to run all the data through a statistics package, to try all the possible combinations and tests and to see if anything pops up. This 'data fishing' or 'data dredging' should be alien to all inquiry (there's an excellent discussion of this on the Bad Science blog http://www. badscience.net/2006/11/just-show-me-the-data/), but we would argue that it is particularly inappropriate to practitioner research, since we don't want to have something (*anything!*) to say about our data in order to publish a paper on it; rather we are interested in what the data can tell us about the situation we're in, about *our* learners and *our* teaching. In the Appendix, you can follow her investigations of patterns, ipsative and cohort targets, gender and ethnicity and birth month as possible explanatory frames.

The summary Table 3.2 indicates both the limits of and the potential for this enquiry. In this round, Jo has partially addressed her questions and can be clear about the kind of evidence she has, while simultaneously recognising that she is generating more questions at every turn. Overall, her quantitative analysis has given her more information about her students than about her interaction with them, suggesting that she could make use of a mixed or qualitative design in the next cycle.

TABLE 3.2 *Summary of Class 9G*

What claims can be made?	What kind of evidence is this?	Questions answered?	New questions
Prior attainment is a pretty good predictor of future attainment	Quantitative measurement, widely recognised measures (*transparency, evocativeness*)	Do some characteristics correlate with attainment?	*Does the standard measure tell us everything we want to know about 9G's progress?*
Birth month is not a good predictor for this cohort The picture on gender and ethnicity is fuzzy	Limited to this cohort, challenges large data studies (*criticalness, empowerment*)		*If birth month is not a key indicator for this cohort, what might be? Can we dig deeper into intersectional experiences? (polyphony)*
Overall attainment is good and most learners make progress. However, it is unclear which stable grades indicate the need to intervene.	Variable depending on the view of progress and norms (*ontological assumptions*)	Where should we focus our attention to raise attainment?	*Are cohort and ipsative approaches mutually exclusive? What might we gain/lose from choosing one or trying to do both? (pragmatic quality)*

An exploratory qualitative approach: How do the learners understand their performance?

At City College, students in the first semester of their Business degree study three rather diverse modules:

- Introduction to Financial Management Systems, taught through lectures and practical workshops and assessed by a multiple choice and short answer exam paper;

- Business Models and Economics, taught through lectures and seminars and assessed by a piece of written coursework; and

- Introduction to Entrepreneurship, taught through collaborative group projects and assessed by portfolio.

All of the modules result in a percentage which is then interpreted against grade boundaries (Table 3.3).

TABLE 3.3 *Marking scheme at City College*

Raw score	Grade
Below 40%	Fail
40–49%	Third Class
50–59%	Lower Second Class (2:2)
60–69%	Upper Second Class (2:1)
70% and above	First Class

Staff acting as personal tutors have regular meetings with students to discuss their results and get together beforehand for an informal briefing as a team. Over coffee and biscuits, the theme of performance emerged as they recalled from previous years that students appear to be interpreting their grades very differently; some see a mark in the fifties as indicative of 'not being up to it', and others see the same mark as 'good – better than I thought I'd do'.

In theory, a 2:2 represents equivalent performance regardless of the module (or discipline) being studied. Studying the learning outcomes documents across subjects and institutions reveals that the descriptors used point to these performances being 'ok': not too many errors or omissions; a basic grasp of the key ideas; no flashes of brilliance or originality. On that basis, students' perceptions of a mark in the fifties as either triumph or disaster are incorrectly calibrated. However, the staff discussion reveals that students are not alone in this: the grading profile of each module is quite different (with the curve of portfolio marks being higher than coursework, for example) depending on the allocation of marks to tasks and the convergence of the assessment. Moreover, it emerges that staff have different ideas about what constitutes 'good enough' performance in the first semester: some are pinning their marks to expectations of what a first year might be able to do; others are looking at mastery of a subject that the students won't be taught again and will need for future modules.

One response to this might be for the staff to attempt to amend their practice into something more consistent, and indeed, this is what Greg suggested, arguing that it is not fair to students that assessment is so variable. Alex agreed about the lack of fairness but said she thought it unlikely that being more prescriptive about marking and feedback would help; instead it might make offering diverse learning experiences more difficult, and how would that be fair to the student body? At this stage, Mohammed pointed out that even if the staff were all in agreement, they still didn't know enough about what the students were experiencing: 'We need more detail!'.

With very little time before the meetings were due to happen, Greg and Mohammed designed a mediated interview (Table 3.4 shows the artefact shared in advance of the interview) to reveal experience naturalistically without too many preconceptions of what that experience might be or how it might be framed. The interview is kept simple and structured, so that the focus of the research – the grades – forms the basis for a free ranging conversation between the student and the interviewer about how they understood the learning experience, the assessment and their own performance. Only the opening gambit 'What do you think about these?' is fixed, and the interviewee then directs the course of the conversation. There is a thirty-minute time limit agreed in advance to make the experience less daunting for the student and the quantity of data less daunting for the staff.

All 200 students are invited to take part in the project, which is presented to them as an opportunity within the tutorial to understand their performance better. They are also offered the option to take part in focus groups after the interviews. Staff find that student engagement with

TABLE 3.4 *City College: Example of grade summary artefact for the mediated tutorial interview*

Student	Intro to Finance Management	Business Models and Economics	Intro to Entrepreneurship	Semester average
Bob Jones	65	52	58	58
We're going to ask	What do you think about these?			
The interview could cover	You will decide how the conversation goes and it is most helpful if you bring your own ideas. If you're not sure how to begin, you could use the topics below and say as much or as little as you like.			

- Your experience on the modules
- Your experience of the assessments
- What you think the grades tell us about
  - what you can do
  - how you have done and
  - how you will do
- Your thoughts and/or feelings about
  - developing business knowledge and skills
  - developing graduate knowledge and skills
- Are the grades fair?

the artefact varies considerably: some are apparently seeing it for the first time in the tutorial, some have clearly given it some thought and a small number have produced written responses to each question. Staff use of the artefact is also idiosyncratic, some 'forget' to use it, others refer to it briefly, some make it the centrepiece of the tutorial, and a subset of these insist that students respond to all of the questions. This provides Greg and Mohammed with some problems when considering the data, which are included with the analysis process in the narrative in the Appendix. The research team conducted a basic content analysis (Table 3.5) which enabled them to start building a map of the responses.

Once the categories are clear and agreed, it becomes possible to group responses from different interviewees under these headings (Table 3.5), both to build up a picture and, simultaneously, to test whether the categories are good enough (Saldana, 2013) and to merge or split them as needed. This is where reflexivity is important since it is easy to get carried away with finding what you hoped for in the analysis phase. This is where counting becomes particularly critical: not because 'numbers rule' and a category is only valid because enough bits of data fit into it but because the reader needs to know which categories are included because they are common and which because they are unusual. You'd want to include both in any

TABLE 3.5 *Content analysis with meaning attributed*

	Intro to Finance Management	Business Models and Economics	Intro to Entrepreneurship	Semester average	Labels
Participant #1	45	58	62	55	
	I was *really upset* when I saw the mark for Finance, I felt it had				Emotion, negative
	dragged down my average although I still got a 2.2. Actually what				Impact on overall grade
	really upset me is that I really *thought I had understood what was*				Emotion, negative
	required of me on this degree, I got the theory on Models and our				Learning, mastery
	firm in the Entrepreneur module came up with some really cool				
	ideas. The 45 *makes me feel like I can't do the basics*, that perhaps				Motivation, confidence
	I'm not suited to this at all.				

holistic account, as they are both part of the narrative. Qualitative accounts that use 'some' or 'many' in place of counts are missing the opportunity to present their theory building transparently. Even with this reflexivity and analysis, Mohammed, Greg and Alex still weren't sure whether the themes they'd identified were a good representation of the students' experiences as a whole or, more crucially, what the students found most important.

A pool of thirty volunteers are available for the focus groups but as time is tight, twelve are selected to represent the various broad levels of performance, and a diamond hierarchy tool is used to rank statements from the interviews (stripped of identifying details, Figure 3.11) with the binary 'reflects my experience/does not reflect my experience'. Preliminary findings from the focus groups are then shared with all 200 students via a document on the Virtual Learning Environment (VLE) for comment (full details in the Appendix).

It's really useful when using a diamond or other visual construction method to take images (still or video) in progress as well as of the finished artefact as this gives greater insight into the thought processes of the respondents (see Figures 3.12 and 3.13).

From this, the team were able to evaluate their students' experience and to consider their next steps, detailed in the summary Table 3.6. Although staff were troubled and moved by students' distress, they found that their analysis discussions began to coalesce around the problem of mismatch between the learning and assessment experiences. This, they felt, was a practical problem that they could engage with, hoping that this would have the secondary effect of reducing students' confusion and unhappiness.

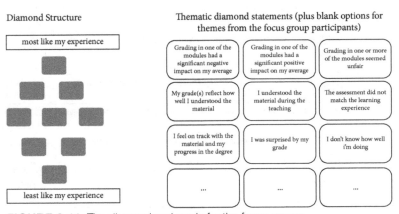

FIGURE 3.11 The diamond and cards for the focus groups.

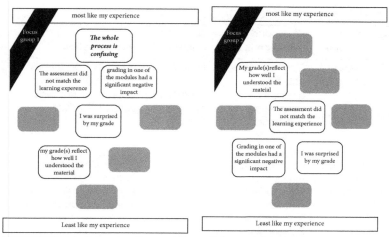

FIGURE 3.12 Exemplar diamond 9s partially completed.

Teanded to appear closer to `most like my experience´

I understood the material during the teaching	The assessment did not match the learning experience

Teanded to appear in the middle

I was surprised by my grade	I don't know how well I'm doing

Teanded to appear closer to `least like my experience´

Grading in one or more of the modules seemed unfair	My grade(s) reflect how well I understood he material	I feel on track with the material and my progress in the degree

Appeared in multiple places

Grading in one of the modules had a significant negative impact on my average	Grading in one of the modules had a significant positive impact on my average

FIGURE 3.13 Key trends in the diamond 9 analysis.

TABLE 3.6 *Summary of City College example*

What claims can be made?	What kind of evidence is this?	Questions answered?	New questions
High levels of distress	Rich qualitative data from a subset of volunteer students (*subjective adequacy, authenticity*)	How do students interpret their grades?	*Is this level of distress tolerable for staff and students? (subjective adequacy, ethics)*
Confusion about assessment among lower-attaining students	Qualitative data triangulated with student characteristics (*emplotment, polyphony*)		*Are we doing enough to develop procedural autonomy? (history of action, empowerment)*
Global interpretations of self from single assessments	Rich qualitative data from a subset of volunteer students (*evocativeness*)		*Are our students particularly fragile? (pragmatic quality)*
Tutor reflection on lack of match between learning experience and assessment		What action can we take to make an impact on the student experience?	*Need for clearer, more personalised and frequent guidance to students – how to achieve this? And/or A critical re-examination of how we teach and what we assess, what is the underlying rationale, pedagogy or convenience?*

A mixed sequential approach: Does learner identity impact performance?

Sandview Primary School serves a mainly working-class community in a large city and is deemed to be 'satisfactory' by the inspectorate in terms of the achievements of its learners when they leave to enter secondary school. Of course, the meaning of 'satisfactory' has slipped during the Ofsted inspection era from the everyday sense of 'fine' to something less positive, while 'good' is often parsed as 'just about good enough' and 'outstanding' as something all schools should aim for. How something can stand out from others if they are all meeting the same high standard is not something that is unpacked.

The head teacher and staff are not satisfied with 'satisfactory': not as part of this 'culture of continuous improvement' and not as a description of their practice. Everyone agrees that they can 'do better', although the students' performance on external tests broadly maps onto national patterns and it is not clear where this 'better' needs to happen. Staff meetings are devoted to discussions, and from these emerge two areas of concern:

- The impression that 'value added' from school entry to age seven is above the average but this levels off between seven and eleven.

- The sense that the confidence and curiosity of the children decline over time and that they are heading into secondary school with rather fixed ideas about their abilities.

This is a difficult conversation, as it appears to be placing responsibility on the teachers who work with the older children, and the head teacher, Ray, becomes concerned that his staff may 'split'. As the tone of the staff meeting hardens, he turns to his deputy, Sue. Sue cuts to the heart of the issue: 'We're all afraid that it might be our fault, but we actually don't know exactly what's going on. It might turn out to be one person or a group of us. It might be lots of factors together. We'll never find out if we don't take the risk of looking closely, so can we agree to be kind and supportive?' Ray chips in: 'Nobody will be fired. We'll all learn something.' Whether or not everyone is completely convinced by this, it does alter the frame for the research that follows.

The first phase is to take that close look that Sue proposed: retrospectively analysing the school's performance data to check whether the 'levelling off' is happening and if so, where. This requires a more fine-grained analysis than simple cohort results and is described in detail in the Appendix. Only 60 per cent of the children tested at eleven were pupils at Sandview at seven, and trajectories were clearly worse for pupils who joined the school later. The second phase of the research could have been 'what's wrong with our incoming pupils?' but, bearing in mind the commitment to learning rather than assigning blame, instead staff choose to focus on 'what do we do well with our youngest pupils?' This appreciative action enquiry has an iterative developmental structure:

1   *Collaborative information gathering*: Colleagues who teach the older children take turns to be participant-observers in the younger learner's classrooms. All the observation notes are typed up and shared.

2   *First-level analysis – shared meaning making*: At a staff meeting where mind maps of key ideas and themes are created. Staff focus on the way in which younger learners (supported by their teachers and independently) spend time setting goals and articulating their awareness of *what, why and how well* they are doing.

3   *Second-level analysis – generating a theory*: From this, the staff develop a theory of change based on growth mind sets and mastery orientation (Dweck, 2017) that might explain the impact of the early years culture and the differences between the groups of learners.

4   *Intervention to test the theory*: Staff devise an intervention programme for themselves in which they track the number and content of their metacognitive conversations with older pupils. The focus is on changing culture through staff modelling, so there are no external targets; rather staff become curious about the *what, why and how well* of their conversational practice. The hypothesis is that by directing attention to this area, staff practice will become more explicit and purposeful and that this will encourage mastery orientation in the learners.

5   *Evaluation of the intervention – exploring evidence of impact*: In addition to the staff's observations and day-to-day conversations with children, the staff chose to use the children's pre- and post-scores on the SDQI, a psychometric test of self-concept (O'Mara et al., 2006).

6   *Evaluation of the theory of change – questioning the explanatory power of the theory*: The staff 'loop back' to their first theory-building meeting in the light of the evidence they have generated and add strength and complexity to their working model of how children understand their learning.

The difference between the map and the journey is explored in detail in the Appendix. By keeping the ideal narrative and the actual events in their awareness, Sandview staff were able to engage with *the history of action* and *emplotment* to demonstrate *transparency*. However, the

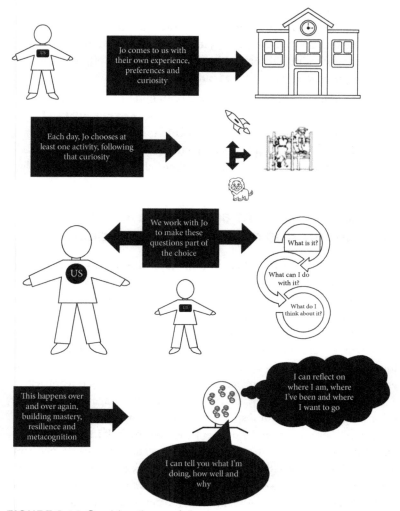

FIGURE 3.14 Sandview theory of change.

process threw up multiple problems in which *pragmatic* and *critical qualities* seemed at odds with one another, with negative impacts on staff *empowerment*. This is often the point at which enquiry projects wither and die, although the commitment of the staff to their theory of change (Figure 3.14) seems to have been a key protective factor.

Two elements that supported the Sandview project and enabled it to tolerate the awkwardness, confusion and uncertainty were the following:

- The *ontologic and epistemologic assumptions:* the staff knew that they didn't understand that it wasn't a simple problem and that they were exploring their way towards a new, partial understanding. Testing and proof are a long way off, so it is safer to propose ideas and raise issues.

- The *subjective adequacy:* there was an underlying commitment to individual learner's intrinsic knowledge and potential and to multiple pathways to achievement. As the staff came to see themselves more explicitly in the role of learners, they were able to grant the same permissions to themselves that they offer to the children.

A mixed concurrent approach: How do different groups of learners use feedback?

At Mooredge Sixth Form College, all A-level history students use the e-learning portal to submit their essays. The tutors in the department mark the work using a rubric derived from the mark schemes of the exam board which is intended to allow the students to see at a glance where they have met, exceeded or fallen short of specific aspects. The rubric gives them a score and there is also an open-text box for the tutor to leave formative comments. Once work has been marked, students receive an email, containing their score and inviting them to view their feedback.

The IT support team have recently published the usage reports for the e-learning portal. Student responses to the email appear to fall into four categories. Approximately 20 per cent click on the link in the email and view their feedback within twelve hours of receipt. Another 35 per cent access their feedback, either through the direct link or by logging on to the portal within seventy-two hours. Of the 45 per cent who have not accessed the feedback at this point, more than half (25 per cent of the student body) will not have read the feedback after one month (Figure 3.15).

The tutor team are quite significantly divided in their formulation of the problem. One group, led by Sam, believe that encouraging students to read the feedback through a combined 'push-pull' approach will bring the numbers up across the cohort; the other group, led by Anna, are concerned that the students not accessing the feedback might be the ones that need it most and who might be least likely to respond to a general intervention. Sam's group are working to Hypothesis A, in which the feedback system and the modes of communication are assumed to

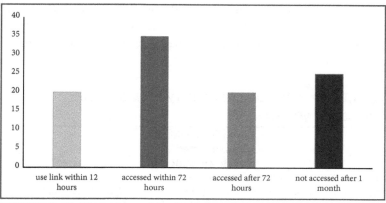

FIGURE 3.15 Student use of feedback (baseline).

be 'good enough' and therefore the focus is on the students. In contrast, Anna's group are working to Hypothesis B, in which nothing is assumed to be 'good enough' and all aspects of the system and all actors within it are potential foci for the enquiry. This difference in positioning could have led to conflict in which one hypothesis triumphed over another or an unsatisfactory compromise in which the essence of each enquiry is diluted by the incompatible elements of the other. Fortunately, the tutor team had recently had a very successful and enjoyable development day looking at historiography, where they reconnected with their disciplinary beliefs in the importance of separate perspectives on key events.

The concurrent design evolved therefore as a purposeful division of effort: both groups use the usage reports as their shared data and then take separate but complementary research routes (Figure 3.16). The

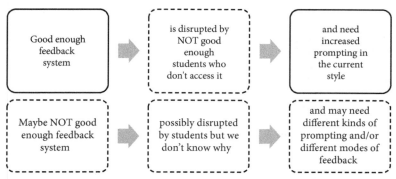

FIGURE 3.16 Formulating hypotheses at Mooredge.

relative simplicity of Hypothesis A and the proposed intervention meant that it was suited to a whole cohort design, while the complexity of Hypothesis B was better suited to a smaller group and a more iterative and fluid design (Table 3.7).

TABLE 3.7 *The complementary routes of the Mooredge enquiries*

Route A: Transparency and incentives (whole cohort)	Route B: Individual responses and narratives (subgroup of students who didn't/still don't access feedback)	Hypothesis being tested
Week 1: Students are reminded in classes that the e-learning portal tracks their use and that staff are aware that some people wait to access the feedback or don't access it at all. The graphs (as shown in fig 3.15) are posted on the portal.		*If students were aware we were checking, they would pick up their feedback in significantly greater numbers.*
Week 2: Usage data checked and shared with students		
Week 3: All students who still haven't accessed feedback sent reminder email.		*Personalised reminder will be more motivating.*
Week 4: Usage data checked and shared with students		
Week 5: Personal tutors use regular meetings to enquire about using feedback. All students are asked whether they find the emails helpful. Students who didn't use feedback in the first set of usage data are asked what has changed. Students who are still not using the feedback are asked about this.		*We don't fully understand the reasons why students do or don't access feedback.*
Week 6: Usage data checked and shared with students		

Week 7: Staff merge the marks database with the usage database.	Staff come together to analyse the conversations they have had with students.	*A1: Higher-performing students are the ones most likely to access feedback, lower-performing students the least.* *A2: Students who access feedback most will show learning gains.* *B1: Students don't access feedback because they don't want to hear it.* *B2: Students don't access feedback because they don't think it will help them.*
Week 8: Usage data checked and shared with students		
Week 9: Both groups come together to share their data and explore what has been learned		

The detailed analysis of the data is in Appendix 1. Sam's group were able to see the impact of their intervention, not just on accessing behaviour as a whole but also on specific groups of students, based on previous behaviour and organised by grades. Hypothesis A1, that accessing feedback correlates positively with grades, has been challenged by the data, and this meant that their hypothesis became more complex, since the rump of 'not good enough' students who continued to resist the feedback consisted of high achieving A/A*and low-achieving D students whose behaviour was relatively unaffected by the campaign and mid-range B/C students who held out despite most of their peers changing their behaviour. Sam's group continued to hold to their belief (A2) that accessing feedback would have a positive influence on grades, but the scope of the project did not include the next round of test data, so the hypothesis remained unchallenged. However, Sam did consider that it would be hard for the A/A* students to show improvement and for that to be attributed to feedback. Anna's group were committed to capturing the *authentic voice* of the students but quickly realised that the voices captured represented only those students who (a) had a considered view about feedback and (b) were prepared to articulate it. The students who did not have a view or chose not to share it were still excluded from the enquiry, and this was a source of frustration for Anna's group and set off many debates about tutorial talk, power, status and access.

When the two groups came together, they were able to dovetail their data and analyses: it became clear that avoidant students were the ones impacted by the personalised emails and that this intervention was a better use of resources than general emails and announcements to all students. The small number of remaining 'feedback avoiders' had quite strongly articulated views which are unlikely to shift in response to behavioural 'nudging'. The staff returned to their original ideas about the efficacy of the feedback system and found that the overall picture was more nuanced and that the positions of the two groups had come closer together. The feedback system was being used by more students, sometimes for perceived intrinsic benefits to their learning. However, more research was needed to answer the emergent questions:

- Does using feedback improve or sustain performance?
- Are non-users right when they say feedback isn't useful?
- If yes, how can we improve it?
  - If no, how can we convince them?
  - If yes and no, how can we have more effective learning conversations?

Where next?

These examples, in particular, the ways in which the data is analysed, are fully explored in the narrative appendices. However, these are exemplar research projects and we imagine that you are reading this book because of your own discomforts, hunches and desire to explore. We hope to have provided some structure and guidance for developing your question, and next, in Chapter 4, we offer you a range of tools to choose from, as well as some discussion of how to judge the quality both of the tool itself – how appropriate to the task? – and how you make use of it.

4 TOOLS FOR ENQUIRY

Understanding this section

The structure of this chapter is unusual for a book of this kind and so we begin this section with a description and some guidance, alongside a discussion of the concept of quality when researching practice.

Elsewhere in this book, we have introduced our use of the term 'tool', with theoretical reflections on the differences between tools (catalytic objects used in *techne* for creative and developmental purposes) and tool-kits (artefacts designed to be reliably operable in a limited number of ways across contexts). We have also set out how the researcher's intent shapes their choice of and use of any enquiry tool, emphasising the primacy of the individual practitioner's professional knowledge: the awareness of their context, reflective focus on the needs of the participants in relation to the research question and 'on the ground' pragmatic choices. Our allegiance to tools rather than toolkits is pretty obvious. So why is this chapter here, looking for all the world like a toolkit?

The answer is that it's not a toolkit, it is a sweet shop. The idea of 'the sweet shop' emerged from our work supporting practitioner-researchers and the desire to offer choice and information without the fear of overload. As detailed in chapter 3, the message was one of choice (pick and mix), supported by clear labelling and a (knowingly parental) exhortation not to overdo it. We began by gathering together basic guides to traditional research methods, then started exploring the use of pedagogic tools as research methods (Baumfield et al., 2009) and added them to the shelves. Innovative methods from other disciplines were imported too (Wall et al., 2013; Woolner et al., 2010), but somewhere along the line we realised that each tool was being customised through use. Sharing those variations made tools more attractive and encouraged further customisations, a process of engaging in and engaging with that increased researchers' confidence (Hall, 2009). This chapter is an attempt to replicate that socially mediated process in print.

Thinking about quality

The judgements around what a successful enquiry process and outcome looks like and what elements make for a good practitioner enquiry practice are somewhat murky. There are lots of places we may go to look for quality markers, but in that this book is arguing for a hybrid crossover space between theory and practice; between methodology and pedagogy, the fitness for purpose is challenging (Wall 2018).

If we look at academic research literature then there are a range of ways standards are articulated. Judgements of reliability and validity would likely be the first that you would come across in delving into the research texts. However, these are terms largely conceived in a scientific model of research where the researcher is distanced from real life and although can be useful in thinking about a tool and its usage, they can also be limiting within a practitioner enquiry frame. In regards reliability, for example, certainly the ability to replicate a research process in its entirety is relatively difficult considering the transient nature of schools; although it might be useful to consider in relation to the specific intention of one tool or aspect. Similarly, validity can be useful in assessing tools or techniques: how sure are you that the data you are collecting is measuring what you intend, how confident are you that you are hearing an honest response? Generalisability might also be close to the top and has similar origin, but arguably less use in a practitioner enquiry scenario, and while writers such as Flyvbjerg (2006) and Larsson (2009) have unpicked the term to broaden it from solely the process of applying a (statistically significant) finding to the rest of the general population, it remains slightly artificial in its usefulness. We are often confused by the apologies felt necessary by the more interpretivist researcher for an inability to claim generalisability, when this was never the intention. Sometimes research is not about generalisation; it is about targeted, rich, deep exploration of one event or individual, and that is important work.

In reaction to these concepts arising from a more positivist/scientific orientation, more interpretivist researchers have generated their own terms with which to explore quality. The assumption being that this research has completely different intent and therefore alternative conceptions of quality are needed. In the literature, it is possible to find discussion centred around key terms initially suggested by Lincoln and Guba (1985) and Guba and Lincoln (1994), such as trustworthiness (including credibility, transferability, dependability and confirmability) and authenticity (with a more ethical and political orientation that considers fairness, ontological authenticity, educative authenticity, catalytic authenticity and tactical authenticity). Additional concepts, with more than a nod to an ethical stance, such as sensitivity to context, commitment and rigour, reflexivity and impact and importance have since been added (e.g. Yardley, 2000; Hammersley, 2007). But again, these concepts are generated from a place of difference, where the researcher is researcher first and, if at all, a participant or practitioner, second. This means that the definitions all presume some sort of distancing at some point. Therefore, while they are useful reference points in the literature, the fit with practitioner enquiry is clunky and often not cognizant of the reality that the practice, the practitioner and the research are so fundamentally entwined.

An alternative viewpoint is to explore the practitioner or professional community for potential answers to this issue of quality. The 'what works' and evidence-based practice agenda (e.g. Hattie, 2008; and for a critique, Biesta, 2010) in education gives some perspective on how we might consider quality in regards teaching and learning. However, this has become tarnished for many by a dominant use of quantitative data and meta-analyses/systematic reviews and a strong political agenda. Of course, this view is also not disassociated with the academic discourse around research methods, but what it does bring is an emphasis on changing or influencing practice. This field gives us notions of confidence and usefulness to be considered. How confident are you that the evidence answers your question, that the process and the evidence combine to find a solution that is strong enough to warrant action? This could be considered from a solely personal perspective: how useful are the answers to you for moving your practice forward (quite a personal judgement of quality)? The more confident you are the more likely the findings are going to prompt strategic thinking and action as a result. The imperative to have professional courage and make significant changes to improve practice. However, making these judgements on your own is problematic and can lead to flawed uncodified thinking, so a more appropriate approach might be to think about these kinds of quality judgements made as part of collaborative engagement with the community.

The question therefore becomes how useful do you and your colleagues find your outcomes (in terms of answering questions and developing practice). This makes a more collaborative community-based approach to thinking about quality that has strong links to the making public part of Stenhouse's (1983) conceptualisation of practitioner research. Of course, how useful depends on complex networks of politics, dissemination process and relevancy which are not necessarily objective (Kvernbekk, 2011). The absence of or limits to objectivity are not an obstacle but rather something that should be openly recognised and embraced, in line with the spirit of reflexivity discussed in Chapter 3. This conception of quality developed as part of a public forum requires an ongoing dialogue with other practitioner enquirers where language and understandings are developed within the community as a shared understanding of practice and research in a dynamic relationship. In addition, there is an ongoing dialogue between an individual's and the communities' ongoing research encounters and the way this experience of undertaking enquiry has a cumulative impact. This drives learning about the approaches and their associated affordances and constraints for different types of intents and contexts forward.

At this point we are aware that we have given many potential ways that judgements of quality can be made and have then introduced levels of doubt about each one in turn. As promised, we return to the five principles from Chapter 1 (Heikkinen et al., 2012; see Table 4.1) and show how we have used them to interrogate the flexibility and contextual sensitivity of each tool.

To conclude this section, we would like to spend a paragraph or two explicitly focusing on ethics. Ethics as a judgement of quality is something Heikkinen et al. (2012) identify, but we feel it is worthy of greater focus and attention here. It is a concept that experience of working within the university system and in partnership with practitioners has made us acutely aware of. Campbell and Groundwater-Smith (2007) in their edited book provide a detailed examination of the ethical dilemmas associated with the meeting of academic and practice-based research highlighting the challenges of different codes of conduct and systems of accountability and how they might come together. As a practical guide, we have found it useful to think about ethics in regards a model of process and output. Ethics is an integral part of professional practice and if considered from a solely output-orientated standpoint, the more predominant focus of university ethics boards (Hammersley, 2006; Hammersley and Traianou, 2012), then this is not sufficiently recognised.

TABLE 4.1 *Five principles for validation of action research*

Validation principles for action research
1. Principle of historical continuity
Analysis of the history of action: how has the action evolved historically?
Emplotment: how logically and coherently does the narrative proceed?
2. Principle of reflexivity
Subjective adequacy: what is the nature of the researcher's relationship with his/her object of research?
Ontologic and epistemologic presumptions: what are the researcher's presumptions of knowledge and reality?
Transparency: how does the researcher describe his/her material and methods?
3. Principle of dialectics
Dialogue: how has the researcher's insight developed in dialogue with others?
Polyphony: how does the report present different voices and interpretations?
Authenticity: how authentic and genuine are the protagonists of the narrative?
4. Principle of workability and ethics
Pragmatic quality: how well does the research succeed in creating workable practices?
Criticalness: what kind of discussion does the research provoke?
Ethics: how are ethical problems dealt with?
Empowerment: does the research make people believe in their own capabilities and possibilities to act and thereby encourage new practices and actions?
5. Principle of evocativeness
Evocativeness: how well does the research narrative evoke mental images, memories or emotions related to the theme?

From Heikkinen et al., 2012, p. 8.

To illustrate this we will use the example of visual research techniques with the intent to elicit the voices of young children (Wall, 2017). Traditional research ethics guidance, as produced by key educational research organisations (e.g. AERA, 2011; BERA, 2011), is useful. Even so, it is worth noting that it mentions neither the specific field of visual methodology nor issues associated with researching young children. The way we include children and their views in research must go beyond accountability and safeguarding to fulfil an agenda that is much more wide reaching and aligned with the UNCRC (1989) and democratic principles (Pope et al., 2010). In the Table 4.2 we have outlined key issues from the field of student voice, researching young children and visual research under the headings of process and output as a way of showing how the different aspects will come together to create a range of considerations that need to be addressed in regards to any ethical engagement. To ensure

TABLE 4.2 *Typology of process and outcome considerations*

	Process	Output
Voice agendas	• Dialogue and participation • Supports devolved models of power • Space to accesses thinking	• Accurate communication of perspectives • Allows a range of voices • Supports 'hidden' voices
Researching young children	• How the process (the tool and the topic) is 'tuned in' to their needs • Reflect familiar pedagogies • Role of the adult as facilitator	• Developmentally appropriate (level of literacy required) • Interpreted in line with the intent of the participants
Visual research	• Create spaces for talk • Mediation of power dynamics between adult and child • Level of scaffold	• Relationship between visual and more traditional forms of data • Accurate interpretation • Quantity versus quality

From Wall, 2017, p. 5.

quality, ethics has to be integrated into the decision-making at all points of the enquiry and be viewed from both a traditional research and a professional perspective.

Choosing tools

Each of the tools is presented here not to show you what it is 'for' but to indicate how it has been successfully used in a number of ways, with the hope that this will stimulate thoughts about how it could be used in your enquiry. Therefore, for each tool, we have provided some information about:

- **Concept** – the synopsis of the tool and the types of intents it might fulfil.

- **Provenance** – since where the tool has come from may shape how it is perceived. For example, Fortune Lines (p. 82) were developed for primary classrooms and while this has not prevented them being used in universities, researchers have had to consider whether the format repels or encourages participants, or whether it privileges certain kinds of response.

- **Use in research** – we don't believe the majority of tools are unquestioningly tied to a particular way of researching (Symonds and Gorard 2010), and therefore this section will explore the range of ways each tool has been used in different types of research. Consideration will be made of the key decisions and potential adaptations that might be appropriate to ensure good fit with specific research objectives. This section will link with the research exemplars in encouraging the researcher to tinker with the tools depending on their intent.

- **Affordances and constraints** – this is demonstrated through the case examples selected to show as diverse a range of practice as possible. Nevertheless, we make no claims to be comprehensive and are sure that readers of this book will find new ways to use the tools to explore practice.

- **Markers of quality** – adapting Heikkinen et al.'s (2012) concepts of quality for researching professional learning, each tool will be considered in light of five criteria for quality in practitioner inquiry:
  - **Recognisability:** when undertaking practitioner inquiry it is important tools have good continuity with normal practice. The *principle of historical continuity* emphasises the narrative in which the inquiry takes place – the narrative of one's own practice, but also the narrative of the learning trajectories of the students and colleagues integral to your inquiry questions. A tool needs to have good fit with the pedagogic, developmental and contextual demands of the practice it is being used to explore.
  - **Metacognitive:** to codify the *principle of reflexivity* to the professional learning realm we have made the productive link to metacognition. An important quality of a practitioner enquiry tool is the way in which it provides new ways of thinking for the practitioner and the community in which they work, the way it facilitates a deeper level of reflective and strategic thinking (Moseley et al., 2005a). As teachers we have good knowledge of what works to get people thinking hard or differently about a concept or idea and this criterion is about tapping into that ability.
  - **Multiple voices:** The extent to which a tool gives participants a voice on issues that pertain to them is important as well as the way they encourage a dialogue between different groups, the *principle of dialect*. Here we draw on ideas of voice and

the associated concepts of power, inclusivity, process and purpose as often discussed in relation to implementing the UNCRC (1989; Robinson and Taylor, 2007; Wall et al., 2018). Although, we would argue these ideas are not tied to children and young people but can easily be translated to other members of any community (Wall and Hall, 2016).

o   **Pragmatic:** combining the *principle of workability and ethics* with pragmatist theories of practice (Dewey, 1999) and research methodology (Creswell, 2003), this criterion focuses on the extent to which a tool is doable within the busy working week of a teacher, whether it is 'easy' to use, has good fit with normal practice or allows the research to complement or mirror the focus of the inquiry.

o   **Evocative:** leaning firmly on the *principle of evocativeness*, this marker of quality is about how a tool might provide new ways of seeing practice, challenge the status quo and encourage productive thinking about practice. To learn professionally then we have to be given a new lens with which to view teaching and learning.

- **Questions researchers should ask** – this relates to the inevitable limitations of any individual tool, so as well as evaluating what a tool can tell us, we need to be asking what it can't tell us and reflecting on whether that is crucial to the enquiry as a whole. This is helpful in deciding what else to add to the 'pick and mix'.

- and **Further reading**.

The tools are in no way a finite list of what is available, but they are chosen to represent a range of data types that may be open to the practitioner. They are organised along two continuums from quantitative to qualitative, and from pedagogical to methodological in regards their origins (Table 4.3). These are rough guides and tools that will bend to the intent of researcher.

The rest is up to you. We recommend when browsing this sweet shop of tools, you foreground what you want to know, what is the question you are asking and what evidence will convince you that you have a good answer to it, and how a tool will work in the context under examination and with the participants you are targeting. Don't be afraid to tinker with and adapt the tools; they are not recipes to follow, but rather a starting point from which to build up a repertoire of techniques with which to undertake enquiry.

TABLE 4.3 *Range of exemplified tools*

Origin intent		Pedagogical				Methodological
Divergent	1.	Fortune lines	7.	Students as researchers	13.	Narrative interviews
	2.	Odd one outs	8.	Arts-based enquiry	14.	Focus groups
	3.	Mind maps	9.	Cartoons and comics	15.	Structured observations
	4.	Pupil views templates	10.	Mapping environments	16.	Standardised questionnaires
	5.	Work samples	11.	Analysis of talk	17.	Small-scale trials
Convergent	6.	Diamond 9s	12.	Surveys	18.	Effect sizes

TOOL 1: FORTUNE LINES

Concept: Fortune lines are a thinking skills technique that supports participants in engaging with a reflection on how they felt about a process over time (Higgins et al., 2001).

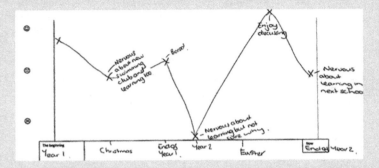

Provenance: The basic premise of a fortune line is a pair of axis with time along the bottom and scale of feelings (this could be as simple as sad to happy, or something more sophisticated depending on participants and intent) up the side. It is used to track how feelings change over time. So, for example, in *Where the Wild Things Are* (Sendak, 1963), children are encouraged to engage with how Max feels at different stages of his adventures. In the research domain this tool is powerful in supporting participants' reflections over time; it is particularly helpful as a scaffold if you are wanting them to reflect over a long duration like a school year or more and practical or difficult periods of learning where you require reflection after the event (see Undrell Moore's example below).

Use in research: Fortune lines can be used as data in their own right, or it can become part of a mediated interview process, where the interviewer uses the opinion line to prompt a reflective dialogue about process. Predominantly it has been the latter, acting as a scaffold for talk with either the spoken explanation only going forward to analysis or a combination of the fortune line and what was said (Wall, 2017). As such the research process is much more in line with the traditional visually mediated interview (e.g. Allen, 2009; Prosser, 2007; Harper, 2002). The child engages with the visual task and the conversation, the main target of the activity. The visual acts as a bridge to their understanding (Harper, 2002); however, if a sample includes young children then mediation process can also help to create a space where dialogue about the child's experiences can be accessed and explored with the visual acting as an aide memoire.

Maybe an accurate representation of the child's responses would only be possible through capturing the talk and engagement with the visual over time (Lodge's (2005) use of an overhead video camera to record the dialogue and the interaction with the visual would be a good starting place).

Exemplars:

Vicky Wasner, an international school in Geneva:
Having worked with a groups of students as researchers to explore the practice of service learning as part of implementing the International Baccalaureate Diploma Programme, Vicky wanted to explore their experiences of the collaborative inquiry process. She used a group fortune line on A1 paper where each student as well as her drew their own annotated line alongside their peers (each colour in the fortune line below representing a different participant). This allowed for an open dialogue, as was the general prerogative of the approach, where all participants could reflect over the duration of the project and compare and contrast similarities and differences in their experiences.

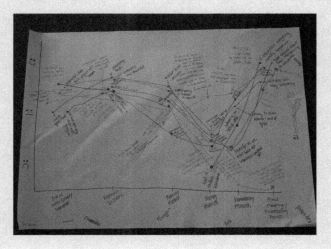

Undrell Moore, School of Dentistry, Newcastle University: He was exploring students' first experience of extracting a tooth from a real live patient. The students had experience on models and pigs' heads, but this was something different. From experience Undrell and his colleagues knew this one experience was extremely formative in the students' development towards being a practising dentist, and so supporting meaningful reflection on the positive, or negative, experiences tied up in this one significant programme event was important. Adapting the fortune line idea after reading of its use in a primary school meant they could annotate the bottom axis with the key moments in the experience (prep operating space, meet the patient, give anaesthetic injection etc.); and using the relatively simple feelings scale from the primary school on the other, the students were encouraged as they were going through the process of extraction to put a simple mark at each stage to show how they were feeling. Therefore having minimum impact but being sufficient to prompt a conversation with a tutor at a later date.

Local authority staff development: The facilitator of this event wanted teachers of different levels of experience to engage with their own professional learning across their careers. She asked them to individually produce their own fortune line starting with when they entered the teaching profession up until the current day – it was interesting in itself when participants identified their start. They were asked to annotate with three lines: (1) how they felt about being a teacher, (2) how they felt about their classroom practice and (3) how they felt about their professional learning. She then asked them to talk through their fortune line in groups. Having the three lines meant that the participants were not only thinking about changes in their learning over time, but also the interaction effect between the identified different aspects of professional life. This led to interesting conversations about how to survive professional peaks and troughs, and how they could better support each other during the natural fluctuations of being a teacher.

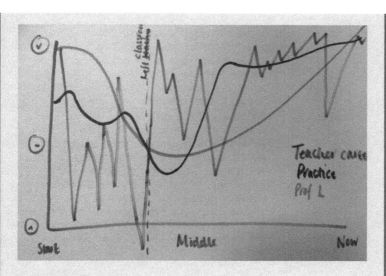

Labels within figure: classroom; Left School; Teacher career; Practice; Prof L; Start; Middle; Now

Quality Criteria

Recognisability	The graph structure is relatively easily accessed by most individuals, even young children, however the process of using this same scaffold as a tool for dialogue is relatively novel. There might need to be some prompting, but once the idea is communicated the tool is conducive to productive thinking and talk.
Metacognitive	Engaging with the affective elements of learning is important but often under-represented in research generally. The fortune line process gives participants a deceptively simple scale on which to talk about how they feel. Add in the dimension of time and very quickly the awareness of change over time, comparison of different feelings at different times and the range of feeling experienced raises the thinking level significantly, even for young children.
Multiple Voices	Bragg and Buckingham (2008) showed that visual-mediated interviews give 'access to a wider range of voices' (p. 121) and when using a fortune line, combining visual and verbal response, this is literal as well as metaphorical. This range of response is all the more important when young children were involved as it provides a 'normal' and meaningful method with which to express themselves.

Pragmatic	Once the scaffold is clear, the advantage of the fortune line is the relative ease with which it can be completed, combined with the breadth of reflection it prompts. Particularly where the learning is practical or experienced based then the tool can be unobtrusively included to support reflection after the event.
Evocative	Feelings about learning change over time. How we feel on a Monday is different to how we might feel on a Friday; how we feel at the start of the day might be different to how we feel at the end; how we feel about English lessons at different points in the school year will vary. This tool is significant in allowing participants to access a sophisticated dialogue around these changes over time and even with a seemingly simplistic feelings scale prompts a level of reflection that often goes way beyond what might be expected.

Frequently Asked Questions

Can this tool be used with young children?	Yes, although as their teacher you probably need to think about how much support they will need to understand what is intended. Think about the extent to which they might have seen graphical representation previously, what links you can make. It might be appropriate to draw the axis with them – 'Imagine this is the start of that thing we did and this is the end; and this is how we feel from happy to sad.'
How does this tool give insight for my professional learning?	Engaging with understandings of learning over time is really important and useful whether it is your own professional learning or how your students develop. The advantage of the fortune line is the way that it scaffolds this engagement. Collecting fortune lines from different individuals to reflect on their experience of the same thing or doing a collaborative version where all contributions are included on the same set of axis means that productive comparisons and insights can be provided.

Further reading

Allen, L. (2009). 'Snapped': Researching the sexual cultures
  of schools using visual methods. *International Journal
  of Qualitative Methods in Education*, 22(5): 549–561.
  doi:10.1080/09518390903051523
Bragg, S. and Buckingham, D. (2008). 'Scrapbooks' as a resource
  in media research with young people. In P. Thomson (ed.),
  Doing Visual Research with Children and Young People.
  London: Routledge.
Harper, D. (2002). Talking about pictures: A case for
  photo elicitation. *Visual Studies*, 17(1): 13–26.
  doi:10.1080/14725860220137345
Higgins, S., Baumfield, V., and Leat, D. (2001). *Thinking Through
  Primary Teaching*. Cambridge: Chris Kington Publishing.
Lodge, C. (2005). From hearing voices to engaging in dialogue:
  Problematising student participation in school improvement.
  Journal of Educational Change, 6(2): 125–146. doi:10.1007/
  s10833-005-1299-3.
Prosser, J. (2007). Visual methods and the visual
  culture of schools. *Visual Studies*, 22(1): 13–30.
  doi:10.1080/14725860601167143
Sendak, M. (1963). *Where the Wild Things Are*. New York: Harper
  and Rowe
Wall, K. (2017). Exploring the ethical issues related to visual
  methodology when including young children in wider research
  samples. *International Journal of Inclusive Education (Special
  Issue: Researching ethically with children and young people in
  inclusive educational contexts)*, 21(3): 316–331.

TOOL 2: ODD ONE OUTS

Concept and Provenance: Not to be confused with the standardised format in tests of knowledge ('find the odd one out in this sequence'), Odd One Outs have their roots in primary Thinking Skills (Higgins et al., 2000), where they are used to draw out the conceptual understanding of a group of learners by identifying things that they have in common and things that are unique to each. It allows for complex relationships to be described, in that there can be some things which all three hold in common (in the centre), things shared by two (described along the planes of the triangle) and singular features (in the corner bubbles).

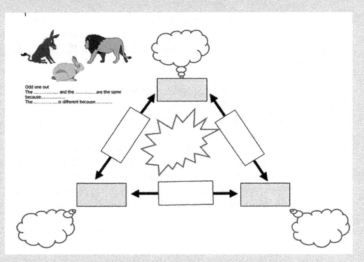

Although there is a symmetry in then attributing the lack of a common feature ('the donkey and the rabbit have long ears') to the third as its unique feature ('the lion has short ears'), it is notable that even very young learners tend not to do this and instead take the opportunity to make more rich and detailed conceptual pictures, so there may be at least seven ideas in play. In the example above, the context and intent of the learners will determine whether their discussion is of taxonomy (types of mammal), habitat (fields and savannah), diet (herbivores and carnivores – though rabbits under stress will eat their young) or imaginative phenomenological approaches (*our all-time favourite*

'The lion is the odd one out because he's looking the other way'). There are no 'right' answers in an Odd One Out exercise and each suggestion requires a minimum of explanation and justification, so it is a particularly powerful way to assess what learners know and think about a topic and to plan a curriculum experience based on need and interest. The contents of the Odd One Out are flexible and three-dimensional found objects as well as drawings, photos and text have all been successfully explored using this format.

Use in research: Practitioners' research use of Odd One Out has often, like Mind Maps, used a pre- and post- capture to illustrate learners' development and change. While this is a valid use of the tool, we feel that the conceptual unfolding that comes from the first experience is not always as rich in the repeat. There is something about the novelty of exploring the relationships that sparks more playful and risk-taking suggestions at the beginning of the experience. We have found that returning to the original Odd One Outs and using them as stimulating and mediating objects in an interview or focus group provides a more detailed picture.

Exemplars:

Nurture Group developing a sense of 'behaving well':
Children in a suburban primary school were offered 'nurture group' time if it was felt that they were finding the classroom difficult to cope with – demonstrated by very withdrawn or very disruptive behaviours. For the nurture group leader, an experienced Higher Level Teaching Assistant (HLTA), it was important that Nurture Group was not simply respite for these children but also an opportunity to build up resilience to the stresses of the classroom. However, it was equally clear to her that because the children in her group responded to stress in very different ways, there would not be a simple solution. She decided to use an Odd One Out as an individual interview support when children first joined the group, asking them to select photos of their classmates (someone not like me, someone a bit like me) alongside their own photo to explore what was easy and difficult about being in school. The children kept their Odd One Out sheets in their Nurture Group folder but the classmates' photos were removed after the interview. These initial interviews revealed children's understanding of how

someone is *supposed to behave* in school and whether their distress came from their own inability to perform in that way or from others' behaviour and, thirdly and crucially, whether their ideas of 'behaving well' were shared and consistently modelled by the teacher. Since all the children had become familiar with the technique, the HLTA went on to use the Odd One Out as a way of discussing difficult incidents with the whole group in circle time and giving them experience of problem-solving alternative strategies. The lack of a single right answer enabled the children to consider their behaviour with less shame and to gradually take more responsibility and extend their options to include being more outgoing or less impulsive.

Lucy Hatt and the definition of 'entrepreneurship': Lucy runs an innovative programme in which students learn entrepreneurship through working in teams to set up and manage real businesses, identifying commercial opportunities, developing plans to exploit these and managing the resulting activities. Lucy's PhD looks at the key learning experiences and 'threshold concepts' associated with becoming an entrepreneur. From the beginning of her doctorate she has struggled with problems of definition and the boundaries between different kinds of 'business education' and 'entrepreneurship education' – are they real and meaningful boundaries at all? She decided to use the Odd One Out format as part of a conference workshop. In her session outline for the conference she offered this challenge to the workshop participants: 'We are perhaps in danger of over using the term and rendering the word's meaning to be so all-encompassing as to become nothing but a trendy label.' The provocation resulted in a very high level of engagement and a large amount of data: although participants were convinced that there were significant differences between business education, entrepreneurship education and the underpinning 'graduate skills' from a generic degree, there was very little consensus about what these differences were and which were the most significant. This might sound like a disappointing result and it would be, if the purpose of using the Odd One Out was to achieve a consensus. However, if the purpose was to confirm Lucy's impression that there was a lack of conceptual clarity in the field, then it was a resounding success. Practitioner-researchers often feel that if something seems unclear, it is because they have not understood it properly and Odd One Outs are a good way to sense-check this among our peers.

What is the question? Starting a collaborative enquiry project: A Special Educational Needs Co-ordinator (SENCO) in a small secondary school wanted to work collaboratively with all the students who had been identified as having additional support needs on a project to understand what 'inclusion' was like and could be like in the school. He started by discussing the project with other staff members, the school management and the governors and came up with a draft plan. As he started to try to recruit the students to become part of the research, he was surprised and disappointed at their lack of enthusiasm. He had a 'lightbulb' moment when filling in a questionnaire at his local cinema: he had started it because he loved films and wanted to contribute but quickly found himself turned off by questions about screening times and popcorn prices: '*These aren't the questions I want to answer*'. He went back into school and explained his mistake to the student group and offered the Odd One Out format as a way to explore their experience. They started with a very broadly framed triad – our school, the ideal school, the worst school – and from that developed triads around particular key ideas: managing break times, support in the classroom, negotiating deadlines, information in a range of formats. The students then democratically produced a hierarchy of issues based on how far the school was from ideal (urgency) and how easily change could be implemented and measured (pragmatic design). Some of the issues were the same as highlighted by staff but the students were considerably more motivated to be co-researchers when they had framed the questions themselves.

Quality Criteria

Recognisability	The simple structure of the Odd One Out means that it is easy to engage learners of all abilities. The discussion of what counts as 'the same' and 'different' is easy to enter *and* quickly becomes quite sophisticated, enabling learners to see that they are engaged in something meaningful and challenging.

Metacognitive	The sharing of conceptual understanding within this very supportive structure allows us to see that our own perspectives and those of others may be valid and commensurable but also that they do not have to converge. Strategic and reflective thinking is prompted naturally in these discussions.
Multiple Voices	While it is important to work around a single Odd One Out in order to facilitate the discussion, all opinions and ideas can be recorded by printing in a large format and/or by providing multiple copies to be completed by individuals at the end of the exercise.
Pragmatic	Odd One Outs are actually quite demanding to produce and require the researcher to do his or her own preparatory work on conceptual clarity in order to pick three stimuli that align well with the research question. For this reason, they tend to be more robust than many questionnaires or interviews and have a greater claim to providing evidence of how learners are engaging with particular concepts.
Evocative	There is a sense of ownership and creativity that participants describe when working an Odd One Out: 'These are *our* ideas' and although there are seven elements to complete, the task appears realistic and achievable.

Frequently Asked Questions

Can I use an Odd One Out format for a large group with individual responses, for example, in an online questionnaire?	You can, although the type of data you will collect will be different from that generated by a group. Individuals working alone are more likely to try to guess what you want as the 'right' answer and you won't capture much of the 'background thinking' that is drawn out of the discussion.
What is the ideal number for the group discussion?	Given that you want time and space for participation, the guidance for focus groups is quite helpful here: groups of 4–6 are optimal; though if you are working with large numbers, you will need one recording device per table to capture the conversations or risk losing whatever is not written down.

How does this tool give insight for my professional learning?	This tool is particular useful in generating a dialogue around hard-to-decipher concepts. By undertaking an Odd One Out with your participants you will start to see the different component parts of these concepts as they understand them. You can decide whether you engage in the activity alongside them or whether you maintain a distance, either way it is a useful exploratory tool.

Further reading

Hatt, L. (2016). What's Distinctive about Entrepreneurship and Entrepreneurship Education? Threshold Concepts and Expertise. Practitioner Development Workshop at 3E (ESCB Enterprise Educators Conference), Leeds. Available at: https://www.ee.ucl.ac.uk/~mflanaga/L%20Hatt%20ECSB%20Paper.pdf

Higgins, S. E., Baumfield, V., and Leat, D. J. K. (2000). *Thinking Through Primary Teaching*. Cambridge: Chris Kington Publishing.

Jones, H. (2008). Thoughts on teaching thinking: Perceptions of practitioners with a shared culture of thinking skills education. *Curriculum Journal*, 19(4): 309–324.

Leat, D. J. K. and Higgins, S. E. (2002). The role of powerful pedagogical strategies in curriculum development'. *Curriculum Journal*, 13(1): 71–85.

TOOL 3: MIND MAPS

Concept: Mind maps, also called concept maps and brainstorms, are a common pedagogic tool used to access students' knowledge and understandings around a topic, either individually or as a group, at the start and/or at the end of a topic. They are useful for eliciting the connections and complexities within a study topic. For practitioner research they are particularly useful in describing, exploring and critiquing complex professional practices. Used often as a self-assessment tool by practitioners mapping their understanding, they can also form the basis for peer coaching, interviews and focus groups.

Provenance: By writing the focus as a key term or question in the centre of the blank sheet of paper, the participant has free reign to put down everything they can think of that's related. This can be done with pens or paper, or there are increasing numbers of software available that do a similar job. The practitioner should think carefully about the nature of the prompt aligning it with what they want to know; questions work well but so do topic titles. A common structure of nodes (things associated with the focus either singular or as a group/category) and links (lines showing associations between the concepts) are commonly used, with the assumption that a change in the ratio between nodes and links shows developing understanding.

Use in research: Mind maps are increasingly being used as a research tool in the academic literature. They enable an immediate survey of participants' understanding about a topic, clear comparison of knowledge held by different groups and/or development of understanding over time by the same group. The clear presentation of the data using conventions that most students are used to, or that are easily explained, provides a commonality to the output which can be explored for its structural elements as well as its content. The structural commonality can be increased using one of the many mind mapping software that are available which limits the artistic quirks (Salzberg-Ludwig, 2008).

Analysing the structure can be done through counting the nodes and links. From this point a range of statistical analysis is possible from simple frequency counts to explorations of complexity via the ration of nodes to links, to comparison of group characteristics (Bowker and Tearle, 2007) and more detailed statistical analysis of changes pre- and post-intervention via, for example, the use of a t-test (Mavers et al., 2002).

Of course, the content can also be explored with key themes generated via an immersive, interpretivist approach to the maps (Pearson and Somekh, 2003). However, there are also examples showing how the completion of a mind map prior to interview supports respondents of all ages in forming their thinking in a way they are happy with. The mind map then becomes a mediating tool for the interview process (Wheeldon, 2011; Wheeldon and Faubert, 2009).

Exemplars:

Duchess High School, Alnwick: Concept mapping was used as a tool to help students make sense of the different sections and concepts within the exam specification. They were used at the end of each module of work in order to develop links, to understand and deepen the metacognition. They were then updated during the final revision sessions before the examination. The student worked in their learning pairs to update and add onto their concept map. Once completed, they then had to explain and justify the links to each other. This encouraged the students to reflect on their learning, deepen understanding and embed knowledge. It is evident from the two examples below that the second demonstrates a deeper understanding of the relationships between the key elements than the first. The ideas are explicit and more connectors illustrate the developing links. This would appear to support the view that the use of the learning pairs has increased the confidence and the capability of the student.

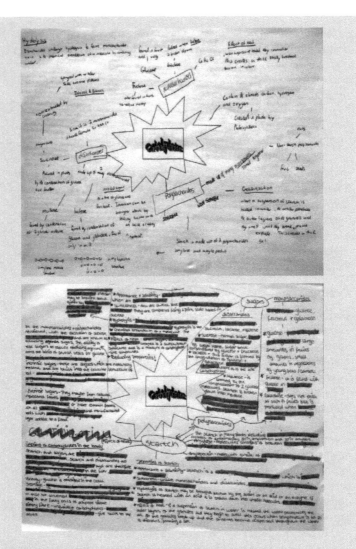

Leaf Lane Infants School, Cheshire: In this class of four-
and five-year-olds, the teachers wanted to explore the children's
understanding of learning. The age of the children meant that it
was pedagogically inappropriate to ask the children to do a mind
map independently and so it was done as a group activity as a
reflection display. To show progression to the young students, but
also for clarity in the enquiry process, then 'traffic light' coloured
bits of paper were used to show what they felt they had achieved

and what they needed to work on. A bonus was that as the key words and photo prompts were added then the display worked as a word bank for the children to access during their learning.

Quality Criteria

Recognisability	One of the key strengths of mind mapping is the familiarity for practitioners and students. The format is one that most can tap into relatively easily and the conventions of nodes and links allow for easy quantitative and qualitative comparisons.
Metacognitive	While simple in construct, mind maps can gain complexity very quickly; as such they are a simple tool that can be used to elicit, summarise and represent respondents thinking relatively easily. If used as part of a mediated interview then they are also supportive of scaffolding complex thinking from relatively young children.
Multiple Voices	As a creative or novel activity, mind maps can often elicit views and voices that might otherwise go unheard. They do not have to be completed as a solitary activity but can be done by pairs, small groups or even a whole class; however, asking individuals to use different colours or providing some sort of code to elicit different contributions might be appropriate.
Pragmatic	Mind maps fit well into normal teaching and learning routines and as such can be used with both a methodological and a pedagogical lens, often at the same time.
Evocative	As a tool for representing complex thinking relatively simply then there is really nothing like a mind map. Not only do they allow the practitioner a quick overview of learners' understanding, but they also visually represent to the learner their own thinking and how this develops over time. This can provide new understandings of the progression made in a topic.

Frequently Asked Questions

Can I combine quantitative and qualitative analysis techniques?	Yes, but think about the different purposes the different techniques are fulfilling within your enquiry. Don't do an analysis for analysis sake, but rather be clear about the intent and how the data will answer your research question. When presenting the two analyses then show how they come together and where there is complementarity in the answer achieved and where there is not.

How many mind maps should I collect?	This will depend on the nature of your enquiry question and the type of analysis that you are completing. For certain statistical tests then there are minimum number requirements for an accurate result. Similarly if you are undertaking a more interpretivist analysis then the number will be limited by how much time you have available to commit to analysis – too many and it will be unmanageable.
How do mind maps support understanding of professional learning?	Mind maps are a useful tool for capturing understanding before and after a topic. Done either as a class, group or individually, they can capture a lot of complex thinking relatively quickly in an accessible form. Then when they are either redone or added to in a different colour or with a complementary emphasis, they clearly highlight changes either quantitatively or qualitatively. They are a child-friendly tool that supports children in giving their perspective and having a role in analysis thus aiding dialogue between student and teacher.

Further reading

Bowker, R. and Tearle, P. (2007). Gardening as a learning environment: A study of children's perceptions and understanding of school gardens as part of an international project. *Learning Environment Research*, 10: 83–100.

Mavers, D., Somekh, B., and Restorick, J. (2002). Interpreting the externalised images of pupils' conceptions of ICT: Methods for the analysis of concept maps. *Computers & education*, 38(1): 187–207.

Pearson, M. and Somekh, B. (2003). Concept-mapping as a research tool: A study of primary children's representations of information and communication technologies (ICT). *Education and Information Technologies*, 8(1): 5–22.

Salzberg-Ludwig, K. (2008). Scholarly research on mind maps in learning by mentally retarded children. In *A paper presented at the European Conference on Educational Research, University of Goteborg*. Available at: http://www.leeds.ac.uk/educol/documents/174867.pdf

Wheeldon, J. (2011). Is a picture worth a thousand words? Using mind maps to facilitate participant recall in qualitative research. *The Qualitative Report*, 16(2): 509.

Wheeldon, J. and Faubert, J. (2009). Framing experience: Concept maps, mind maps, and data collection in qualitative research. *International Journal of Qualitative Methods*, 8(3): 68–83.

TOOL 4: PUPIL VIEWS TEMPLATES

Concept: Pupil views templates (PVTs) have been designed to help develop talk about learning while also supporting pupils in thinking about their learning and thinking, their metacognition. For practitioner research, using PVTs highlights the distinction between the behaviours we observe in learners (which are only a proxy indicator of what they are learning) and how the learners themselves characterise those behaviours. These conversations reflect back to the teacher the cultural 'givens' of the classroom, thereby giving the teacher the opportunity to consider 'is that what I intended?'.

14. Pupil Views – Working with an interactive whiteboard

Name:
Age:

Provenance: The templates use the semiotics of a cartoon (Wall, 2008), combining images of learning scenarios that pupils recognise and the structure of thought and speech bubbles to build a bridge between their experience, which is easier to talk about, and their thinking about their learning, much harder to articulate. The familiar design means that the pupil can engage with the tool, for example, by drawing in the faces of the teacher and pupils, adding features of their classroom to the image, drawing what was on the board. This activity provides a thinking space which supports discussion and reduces any tension or implication that there is an expected or a correct way to complete the template helping to ensure that the children can express their own thoughts and opinions.

Use in research: The template forms the basis of an interview about learning and the centre of a three-way interaction between an adult (likely to be the teacher), the pupils and the template (Wall and Higgins, 2006). The teacher (or other adult) has an important role, in that they help to initiate the discussion about the chosen learning situation and to a certain extent will steer the dialogue that develops (Varga-Atkins and O'Brien, 2009). The extent to which this role is structured is open for negotiation, for example, in a research project where reliability was necessary then a script was provided (Wall, 2008); alternatively, it can be more unstructured. The template serves as a reminder of the learning context under discussion and is a stimulus for this; however, as part of the process, it is also annotated by the children and therefore becomes a record of the discussion and a stimulus for further talk and ideas of their own (Baumfield et al., 2008). The templates have good potential for gaining insight into the voices of marginalised groups, for example, young children (Wall, 2008), immigrant children (Kirova and Emme, 2008) or children with special education needs (Byrnes and Rickards, 2011; Lewis et al., 2008).

Exemplars:

Victoria Symons and Deborah Currans, Wooler First School: Victoria and Deborah were very concerned about the power dynamics that would be implicit in them doing interviews with the children in their school. This was particularly pertinent for Deborah as head teacher. They considered having the children interview each other and this worked with the older children, but not so much with the younger ones – interviewing needs a certain amount of maturity, knowledge and skills. So, they chose PVTs as a method for facilitating the opinions of children across her first school (4 to 9 years) with less adult involvement.

Gill Maitland and Diane Murphy, Duchess' Community High School: Working with Year 10 (14–15 years), Food Technology PVTs were used to compare students learning in different grouping arrangements: groups, pairs and individually. They found that the PVTs not only provided useful insight for them as teachers, allowing them to identify what the students were thinking and gain a better understanding on how groups worked together, but also helped the students to frame and justify their learning. This combination of feedback for both staff and students was essential in taking their engagement with cooperative learning strategies forward.

Kirstin Mulholland, Newcastle University: Kirstin, as part of her EdD, explored her class of eight- and nine–year-olds' perceptions on learning in maths using thinking skills. She used the PVTs as a way of capturing the children's thinking but also as a way to measure their metacognitive development. A blank template was chosen, where the child could draw the learning scenario they wanted to reflect on, and used systematically throughout the research period (two academic years). Class-level trends were explored using a deductive coding scheme for metacognition (see Wall and Higgins, 2006), but also in-depth analysis of individual case study children were tracked across the investigation. This allowed, when combined with other data (work samples, practitioner observations, attainment data etc.), an accurate picture of the intervention at class as well as student level.

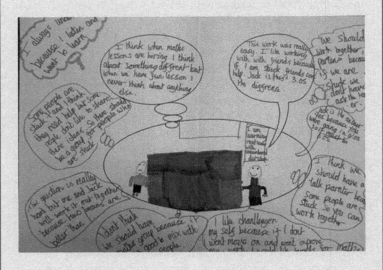

Quality Criteria

Recognisability	The semiotics of PVTs means that it fits well as a school-based task. Participants from a range of cultures including young children have understood the cartoon format, meaning it is a very inclusive tool. The structure of speech and thought bubble helps move dialogue about learning from the concrete, what was being said in this learning scenario, to the more abstract and complex, what are they thinking?
Metacognitive	The use of the thought bubble automatically facilitates the participant in engaging with the learning and thinking process. This is therefore inherently metacognitive, but an important consideration when reading the comments is whether because an individual has written a comment in the thought bubble, indicating a thought, does this mean that they are able to be metacognitive; is it more that the structure of the PVT facilitates a pseudo-metacognitive response?
Multiple Voices	PVTs can be completed individually or as part of a group with the outcome being an individual or group template. All decisions have pros and cons in regards the nature of the voice being elicited. The discussion can be recorded or just the written output on the template collected. The latter is more manageable if working with larger samples, but the former allows for in-depth study of participants' perceptions of a topic.
Pragmatic	The strength of PVTs is the capacity to fulfil both pedagogic and research agendas. The tool can be used to create insight on the learning perceived by students while also providing data robust enough to facilitate a confident answer to an enquiry question. They encourage tight feedback loops between the teachers' and students' learning, resulting in a catalytic relationship, moving talk about metacognition forwards.
Evocative	Previous work has shown the structure is supportive of children engaging with learning and teaching in a productive and authentic way. This has meant that not only have teachers gained insight into their students' awareness of their own learning, but it has also allowed, even very young children, to engage in complex dialogue about learning (Wall, 2008). This process has given participant teachers better understanding of their students' capabilities.

Frequently Asked Questions

Do PVTs work with older children and adults?	Yes, although they might have to be scaffolded differently i.e. the nature of the prompt provided, the amount of support given and autonomy encouraged. This may mean that the task can be undertaken with larger groups.
Is the evidence in what is written in the thought/ speech bubble or in the talk elicited by the activity of completing the template?	Either, it depends on what you want to know and the evidence that will convince you that you have achieved an answer to your research question. As a general rule if you have a smaller sample then you can deal with more data complexity and so the latter is possible; with a larger sample then the sheer volume of potential data might encourage you to go for the relatively simple data represented by the written comments.
How do PVTs support professional learning?	PVTs are designed to support students to express their thinking about a particular teaching and learning scenario (captured by the image). The thought and speech bubble structure facilitates a move into the metacognitive realm, so how they learn in that moment. This means that the templates provide insight into the children's perspectives on teaching and learning, that might otherwise have been missed in normal classroom dialogue.

Further reading

Baumfield, V., Hall, E., and Wall, K. (2008). *Action Research in the Classroom*. London: SAGE.

Baumfield, V. M., Hall, E., Higgins, S., and Wall, K. (2009). Catalytic tools: Understanding the interaction of enquiry and feedback in teachers' learning. *European Journal of Teacher Education*, 32(4): 423–435.

Byrnes, L. J. and Rickards, F. W. (2011). Listening to the voices of students with disabilities: Can such voices inform practice? *Australasian Journal of Special Education*, 35(01): 25–34.

Kirova, A. and Emme, M. (2008). Fotonovela as a research tool in image-based participatory research with immigrant children. *International Journal of Qualitative Methods*, 7(2): 35–57.

Lewis, A. N. N., Newton, H., and Vials, S. (2008). Realising child voice: The development of cue cards. *Support for Learning*, 23(1): 26–31.

Long, L., McPhillips, T., Shevlin, M., and Smith, R. (2012). Utilising creative methodologies to elicit the views of young learners with additional needs in literacy. *Support for Learning*, 27(1): 20–28.

Maitland, G. and Murphy, D. (2008). *How can Cooperative Learning Strategies Support A4L, Group Work & Social Interaction?* London: Campaign for Learning.

Mulholland, K. (2016). '"I think when I work with other people I can let go of all of my ideas and tell them out loud": The impact of a Thinking Skills approach upon pupils' experiences of Maths, e-Thesis, Newcastle University.

Prosser, J. (2007). Visual methods and the visual culture of schools. *Visual Studies*, 22(1): 13–30.

Symons, V. and Currans, D. (2008). *Using Marking Ladders to Support Children's Self-Assessment in Writing.* London: Campaign for Learning.

Varga-Atkins, T. and O'Brien, M. (2009). From drawings to diagrams: Maintaining researcher control during graphic elicitation in qualitative interviews. *International Journal of Research & Method in Education*, 32(1): 53–67.

Wall, K. (2008). Understanding metacognition through the use of pupil views templates: Pupil views of Learning to Learn. *Thinking Skills and Creativity*, 3(1): 23–33.

Wall, K. and Higgins, S. (2006). Facilitating and supporting talk with pupils about metacognition: A research and learning tool. *International Journal of Research and Methods in Education*, 29(1): 39–53.

TOOL 5: WORK SAMPLES

Concept: Schools are data-rich environments and teachers routinely ask children, even young children, to complete tasks that produce written output of one form or another. For us, it seems common sense that using this output of the teaching and learning process in some way can be useful as part of an enquiry focused on student outcomes. For practitioner-researchers, treating the work samples as 'data' has a creative and unfolding impact: we are encouraged to look at the work sample as an *artefact*, engaging critically with the apparent and underlying meanings; we have the opportunity to consider our assessment and feedback practices through a close analysis of our mark-making; we can use the sample as the basis for a discussion with other teachers about the purpose and effectiveness of the task and we can use it as a mediating tool to talk to students about their content knowledge, understanding of the task and learning identity.

Provenance: The provenance for this type of evidence comes from the assessment literature rather than from the research literature per se. There is much dialogue around the advantages and disadvantages of using teacher assessments and coursework alongside more traditional tests and exams as a way to assess children and young people's achievement (e.g. Black, 2001; James and Pedder, 2006), and similar arguments would be relevant here. The key advantage is that it is pragmatic, using evidence that is bring produced already.

Use in research: Because of access, the use of work samples is relatively rare by more traditional researchers (those researching from outside the school). Where work samples have been used then there is great range in the way the work is assessed from a relatively closed and summative way (usually analysing the grades/mark awarded using statistical analysis: e.g. Boston, 2014) to something rich and in-depth with a more formative approach (e.g. Downton and Wright, 2016). The use of assessment language is intended as the crossover between when work samples are being used with a purely academic intent and when they are being used for research remains difficult to unpick.

A useful reference point is the work in 1992 of Arter and Spandell who describe in-depth the advantages and limitations of portfolios of student work. Building on this, McConney et al. (1998) describe teachers' methodology for engaging with work samples using very research-orientated terms such as validity and reliability. In both the line is very fine between what is pedagogical and methodological, but that fits very well with the intent of this book. It is interesting to note that there is a complementary relationship between overarching trends in policy and the promotion of teacher assessment generally and the use of work samples as a research tool, hence needing to go back a significant period of time to find these references.

An important ethical consideration when using work samples is getting permissions for use. If you are using a child's work for purposes outside of normal teaching and learning practice, then you must make sure that consent is gathered from the children and their parents. This can be retrospective, but still must be ensured.

Exemplars:

Scottish Nursery: In a nursery for three- to five-year–olds, the children are asked to sign in next to their names every morning when they arrive. It fulfils a range of literacy skills from name and letter recognition through to the writing their name out in full. There is no pressure on the activity, and if the children choose to colour in the box or 'emergent write' on the sheet, that is also fine. Over the academic year however clear progression can be seen from the start of August through to June in every child's ability. The nursery staff simply photographed the sheet every Wednesday (they could have done it every day, but this was felt to be too much data to be manageable). At the end of the year, they were able to show the children and have a conversation about their progression through the year.

BLUE GROUP SIGN IN SHEET	
Edward	
Freya	
Corner	
Mathew	
Layla	
Sarah	
Liam	

Wilbury Primary School, Enfield: Elaine and Ann were exploring the impact of a peer assessment on seven- and eight-year-olds writing. Over three cycles of enquiry they investigated the attitudes of children involved, children's thinking about their learning and progression as demonstrated by individuals' written work. They did not want to add to the burden of the children and so regularly collected written work samples over the academic year. Each sample was copied and a sticker used to annotate it with key information such as nature of task, amount of time allocated, objectives and child's targets alongside the teacher assessment completed based on national curriculum levels. This meant a quantitative analysis of progression based on attainment could be undertaken across the class, as well as a more detailed analysis of the narrative of improvement across different groups.

The Roseland School, Cornwall: Mandi was interested in how to engage a large class of final year, fifteen- to sixteen-year-old, boys in English. The class were predicted to do well in their GCSE exams, but she felt that she needed the teaching and learning to be active and varied to address the needs of the class. One technique used was presentations, where working in small groups slides shows were prepared, shared and then improved based on peer feedback. The teacher used the PowerPoints as evidence of the progression made and the extent to which the students understood the expectations of the curriculum being followed.

Quality Criteria

Recognisability	The crossover between the normal assessment practices and the use of work samples as a research tool in regards the language and the skill set is an advantage. Teachers just need to see it as a valid transfer from one domain into the other.
Metacognitive	A piece of work completed in the classroom is more or less representative of what a student could do on that day, with due consideration of all the things that could have influenced that. Different types of work, how open or closed the task, or how much of their 'working' was captured, will represent the thinking behind that outcome more or less accurately, but it is the teachers reaction to that which provides insight.

Multiple Voices	There is directness to using work samples in your enquiry. If the work samples are reproduced as evidence then it gives the children and young people a very obvious voice in the outcome of the research. Also the fact that they are drawing on your expertise as a practitioner, using a skill set that all teachers are very familiar with, then they give teacher-researchers a level of confidence that they might not feel with other less usual types of evidence.
Pragmatic	Work samples are inherently practical; they are a tool straight from the teachers' normal repertoire and as such should not require too much adaptation. Rather it is a matter of adding clear strategy to their use in relation to the research questions being asked – this matching is essential in ensuring the narrative if the research is clear.
Evocative	As work samples come directly from the classroom then they foreground the practice under investigation and evoke the teaching and learning experience very immediately to the reader. They use a technique that is one of the cornerstones of teaching practice and transfer that voice to a research objective, as such they give teachers a confidence and insight second to very few sources of evidence.

Frequently Asked Questions

Should we use quantitative or qualitative assessment techniques?	This is really up to you; both have advantages and disadvantages. The decision lies around the decision between closing the outcome down, enabling the inclusion of larger populations and the potential of statistical analysis, or opening it up but focusing on fewer individuals in depth.
Should I use a one off assessment technique or collect work samples over a longer period of time?	The response is similar to above and has the same pragmatics in regards the research. But using your pedagogic knowledge it also draws a decision between a more summative approach and a more formative, progression orientated set of data. Use your teacher instinct to think about what will answer your research question effectively.

How do work samples support understanding of professional learning?	As work samples have their origins so firmly in an individual's practice, then they have an immediacy in speaking to the outcomes of an enquiry. Their use gives a direct connection between the research process to classroom practice. For effective research use there needs to be a systematic nature to their collection, who have they been collected from and why, and the assessment should have clarity and rigour to allow for accurate comparisons and/or effective communication of outcomes.

Further reading

Arter, J. A. and Spandel, V. (1992). Using portfolios of student work in instruction and assessment. *Educational Measurement: Issues and Practice*, 11(1): 36–44.

Black, P. (2001). Dreams, strategies and systems: Portraits of assessment past, present and future. *Assessment in Education: Principles, Policy & Practice*, 8: 65–85.

Boston, M. D. (2014). Assessing Instructional Quality in Mathematics Classrooms through Collections of Students' Work. In *Transforming Mathematics Instruction*. New York: Springer International Publishing, 501–523.

Downton, A. and Wright, V. (2016). A rich assessment task as a window into students' multiplicative reasoning. Paper presented at the Annual Meeting of the Mathematics Education Research Group of Australasia (MERGA) (39th, Adelaide, South Australia, 2016).

James, M. and Pedder, D. (2006). Beyond method: Assessment and learning practices and values. *Curriculum Journal*, 17: 109–138.

McConney, A. A., Schalock, M. D., and Del Schalock, H. (1998). Focusing improvement and quality assurance: Work samples as authentic performance measures of prospective teachers' effectiveness. *Journal of Personnel Evaluation in Education*, 11(4): 343–363.

Concept: Often when we rank items we are more confident of what goes at the top and what goes at the bottom, and the middle is a bit more vague. Ranking items into a diamond helps respondents deal with this grey area, while also opening up a dialogue with others about the ordering process. Since practitioner research deals with complexity and multiple competing agendas, Diamonds can help to tease out the relationships between elements and help collaborative researchers to establish democratically what participants want to prioritise.

Provenance: A pedagogic approach linked to the tradition of thinking skills (Rockett and Percival, 2002) that has increasing recognition as a research tool that is useful in scaffolding responses (Baumfield et al., 2012).

Use in research: Diamond ranking has been used as part of a mediated interview (with children: O'Kane, 2010 and adults: Towler et al., 2011) and as a tool with primary teaching and learning objectives and with a more formal research intent, such as a survey (Towler et al., 2011). There is good potential to use this tool with a population that includes a range of ages and abilities (Woolner et al., 2010). It has flexibility in allowing more or less structure to be introduced by the researcher to the responses elicited. By giving the respondents nine items (these could be quotes, images or physical objects) and a clear outline of a diamond then the activity is relatively closed and the researcher can assign numerical rank to each item as graded by the respondents (Clark, 2012). However, the task can be opened up by increasing the number of items given (the respondents then need to discard items not perceived as relevant), by decreasing the number of items and giving blank place holders (the respondents then have the space to introduce their own place holders), by being flexible about the ranking output (does it have to be a diamond: is it more important that there respondents engage in conversation comparing the items?), by asking the respondents to choose their own nine objects based on a theme (e.g. by asking respondents to take nine photographs before the diamond ranking activity) or by using diamond ranking to validate research interpretations by giving the findings or quotes from a previous round of data collection as the items to be ranked and asking for respondents' views. Data tends to come from the rank of the items and/or from the rationales given for the rank (either written on a physical version of the diamond or spoken and recorded in some way). Obviously the elicited data can vary depending on the researcher's choices from numerical ranking, through to a more traditional looking interview transcript of the decision-making process. The way in which the activity is structured and, as a result, the data that arises will be somewhat dependent on the nature of the population (aptitudes, ability and quantity/sample) being surveyed. At analysis stage, an important consideration is the extent to which the actual diamonds are used as part of the analysis, alongside the quantitative and/or qualitative data is important. This type of approach has been shown to have good fit with participatory approaches and partnership working (O'Kane, 2010; Wall et al., 2012).

Exemplars:

Lucy Fisher, Carterhatch Junior School, Enfield: Lucy wanted to explore how explicitly involving Year 4 (eight- and nine-year-olds) in investigating barriers and aids to their learning might have an impact upon their learning. Her approach was aligned with partnership working and facilitating the students to become active enquirers into their own learning. She began by planning a series of short and active 'Learning Lessons' that initially encouraged the children to think about learning in general. She moved on to focus on the 'learning environments' and the children were asked to sort through pictures by diamond ranking them. They did this activity initially as a group, however many children did not agree with others in their groups and expressed a wish to do the activity individually too. Over the next couple of weeks, she was able to take small groups of children out of class around the school, identifying the different learning environments that were available to them using the diamond ranking activity as a starting point.

Pele Mobaolorunduro, Geoff Davison, Mo Pamplin and Dean Britton, School of Health, Care and Early Years & Learning Services, Lewisham College: In Lewisham FE College four team members wanted to explore student perceptions of the jump between level two and level three study and think about the most appropriate ways for staff to support students making this important transition. One element of the data collection was for students to diamond rank their confidence and familiarity with a range of study skills (e.g. note taking, time management etc.). Results were achieved by reviewing the diamond ranking activity and giving a score of 5 to the single skill placed on the top row, 4 to the two skills in row 2 and so on. The mean and modal score for each skill were then extracted, although this placed the skills in very similar ranking positions, with the two extremes unaffected. The team concluded that students managed to complete their studies at level two, and progress to level three, without properly developing the study skills needed to be effective learners. It was not that the students did not have an awareness of the importance of more sophisticated skills, recognising the advantages to being organised and planning their time and resources; they just did not use them. As a result of the activity scaffolded by the diamond ranking activity the team recognised that attention needed to be paid to enhancing students' personal responsibility and organisation, to ensure that ownership of these kinds of study skills is fully taken on by the students.

Rachel Dunn, Northumbria University: Rachel's research looks at the training of lawyers and the role that practical experience plays in developing key skills. Her initial discussions with students and tutors about which skills are important led to the development of a larger diamond with sixteen options, at least two of which were always left blank for participants' own ideas. Rachel conducted single diamond exercises with employers, academic staff and students in the UK, Poland and the Czech Republic as well as repeated diamonds with groups of Northumbria students. Each exercise was video-recorded and transcribed, so Rachel had the final.diamonds, the evolution of each diamond and the discussions to analyse, enabling her to rank skills quantitatively, to track the movement of cards during discussions to assess group process and to explore the transcripts to understand the reasoning behind the hierarchies.

Quality Criteria

Recognisability	Diamond ranking is a strategy that can be used both from a teaching and learning or a research intent, or to bridge the two. The semiotics of the ranking process means that it fits well as a school-based task – for staff and students. The structure of the diamond and therefore the process of ranking the items are relatively self-explanatory but are inherent of space for discussion and productive dissonance. As such it is a relatively simple start to what can become quite complex ideas.
Metacognitive	Diamond ranking originates from the Thinking Skills tradition, as such it facilitates concept elicitation due to its potential for open-ended discussion. The nature of the task means that respondents can have time to consider ideas and think about their assumptions and attitudes to the topic. This means that the activity is more likely to be metacognitive.
Multiple Voices	Diamond ranking can be done individually or as part of a group. Recording discussion allows for in-depth study of participants' perceptions and higher-order thinking about a topic. However, when done independently and on a larger scale then it can also enable the surveying of a wide range of perspectives which can result in the calculation of group means and their range of opinion on a topic.
Pragmatic	The flexibility of the process means that the practitioner can add or remove structure and play with the number and type of objects to be ranked; this means that it is adaptable to a wide range of participants' ages and abilities and research intents. It can be used in a survey to gather quantitative data of the ranking process or it can be used in a more discursive setting as part of an interview. It is adaptable depending on the intent of the practitioner.
Evocative	As the completion of a diamond 9, particularly within a group setting, allows space for thinking around a topic and the consideration of other viewpoints, this means that there is the potential for movement in the respondents' thinking. The snapshot aspect allows for the possibility of change and reflection on current context.

Frequently Asked Questions

What is the merit of including blank cards?	Blank cards make the exercise both more participatory and more divergent, so are a good thing if you want to explore concepts but problematic if you want to test an existing theory. You'll need to decide what is most important to you.
My participants don't want to make a diamond. Does this matter?	There's always one. If you are recording the conversation and interested primarily in the thought process, it's not *as vital*, although it will cut down your data set of completed diamonds to compare. If your participants are adamant that the cards are all equally important and want to put them in a straight line, it may be worth asking if they think they can all be *tackled* simultaneously in order to draw out the hierarchy.
How does diamond ranking support professional learning?	Diamond ranking can be a relatively quick and structured way of getting a response from quite large groups of individuals. The more that you close the task down, i.e. quantify the responses, the quicker it is do. It is equivalent to a visual survey asking for a ranking of concepts/ideas/responses. Of course if you complicate the task, using some of the ideas above, then this maybe negates the ease slightly, but still the structure allows for analysis across large samples relatively quickly. If your enquiry is wanting to survey the class or year group school about their attitudes to a change in timetable or school building, for example, then diamond ranking could be novel and pedagogically appropriate way to go about it.

Further reading

Baumfield, V., Hall, E., and Wall, K. (2012). *Action Research in the Classroom* (2nd Edition). London: SAGE.

Clark J. (2012). Using diamond ranking as visual cues to engage young people in the research process. *Qualitative Research Journal*, 12(2): 222–237.

Hopkins, E. (2008). Classroom conditions to secure enjoyment and achievement: The pupils' voice. Listening to the voice of every child matters. *Education*, 3–13 36(4): 393–401.

Niemi, R., Kumpulainen, K., and Lipponen, L. (2015). Pupil as active participants: Diamond ranking as a tool to investigate pupils' experiences of classroom practices. *European Educational Research Journal*, 14(2): 138–150.

O'Kane, C. (2010). The development of participatory techniques: Facilitating children's views about decisions which affect them. In P. Christensen and A. James (eds.), *Research with Children: Perspectives and Practice*. London: RoutledgeFalmer, 136–159.

Rockett, M. and Percival, S. (2002). *Thinking for Learning*. Stafford: Network Educational Press.

Towler, C., Wooler, P., and Wall, K. (2011). "In college it's more explicit. Outside college it's just your life": Exploring teachers' and students' conceptions of learning in two further education colleges. *Journal of Further and Higher Education*, 35(4): 501–520.

Wall, K., Higgins, S., Hall, E., and Woolner, P. (2012). 'That's not quite the way we see it': The epistemological challenge of visual data. *International Journal of Research and Methods in Education*, 36(1): 3–22.

Woolner, P., Clark, J., Hall, E., Tiplady, L., Thomas, U., and Wall, K. (2010). Pictures are necessary but not sufficient: Using visual methods to consult users about school design. *Learning Environment Research*, 13(1): 1–22.

TOOL 7: STUDENTS AS RESEARCHERS

Concept: 'Students as researchers' (SaR) is a model with direct parallels to practitioner research, where students take control of the research process from inception to dissemination. There is often an ethos of partnership working underpinning the activity although the extent to which power is truly handed over varies depending on intent and age of participants.

Provenance: Arising from student voice work, SaR aims to facilitate student perspectives that have increased authenticity and warrant that are more likely to be listened to by adults in power. By engaging in research then the aim is to create an increasingly informed and robust student voice that can engage in creative productive discourse with teachers creating new insight on old debates and generating new ways of looking at the lived experience of children and young people.

Use in research: SaR is a relatively new and developing research approach. It combines theory around pupil voice (Ruddock et al., 1996), participation (Hart, 1992), and enquiry methodology (Cochran-Smith and Lytle, 1999) and pedagogy (Leat and Reid, 2012). Projects using SARs aim to gain better understanding of students' perspectives through facilitating enquiry-based research whereby the students can investigate the topic for themselves to gain deeper understanding (Kellett, 2010; Thompson and Gunter, 2006). The ideal is teachers, researchers and students learning together and co-producing knowledge. There is increasing evidence of how such an approach can be effective with young students as well as students with special needs.

Handing control of the enquiry over to students can be perceived of as risky but we have observed, in the majority of cases, the more students are trusted (with appropriate scaffold and training: Kellett, 2005) the greater the reward (Bragg, 2007). One of the most successful student councils we have seen was made up of primary children from the age of four to eleven and was given a budget of £3000 to spend on what they (and the student body) felt the school needed. That was the only input from the teaching staff and the children were trusted to spend the money wisely; needless to say they met the challenge and the benefits to the individuals and the school community were huge. Fielding's (2001) typology of pupil involvement is useful in thinking about the level of control and participation and indeed the consequences of giving pseudo-control for a research agenda without true understanding of the consequences.

Exemplars:

John Welham, Camborne Science and Community College, Cornwall: John wanted an authentic students' perspective on the school's approach to metacognitive-based pedagogies. He 'contracted' a group of twelve/thirteen-year-old researchers to engage with a three-year process, so until they left the school at sixteen, of enquiry. Each academic year the students had increased decision-making powers over the research intent, process and dissemination of findings. The first year started with the design and implementation of a learning log; in year 2 the students undertook interviews and questionnaires with peers; and in year 3 they co-designed and evaluated a curriculum based on their findings with staff. The intervention yielded some fascinating insights into students' perceptions of learning, target-setting and the whole exam preparation process.

James Mannion, Sea View, Sussex: For drugs education, rather than the usual format of giving information about various drugs along with a prohibitive message, the PSHE teaching team wanted to get students to investigate the topic in a way that was meaningful by carrying out an original piece of research. First students did a literature review, where they looked at local and national news stories involving young people, drugs and alcohol. From this a decision was made to investigate people's attitudes to drugs to try and understand why so many people do things that are essentially bad for them. This involved writing a questionnaire (after researching and discussing what makes a good questionnaire and thinking about attitude measures) and getting people to complete it, across a spread of ages. Research ethics was discussed a lot; for example, they weren't allowed to ask questions which might lead people to incriminate themselves or others. They also had to gain written consent from participants, explaining what the research was for, that their answers would be anonymised and treated confidentially etc. The end result was a report summarising findings and sharing what they had found out. A PSHE lead from the local authority was blown away by the maturity and proactive way in which the students managed their own learning.

Louise Brown and Dawn Hunter, Amble First School, Northumberland: Across the whole school there was a desire to build children's capacity to learn new language and describe their learning, to raise self-esteem and build confidence and to encourage inclusive and active participation in learning. In reception classes (4–5 years) this was done using an approach Dawn and Louise called 'Learning Detectives'. Children were encouraged to detect good learning, wearing a deer stalker hat if they liked, using this prompt sheet. The children shared their findings with the rest of the class at the end of their investigation. This supported children in engaging with the language of learning and over time the identification of learning became unprompted and part of normal practice.

Quality Criteria

Recognisability	For a teacher engaged in a practitioner enquiry then using a similar approach with students can seem like an obvious step. The fit with enquiry-based pedagogies also encourages this. The trick is to ensure that power is truly handed to the students rather than pseudo-decision making, if the teacher retains all the control as in 'normal' teaching then there is the potential for a backlash.
Metacognitive	In a SaR approach students are required to take ownership of their learning through objectives, process, outcome and evaluation. The research process encourages multiple higher-order thinking skills and techniques that are supportive of lifelong learning. The trick is to support the students so they recognise this metacognitive element as equally important to the research outcomes.
Multiple Voices	Engaging a SaR group, if done well, should support voice agendas, but beware bias in student selection. Perceptions of the technicality of research can mean the involvement of more able and/or motivated students. To ensure multiple representative voices then a key role for any facilitator is to provide scaffolds that support the process without inhibiting student participation.
Pragmatic	A strength of SaR is the fact that it fulfils both research and pedagogic objectives. The skill set inherent in research mirrors many facets of advanced study. In addition, asking students to invest time and thought to a project, if handled sensitively, generates 'buy in' from the student body. This can support change management.
Evocative	Students involved in a SaR initiative are not just being encouraged to have a voice, but rather to have an informed voice, to ask questions about a topic of interest and generate an evidence-based opinion on that basis. These are fundamental skills of political engagement in a democracy. Its more about whether the school system is ready to listen and act on these voices once they start.

Frequently Asked Questions

How much control should I give to the students?	The answer to this question is really as much as possible and where it's unrealistic to give more power, and this is understandable in a school setting, then this needs to be discussed with the students so they understand the boundaries and rationale.
How much research training is needed for the students?	By engaging in the process of research then even young students will quickly start to think about key questions, such as what makes good data? Ethical approaches? What is quality? They learn by doing and will often apply the same investigative skills to finding out about the research process that they are using to explore the target topic.
How does a student as researchers approach support understanding of professional learning?	Involving SaR in your enquiry means engaging in an informed dialogue with students about practice. You will of course benefit from their perspective, but by them being involved in the actual research, then you are more likely to be involved in a process of co-constructing understandings of practice. This collaborative process has value for both parties in that it provides insight that supports learning and teaching, but the dialogue ensures a tighter feedback loop between student and teachers which has to be a good thing.

Further reading

Bragg, S. (2007). 'But I listen to children anyway!'—Teacher perspectives on pupil voice, *Educational Action Research*, 15(4): 505–518.

Brown, L. and Hunter, L. (2008). *Developing a Language for Learning to Support Assessment for Learning*. Available at: http://www.campaign-for-learning.org.uk/cfl/index.asp

Cochran-Smith, M. and Lytle, S. L. (1999). Relationships of knowledge and practice: Teacher learning in communities. *Review of Research in Education*, 24: 249–305.

Fielding, M. (2001). Students as radical agents of change. *Journal of Educational Change*, 2(2): 123–141.

Hart, R. A. (1992). *Children's Participation: From Tokenism to Citizenship. Innocenti Essays No.4*. Florence: UNICEF International Child Development Centre.

Kellett, M. (2005). *How to Develop Children as Researchers: A Step by Step Guide to Teaching the Research Process*. London: SAGE.

Kellett, M. (2010). Small shoes, big steps! Empowering children as active researchers. *American Journal of Community Psychology*, 46(1–2): 195–203.

Kellett, M. (2011). Empowering children and young people as researchers: Overcoming barriers and building capacity. *Child Indicators Research*, 4(2): 205–219.

Leat, D. and Reid, A. (2012). Exploring the role of student researchers in the process of curriculum development. *Curriculum Journal*, 23(2): 189–205.

Mannion, J. and Mercer, N. (2016). Learning to learn: Improving attainment, closing the gap at Key Stage 3. *The Curriculum Journal*. doi: 10.1080/09585176.2015.1137778

Ruddock, J., Chaplin, R., and Wallace, G. (eds.). (1996). *School Improvement: What Can Pupils Tell Us?* London: Fulton.

Thomson, P. and Gunter, H. (2006). From 'consulting pupils' to 'pupils as researchers': A situated case narrative. *British Educational Research Journal*, 32(6): 839–856.

Welham, J. (2010). *Why do some student engage more fully with L2L than others?* Available at: http://www.campaign-for-learning.org.uk/cfl/index.asp

TOOL 8: ARTS-BASED RESEARCH

Concept: Arising out of the interpretivist research paradigm and drawing on arts-based therapy, arts-based research uses systematic creative and artistic techniques to facilitate the process of thinking and to support expression of experience. Arts-based research is often seen as particularly useful in relation to subjects that are challenging to articulate either because they are deeply personal, are hard to verbalise or are emotionally significant, or for giving voice to those who are marginalised.

Provenance: Motivated by the idea of 'new ways of seeing and saying' (Eisner, 1997, p. 4), arts-based approaches have established a role for exploring difficult topics, to managing diversity of content and supporting a range of expression when undertaking meaning-making and issues related to ideas and agency (Sullivan, 2010). They can be used at all stages of a research project – data collection, analysis, interpretation or dissemination (Leavy, 2008). The range of techniques represented in this category are wide ranging from drawing, painting, collage, experimental writing forms, poems, dance, drama, musical composition, sculpture, photography and film making (to name a few); the commonality comes from the commitment to an artistic process and a foregrounding of creative understanding as a result (Sullivan, 2010).

Use in research: In 1994, Gallas described how children viewed the world and how the language they used was multi-modal. The potential of arts-based research is to tap into some of these less acknowledged languages. With strong overlaps to visual methods, a significant difference of arts-based research approaches is the emphasis on process and the way that making art is supportive of reflection and introspection, therefore facilitating a level of sustained engagement with the topic that might otherwise be absent (McNiff, 2008). The process of undertaking sustained enquiry into a topic via the medium of making art is seen by its proponents as inherently cognitive, but also as disruptive of 'normal' thinking (Leavy, 2008). To achieve this takes a greater creative commitment than might be presumed with a more traditional research approach. In addition, the response to a piece of art can also be used for research purposes, and can be evocative and supportive of eliciting a range of views. Indeed it can be seen as particularly interesting when eliciting perspectives from those outside the artists' community (McNiff, 2008).

One of the main challenges for this area of research is codification against more traditional forms of research, particularly around judgements of quality, with interrogations of validity, trustworthiness and authenticity being particularly important (Leavy, 2008). The role of the researcher and of the researched are often merged with a collaborative intent towards meaning-making and better understanding. This can be fraught with risk, professional and personal, as the artistic aspects of the research require a critical community that is supportive of the process while also being aware of potential judgements being made (Cahnmann-Taylor and Siegemund, 2008). Similarly the nature of the outputs of this kind of research might not fit with usual forms of research output, such as write-ups and printed forms of dissemination, as such there is a prerogative to follow through with the creative ideas and try something different, while embracing the alternative audience that might be reached (Smithbell, 2010).

Exemplars:

Helen Burns, Baltic Centre for Contemporary Art: A group of eight- and nine-year-olds were introduced to the world of contemporary sculpture by exhibitions at the Baltic. They were facilitated in using the art as metaphor for their thinking and learning. Over time the students were guided, by a local artist, through the process of developing and producing a piece of art that represented their understanding of themselves as learners. The children were encouraged to talk about their sculptures and exhibited them at a private viewing at the Baltic.

"A war robot with lots of dents...{representing} not giving up because even though your team might, it doesn't mean you should."

"Before, I gave up but now I know not to {because} I might be faced with a really hard Test"

Frances Breslin Davda, Strathclyde University: As part of data collection, children aged six to eight were asked whether they had ever *not* asked a question because they were too shy or embarrassed. To help the children feel comfortable and to encourage them to think about their experiences, Frances used a puppet (Jack) and discussed why Jack might choose not to ask a question if he wanted to find something out. To keep the children engaged, so children without writing or oral skills could participate, and so no one had to reveal their answer in front of their classmates, children were asked to put a tick on a folded piece of paper if yes, they had ever not asked a question, and a cross if no they hadn't, and then place their paper in a pirate's treasure chest. The treasure chest stimulated a lot of excitement and discussion from the children, and the researcher used the chest to explain to the children that their answers were as valuable to researcher as pirate's treasure, and that Frances would honour their anonymity, the same way pirates would never tell where their treasure is hidden.

Quality Criteria

Recognisability The techniques and forms included under the heading of arts-based research are varied and as such a range of tools can be offered to suit different dispositions and intents. Tools are likely to be familiar to participants and often perceived of as fun, offering a way in, but also could elicit an emotional response (positive or negative) to their use.

Metacognitive	The process of producing a piece of art has explicit implications for cognitive engagement. It creates time for thinking and space for dialogue as the art work progresses and develops that are supportive of deep engagement with challenging topics.
Multiple Voices	One of the perceived strengths of arts-based research is the fact that it opens up new forms of expression as well as providing a base for a process that is supportive of a different way of thinking. As such it is argued to gain access to domains of experience that might be difficult, and/or facilitate voice from individuals for whom traditional forms of expression may be challenging.
Pragmatic	The enquiry process advocated under arts-based research is one that has much commonality with successful teaching and learning, as such it can provide a bridge between pedagogy and methodology in providing supportive spaces that allow participants (and researchers) to engage with thoughtful responses to difficult provocations.
Evocative	An arts-based approach provides a lens through which difficult subjects and hard-to-reach participants can be addressed and considered. The types of data produced, the art work or performance aspects, provide the basis for original ways of disseminating that can often prompt emotional responses from an audience that might otherwise have remained disengaged.

Frequently Asked Questions

Does the data come from the process or output?	The answer to this depends on your intent, as either would be appropriate. Data from process would include the conversation generated by the process of undertaking art and the output would be the piece of art, whatever that might be. Of course you could choose to use both.
How do I decide on themes or categories for analysis?	Once you have decided on the data that you are taking forward, then you need to think about the analysis technique that is most appropriate. For text-based output then there is a lot written about how to analyse; if it is the art that is taken forwards then you probably need to be a bit more flexible and creative using interpretivist techniques as well as some media analysis and/or art appreciation. Whichever, some sort of validation from the participants would be beneficial to ensure that the analysis fits with their perceptions.

How does this tool give insight for my professional learning?	Arts-based methods are particularly useful for facilitating dialogue around difficult or challenging topics, with students or colleagues, where thinking maybe hard to articulate or problematic to say out loud. The art process provides a thinking space around which those thoughts can be considered before they are made public. In addition, they can mediate power dynamics by changing the emphasis of an exchange. With both of these advantages however are ethical implications around the extent to which you are putting respondents at ease and supporting them in talking about things they might otherwise not want aired – be careful you are not overstepping the line and there is an option for retraction if your participant is not happy.

Further reading

Burns, H. (In press). Imagining Better Learning: A theoretical exploration of our understanding of imagination, its role in cognition and metacognition, its relationship with visual-art and what is implied for visual-arts-pedagogies, EdD Thesis, Newcastle University.

Cahnmann-Taylor, M. and Siegesmund, R. (2008). *Arts-based Research in Education: Foundations for Practice*. New York: Routledge.

Eisner, E. (1997). The promise and perils of alternative forms of data representation. *Educational Researcher*, 26(6): 4–11.

Gallas, K. (1994). *The Languages of Learning: How Children Talk, Write, Dance, Draw, and Sing Their Understanding of the World*. New York: Teachers College Press.

Leavy, P. (2008). *Method Meets Art: Arts-based Research Practice*. New York: Guilford Press.

McNiff, S. (2008). *Art-based Research*. London: Jessica Kingsley Publishers.

Smithbell, P. (2010). Arts-based research in education: A review. *The Qualitative Report*, 15(6): 1597–1601.

Sullivan, G. (2010). *Art Practice as Research: Inquiry in Visual Arts*. London: SAGE Publishing.

TOOL 9: CARTOONS AND COMICS

Concept: Comics and cartoons aim to support respondents in giving a narrative response using words and pictures. McCloud (1993) defines cartoons as 'juxtaposed pictorial and other images in deliberate sequence, intended to convey information and/or to produce an aesthetic response in the viewer' (p. 9).

Provenance: The use of cartoons and comics in research and pedagogy has a growing tradition, for example, work on concept cartoons (Keogh and Naylor, 1999) and PVTs (Wall and Higgins, 2006); however the image used in these cases represents a static point in time. Galman's (2009) work has shown how graphic novels can be useful in supporting students in developing a flexible narrative: 'To create a performance ... a drama of their words' (p. 213). So combining these ideas, cartoon storyboards were designed (Wall et al., 2016) to explore participants' stories and reflections.

Use in research: This technique is really useful when a narrative response or interpretation is useful. For example, when your enquiry is about a process such as learning (Wall et al., 2016) or a journey such as migration (Cameron and Theron, 2011), and indeed there is a significant body of work around using cartoons to engage with autobiography, adult-life journeys etc. (e.g. Watson, 2008). Therefore, the prompt used with participants at the start of the activity should encourage the telling of a story over time and encourage the identification of stages in the story to represent the passing of time appropriately; although be careful not to impact too much on the response.

The technique has been shown to be sensitive to difficult topics and enabling of contributions that might otherwise be challenging to gather. As cartoons might be perceived as non-mainstream then asking participants to engage with their production can grab attention and encourage a level of engagement that might otherwise be unusual; for the same reason it can offer dissemination routes to hard-to-reach audiences. However, it is important to be aware that there is an inherent level of skill in being able to represent your thinking in pictorial form and there is added complexity of storytelling in the cartoon format (although the inclusion of words can help with this: Wall, 2017) and so providing scaffolds, such as framing and/or (verbal/artistic) prompts, might be appropriate to support completion. That is not to say it is not possible for even young children to participate in such an activity (Wall et al., 2016), but recognition of the cognitive load and impact of the medium should be considered in relation to the data collected (Wall, 2017).

Cartoons do not have to be used as part of the data collection and the process of drawing out a narrative allows a more accessible way of presenting complex ideas; this can be seen in the tradition of graphic facilitation, commonly used in the corporate world as a way to synthesise understandings and also to disseminate outcomes. However, with a research eye, thinking about how a cartoon approach can give a new perspective of an interview transcript or piece of theory (see the example of Chris Bailey and Katy Vigurs below) and as such can be a novel way to get validation of outcomes from hard-to-reach audiences.

Exemplars:

Katy Vigurs, Staffordshire University: Katy used interview transcripts from a project (funded by the Society for Research into Higher Education) to show the financial pressures faced by many young people in higher education. The overarching narratives that emerged were inherently visual and she employed students pursuing BA in Cartoon and Comic Arts to transform the findings into graphic representations in the form of a thirty-page comic book. This comic book has enabled the research to reach a much-wider audience, particularly students and their families, informing decision-making about their finances and graduate futures (Priego, 2016; Vigurs et al., 2016a, b).

Chris Bailey, Sheffield Hallam University (www. mrchrisbailey.co.uk): Chris's doctoral study involved an exploration of the 'lived experience' of a group of children playing collaboratively to create a 'virtual community', in an after-school Minecraft Club. When reflecting on the participant-produced video data, Chris found that traditional methods of transcription that relied purely on the written word did not authentically reflect the lively and creative nature of the children's play, in and around the videogame. He therefore developed a transcription method involving comics that included the visual elements of the videos. Seeing the value of working multimodally led Chris to extend his use of comics to other aspects of the project, using illustration as a means of developing theory and responding to data, through a process of thinking and representing ideas.

'INVESTIGATING THE LIVED EXPERIENCE OF AN AFTER-SCHOOL MINECRAFT CLUB'

CHRIS BAILEY, SHEFFIELD HALLAM UNIVERSITY

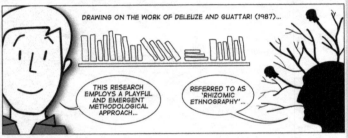

Maths Teacher, Preston Lodge High School, Scotland:
This teacher was interested in how children in lower and
middle groups could be encouraged to approach challenge in
maths with a positive, 'can do' mindset. It was noted that they
often gave up and were not happy moving out of their comfort
zone; as a result this was holding back their achievement. As
part of the exploratory stage, 'what's going on?', the teacher
asked the students to draw a cartoon story of how they

approached a maths problem. The children in two classes were asked to complete the task. They were encouraged to be as honest as possible and that their answers would only be used to investigate how to make practice better for all. They were given a strip of six boxes and asked to use as many as needed.

Quality Criteria

Recognisability	The cartoon format is generally well-understood and has universal appeal across age groups. The combination of words and pictures in frames telling a story is also relatively well-known; indeed in our experience participants have needed little encouragement to use and adapt a 3x2 box template to fit the story that they want to tell in the way they want to tell it.
Metacognitive	The focus on storytelling adds the dynamic of time to any response. While it adds complexity and therefore cognitive load, the semiotics of cartooning and associated structure give adequate scaffold for this. Indeed, engaging with this encourages deeper reflection on the topic as participants engage with how best to tell their 'story'. If the story being told also happens to be about the process of learning, then the potential for metacognition increases.
Multiple Voices	The voice element of this technique is primarily about giving voice to those who might not otherwise be heard or by sharing research outcomes with hard-to-reach groups. Cartooning is not for all, but for some it is a great way of expressing a narrative response. It also allows communication of ideas in a way that is not dominated by literacy or numeracy skills and as such allows the elicitation of voice with hard-to-reach groups.
Pragmatic	By giving scaffolds, such as framing, and assurances that quality of drawing is not the key aspect of the task then cartoons can be used with a range of students. Alternatively by using artists or students of art, like Katy did, you can generate an outcome for a range of purposes.

Evocative	By focusing on a drawn narrative then cartoons and comics are adding something different to the research process, and this is likely to elicit some kind of response because of its difference to what is normally done. This can lead to strong reactions but if harnessed in the right way can elicit new perspectives and ways of viewing old ideas.

Frequently Asked Questions

I am not very good at drawing, does this matter?	No, the use of drawing and words combined means that a narrative can be expressed relatively easily, plus structures and prompts can be given, for example, speech and thought bubble shaped post-it notes, to help the process seem less scary. Alternatively use 'experts' or more experienced artists to do the drawing in partnership with the participants.
If I use cartoons as data, how do I manage the data set?	The data produced from using this technique is relatively complex and as such a balance will need to be struck at the design stage regarding the number of respondents and the method of analysis. The data fits well with inductive analysis processes of multiple readings and thematic generation, but a large sample can be generated relatively easily and therefore such an open process might be overwhelming. As a researcher, be aware of the task that you are setting yourself and balance your data set and analysis techniques accordingly.
How can cartoons and comics support research into professional learning?	Cartoons and comics have a number of advantages. First, they are a tool many children and young people find motivating in regards providing a response to support your enquiry. Asking for a response in cartoon format may well achieve higher response rates and greater engagement (validity) by your respondents. They also provide a format for your data that is easily communicated back to your students. In regards to encouraging a dialogue about your enquiry and closing feedback loops in your teaching and learning, they are a very effective tool.

Further reading
Bailey, C. (2016). Free the sheep: Improvised song and performance in and around a Minecraft community. *Literacy*, 50(2): 62–71.

Cameron, C. A. and Theron, L. (2011). With pictures and words I can show you: Cartoons portray resilient migrant teenagers' journeys. In L. Theron et al. (eds.), *Picturing Research: Drawing as Visual Methodology*. Rotterdam: Sense Publishers, 205–217.

Galman, S. A. C. (2009). The truthful messenger: Visual methods and representation in qualitative research in education. *Qualitative Research*, 9(2): 197–217. doi:10.1177/1468794108099321

Keogh, B. and Naylor, S. (1999). Concept cartoons, teaching and learning in science: An evaluation. *International Journal of Science Education*, 21(4): 431–446. doi: 10.1080/095006999290642

McCloud, S. (1993). *Understanding Comics: The Invisible Art*. New York: HarperCollins.

Priego, E. (2016). Comics as research, comics for impact: The case of higher fees, higher debts. *The Comics Grid: Journal of Comics Scholarship*, 6(1): 1–15. doi:10.16995/cg.101

Vigurs, K., Jones, S., and Harris, D. (2016a). *Greater Expectations of Graduate Futures? A Comparative Analysis of the Views of the Last Generation of Lower-Fees Undergraduates and the First Generation of Higher-Fees Undergraduates at Two English Universities, Research report for SRHE* (Society for Research in Higher Education). Available at: http://eprints.staffs.ac.uk/2502/

Vigurs, K., Jones, S., and Harris, D. (2016b). *Higher Fees, Higher Debts: Greater Expectations of Graduate Futures? – A Research-Informed Comic*. Stoke-on-Trent: Staffordshire University. Available at: http://eprints.staffs.ac.uk/2503/

Wall, K. (2017). Exploring the ethical issues related to visual methodology when including young children's voices in wider research samples. *International Journal of Inclusive Education*. doi:10.1080/13603116.2016.1260845

Wall, K., Hall, E., Higgins, S., and Gascoine, L. (2016). What does learning look like? Using cartoon story boards to investigate student perceptions (from 4 to 15) of learning something new. In M. Emme and A. Kirova (eds.), *Good Questions: Creative Collaborations with Kids*. Thunder Bay, ON: National Art Education Association.

Watson, J. (2008). Autographic disclosure and genealogies of desire in Alison Bechdel's Fun Home. *Biography*, 31(1): 27–58. doi:10.1353/bio.0.0006

TOOL 10: MAPPING ENVIRONMENTS

Concept: Learning and teaching are arguably defined by space and place. To map out where and when learning happens in an attempt to better understand the learning environment and its relationship with effective learning. It is likely to be useful for both the practitioner-researcher and the students. Of course, there is a healthy tradition around mapping thinking, but please see our section on mind mapping for this.

Provenance: Roger Hart, long-term advocate of child participation, often argued that map-making was an effective way for children to communicate their understanding of their environment (e.g. Hart, 1992). Relatively young children have been shown to be able to engage with maps (Blades and Spencer, 1987) and as a result they become a useful tool to engage in conversations about the learning environment they experience.

Use in research: Research shows that teachers and learners are aware of the physical environment and often have strong opinions about it (Burke and Grosvenor, 2003) that influence their attitudes and views to the learning experience as a whole. However, there is often a difference between what the students experience and what the teachers experience, and this can lead to dissonance that is useful to resolve. Maps can help identify any difference, but also can be a tool to support dialogue to resolve any resulting tensions (Woolner et al., 2010).

Mapping can include the literal use of community/school/classroom maps (Woolner, 2014; Woolner et al., 2010). This can involve participants in a process of adapting and annotating pre-made maps or aerial photographs (Blades and Spencer, 1987). Alternatively, it can involve participants in a process of map-making from scratch or with some scaffolding (Passini, 1984). We also include examples of learning walks or the Mosaic approach (Clark and Moss, 2011) – moving around the space to identify key area of interest; the participant may not be involved in map-making per se but it is likely that the researcher will engage with maps when recording or analysing the data.

In regards to the data, then the practitioner-enquirer can choose whether it is the actual maps that go forward to analysis, or the participants' reflections on them as captured via an interview process, either while the map is being created/annotated or retrospectively after the task has been completed. Lodge (2005) had an interesting process where she set up a video camera above the map, located between the interviewee and interviewer. This meant that not only was the dialogue around the map captured, but also any visual use of the map (e.g. pointing to specific elements) to elaborate the spoken word. The location of the video camera above the table had the added advantage that the children were not in shot and therefore anonymity was maintained.

Exemplars:

Pam Woolner and a team from Newcastle University: used two complementary tasks on school maps to explore how different groups of users used and perceived the physical space as part of a school redesign. One activity involved each person mapping his/her location during a typical day, adding stickers (colour-coded for 'places I like' and 'places I don't like'), and adding any other comments or annotations. In general, the students' mappings covered much of the building, while teachers and most other staff tended to stay in more limited areas. For example, in the maps reproduced, the Year 8 student visits many more places (left) than the science teacher (right) during a typical day (Woolner et al., 2010). This difference in experience prompted much discussion about potential solutions and improvements.

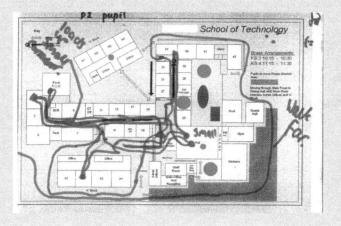

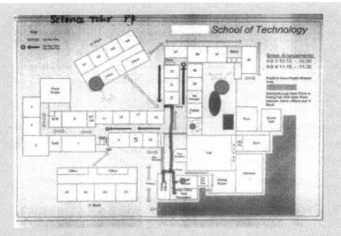

Infant School, Enfield: As part of an enquiry into how children used different spaces around the classroom, children move around the indoor and outdoor space with an adult taking photos with the tablet of their 'favourite places to learn'. The adult prompted the children as they took each photo regarding why it was a good place to learn and what the good learning was. This approach draws from Clark and Moss's (2011) Mosaic Approach and although the children did not create or use a map, the teacher was able to construct a map of their learning space and where the children perceived learning happening. The resulting map combined the images and the rationales of the children, meaning the teacher could explore different children's perceptions, the types of learning they were identifying as important (inside and outside of the classroom) and how the different spaces were used individually and in combination.

Quality Criteria

Recognisability	Maps are a tool that the majority of individuals, including quite young children, instinctively engage with, although it is rarely considered from a research perspective. As a visual representation of how space is used and perceived then maps provide new and useful ways to engage with a range of participants.

Metacognitive	The physical environment impacts on how we learn, but is rarely explored. Maps and map-making help to open up discussions about what makes a good learning environment and how we might learn differently in different spaces.
Multiple Voices	Within a school setting we learn alongside a whole community; exploring different perspectives on the spaces that we inhabit is helpful in developing a dialogue that is mutually respectful of how we learn. Maps are catalytic of such talk, showing quickly and simply how we each use a space and allowing comparisons.
Pragmatic	Once mapping as a tool has hit your radar, then it is relatively easy to do. In the age of Google Maps then maps of different locations and at different scales are relatively easy to get hold of. This is a tool that is relatively easy to use and with younger children you're probably hitting geography curriculum outcomes too.
Evocative	Most individuals do not engage very often with the physical space that they inhabit. Maps therefore as an enquiry tool help participants to engage in a novel way with the everyday. This encourages productive thinking and often new perspectives on old debates.

Frequently Asked Questions

When should I use a pre-drawn map and when should I use map-making?	The key here is to think about the intent with which you are using the mapping process and how linked do you want your participants' thinking to be to what they have already experienced. By using a pre-drawn map then you are providing some context/limit to the responses and you need to decide whether this literal association is useful or not.
How do I analyse maps as an output of an inquiry?	Maps, especially if totally free drawn by participants, are complex data and therefore choosing an analysis process that will cope with this complexity is important. If you have a lot of maps, then a top-down approach counting key aspects predetermined by experience and/or reading across the full range might be appropriate. If you have a small number then doing something that is more bottom-up will work, so trying not to have preconceived ideas and allowing the data to dictate what you think are the commonalities and differences across the sample.

How does this tool give insight for my professional learning?	By using a tool like mapping to engage in an enquiry about the space in which you learn and teach, you are starting to think about how the physical environment might impact. This is something that is often taken for granted and therefore remains implicit in most teachers' and students' experience; when foregrounded it often brings new ways of looking at old debates with productive challenges for developing practice.

Further reading

Blades, M. and Spencer, C. (1987). The use of maps by 4–6-year-old children in a large-scale maze. *British Journal of Developmental Psychology*, 5(1), 19–24.

Blades, M. and Spencer, C. (1987). Young children's recognition of environmental features from aerial photographs and maps. *Environmental Education and Information*, 6(3): 189–198.

Burke, C. and Grosvenor, I. (2003). *The School I'd Like*. London: RoutledgeFalmer.

Clark, A. and Moss, P. (2011). *Listening to Young Children: The Mosaic Approach*. Jessica Kingsley Publishers.

Lodge, C. (2005). From hearing voices to engaging in dialogue: Problematising student participation in school improvement. *Journal of Educational Change*, 6(2): 125–146. doi:10.1007/s10833-005-1299-3

Moos, R. H. (1979). *Evaluating Educational Environments*. San Francisco, CA: Jossey-Bass.

Passini, R. (1984). Spatial representations, a wayfinding perspective. *Journal of Environmental Psychology*, 4(2): 153–164.

Woolner, P. (ed.). (2014). *School Design Together*. Abingdon, Oxford: Routledge.

Woolner, P., McCarter, S., Wall, K., and Higgins, S. (2012). Changed learning through changed space: When can a participatory approach to the learning environment challenge preconceptions and alter practice?. *Improving Schools*, 15(1): 45–60.

Woolner, P., Hall, E., Higgins, S., McCaughey, C., and Wall, K. (2007). A sound foundation? What we know about the impact of environments on learning and the implications for building schools for the future. *Oxford Review of Education*, 33: 47–70.

Woolner, P., Clark, J., Hall, E., Tiplady, L., Thomas, U., and Wall, K. (2010). Pictures are necessary but not sufficient: Using a range of visual methods to engage users about school design. *Learning Environments Research*, 13(1), 1–22.

TOOL 11: ANALYSIS OF TALK

Concept: We make our understanding of the world public through our talk. This might be our understanding of facts or concepts, our understanding of appropriate ways of communicating in a particular social situation or a metacognitive understanding of ourselves and the processes we're engaged in. For practitioner research, talk offers many of the answers to our questions, as well as posing new ones as the analysis develops: as Walsh and Mann (2015) argue, it is a way to make reflective practice 'data-led'. It is also time- and resource-consuming: anything more than a initial impressionistic look at talk will require recording, repeated listening and transcription.

Provenance: It is likely that you'll be interested in *what is said* – calling for a content analysis – and also *who speaks, when and for how long* – calling for an interaction analysis – and possibly also *whether and how ideas are developed collaboratively through the talk* – which calls for a discourse analysis. The kind of study being undertaken will also shape the form of analysis: if we want to know how children organise their group work we might take several recordings of the first five minutes of group tasks and look at them from an open, immersive perspective to see what themes emerge; whereas if we want to know whether student mental health nurses have absorbed and are able to use key professional vocabulary, we might take several recordings of the first five minutes of patient review meetings and selectively code the terms used: '*correct, incorrect, lay equivalent substituted, ambiguous*'.

Use in Research: Analysis of talk draws on research from sociolinguistics, anthropology and sociology, with greater use of particular approaches depending on the intent of the researcher. There is a very large literature on how to go about this which we have suggested below that you enter by way of Neil Mercer and Steve Walsh's work as they make sense of the technicalities with a pragmatic view of the needs of the practitioner.

Sinclair and Coulthard (1975) first identified a prototypical form of teacher-led talk. They called it the IRF sequence consisting of three moves – an *initiation*, usually a teacher question, a *response*, usually from the student, and then a *follow-up*, where the teacher provides some kind of feedback. A range of research has followed up this IRF sequence (e.g. Dillon, 1994; Nystrand et al., 1997; Wells, 1993; Wood, 1992; Nassaji and Wells, 2000) and suggest it can take a variety of forms and functions leading to different levels of pupil participation and engagement, particularly through the use that is made of the follow-up move. For example, Hardman et al. (2003) showed how effective teachers were more likely in the feedback move to use uptake questions ('that's an interesting response from John, can anyone add anything to his answer?') and probe moves ('I like that thinking, can you tell me a bit more about what you mean?').

There's a key consideration about how 'naturalistic' the talk you capture is and the nature of the claims you can make about its authenticity. Any ethically recorded talk is by definition not private speech, so the speakers have a self-consciousness and also a sense of performance (even if what they think is required is not what the researcher is after). This is where the sociological perspective and discussions of explicit and implicit power are useful: there are things I can say in this space because I am the professor; there are things nobody can say; there are signals we can all give that something can be said; a more sophisticated and nuanced talk culture can be developed. This is a reflective conversation that needs to happen internally for the practitioner and researcher; it can be even more catalytic and valuable to have it with the participants.

Exemplars:

Stacey Cartner and Katy Richards, Hebden Green Community School: Hebden Green contains less than 100 pupils with a variety of learning and physical disabilities. Learners receive a curriculum that is tailored to their individual requirements from three to nineteen years. Katy and Stacey wanted to develop question and answer sessions. In doing this they hoped to develop learners' readiness to engage and interact with both staff and peers; to develop learners' ability to reflect on the activity and discuss their ideas; and to develop a range of strategies and resources to improve learners' communication with staff and peers. They decided to focus on literacy sessions in Key Stage 1 (children aged four to eight years). They felt the use of drama and role play would be the best vehicle for improving questioning techniques; as, if the children were in character, then they would find it easier to say/show/act how certain characters might be feeling at a certain time and be able to explain why using the context of the story.

They videoed lessons before and after a series of lessons focusing on the types and style of questioning used. In the pre-intervention video it showed teachers were mostly asking the children knowledge questions with yes/no or definite answers. To move away from this and ask a wider range of evaluative and reasoning questions they looked at their planning and tried to incorporate a wider range of questions into literacy lessons each day. After a term of this increased questioning, another lesson was planned to be videoed. The children chose suitable costumes for each character which lead to a discussion about who would be most suitable to play each character. This second video showed a greater range of questions which received a wider range of responses from the children. The next challenge was to make sure that all of the children had access to answering these questions, even though some are non-verbal.

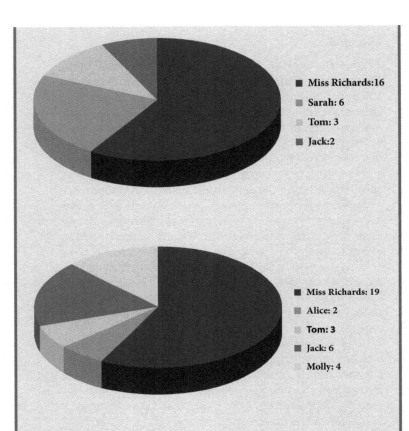

Miss Richards:16
Sarah: 6
Tom: 3
Jack:2

Miss Richards: 19
Alice: 2
Tom: 3
Jack: 6
Molly: 4

The Cambridge Primary Review Network and Wooler First School: Students acquiring and using talk for empowerment: In 2010–2012 the North East Regional Group of the Cambridge Primary Review Network (Alexander, 2010) set up a series of 'learning walks' in which groups of up to seven practitioners spent a morning or an afternoon in a setting. The key focus of each walk was identified by the host organisation – usually posed as a question for the participants to explore as they move around, linked in to one or more of the CPR aims. A collaborative reflection from each learning walk, co-ordinated by one of the university team, appeared on the Regional Network website. In this instance, the visit took place in November and the talk was recorded in shorthand by the researcher, resulting in less accurate data capture than a recording.

Part of our visit involved individual children giving us mini-tours of their classroom. What we as visitors particularly noted was the way in which these very articulate and charming children encouraged their peers to talk to us about what they were doing. They tended to begin by using open questions – *'Waddya want to tell the wifies [female visitors] about what you're doing?'* and then continued to draw out the conversation, encouraging elaboration – *'Willya say a bit more about how you chose the pictures? Why're these the best?'* and providing scaffolding prompts, particularly in respect to process – *'What's the peasy [easy] bit about this? What's been dead hard?'*. One class were conducting enquiries into aspects of Victorian children's lives and producing posters and on each table, they were able to explain what they had learned, how they had learned it and how they were going to communicate that most effectively. At the end of the morning, Victoria Symons, the class teacher, held a plenary in which she asked these key process questions and it became apparent that our guides had internalised these forms of talk and used them to encourage each other to show their skills and understanding.

Quality Criteria

Recognisability	While most practitioners recognise the value of talk, most humans automatically filter and edit what they hear from others and what they think they are saying themselves. For this reason, listening to recordings and reading transcripts are initially uncomfortable; we sound incoherent and unpolished. Working through this stage is important to come to an agreed standard for 'good enough' talk in a setting.
Metacognitive	The analysis of what is said, by whom and how leads inevitably to fundamental reflective questioning of the purpose(s) of our talk. By bringing this in to the forefront of awareness, we are able to make small changes. Leaving three seconds of silence rather than one can radically change the dialogue and who participates.

Multiple Voices	With the caveat about naturalistic or authentic voices in mind, it's clear that a focus on talk is likely to make space for multiple voices. Indeed, the discovery of very high levels of uniformity in talk would be a thing to examine in more detail – have the ideas been absorbed or are they being parroted?
Pragmatic	Talk is going on all the time, although the majority of it may be formulaic. Voice recorders are installed on most laptops and smartphones and listening back to an interaction together can be the basis for developing an enquiry as well as talking about talking with participants.
Evocative	The live or unedited transcribed voices of learners speak volumes to the listener, providing rich case examples of meaning being made. The interpretation is, like most qualitative work, dependent for its warrant on the transparency of the analysis and coding.

Frequently Asked Questions

What if someone doesn't want to be recorded in a session, can I not record at all?	You have to make a contract that you can keep to. If you are recording a small group discussion, editing out one person's contribution will make nonsense of the data but you might be able to edit a larger group discussion. There can't ethically be a conflict between someone participating in a discussion and the research, so you can't just advise them to keep quiet (unfortunately that's a real example).
There're so many ways to analyse talk, won't I be overwhelmed?	As with most analysis, it's sensible to proceed in stages. You might want to consider your process hypothesis: if the content is driving the interaction, you might look at markers for 'natural' talk (such as overlapping speech) and code those onto the transcript before checking the content analysis. This will mean that you are consciously looking for one pattern at a time.

Further reading

Alexander, R. J. (ed.). (2010). *Children, Their World, Their Education: Final Report and Recommendations from the Cambridge Primary Review.* Routledge.

American Educational Research Association (AERA) Annual Meeting, New York. Text in this section drawn from draft paper. Available at: https://iu.app.box.com/s/a1tmd8jcs6cqm6wpv86mp913embmwg3r (accessed May 2018).

Bae, H., Glazewski, K. D., Brush, T., and Kwon, K. (April, 2018). Fostering Transfer of Responsibility in the Middle School PBL Classroom: An Investigation of Dialogic Scaffolds. Presented at American.

Dillon, J. T. (1994). *Using Discussion in Classrooms.* Milton Keynes: Open University Press.

Hardman, F., Smith, F., and Wall, K. (2003). Interactive whole class teaching in the National Literacy Strategy. *Cambridge Journal of Education,* 33(2): 197–215.

Mercer, N. and Hodgkinson, S. (eds.), *Exploring Talk in School: Inspired by the Work of Douglas Barnes.* London: SAGE Publications Ltd.

Mercer, N. and Sams, C. (2006). Teaching children how to use language to solve maths problems. *Language and Education,* 20(6): 507–528.

Nystrand, M., Gamoran, A., Kachur, R., and Prendergast, C. (1997). *Opening Dialogue: Understanding the Dynamics of Language and Learning in the English Classroom.* New York: Teachers College Press.

Sinclair, J. and Coulthard, M. (1975). *Towards an Analysis of Discourse: The English Used by Teachers and Pupils.* London: Oxford University Press.

Walsh, S. and Mann, S. (2015). Doing reflective practice: A data-led way forward. *ELT Journal,* 69(4): 351–362.

Wells, G. (1993). Re-evaluating the IRF Sequence: A proposal for the articulation of theories of activity and discourse for the analysis of teaching and learning in the classroom. *Linguistics and Education,* 5: 1–37.

Wood, D. (1992). Teaching talk. In K. Norman (ed.), *Thinking Voices: The Work of the National Oracy Project.* London: Hodder & Stoughton.

TOOL 12: SURVEY

Concept: Surveys are often assumed to be questionnaires; that is not our intention (if you want to think about using questionnaires then see the specific tool advice elsewhere in this book). Rather, we would like to follow Bryman (2008) who describes survey or cross-sectional research as a design (rather than a data collection tool) where the intent is to explore trends across a population. Within education such tools to explore practice with this lens, to take a snapshot of attitudes, behaviours or achievement across groups, classes or school populations, are very useful. This tool summary can be read alongside a number of other techniques we have included that could be used with the intent to survey, for example, PVTs, diamond ranking or work samples.

Provenance: To survey a population, to explore the existence (or not) of a characteristic or behaviour, across an identified demographic is a process underpinning many enquiries. The survey can be a one-off (how do our final year students feel about leaving?), it could be a before and after/pre- and post-measure (how do behaviours change after a bullying intervention programme?) or it might be something more longitudinal (how do self-assessments of learning change over the term in the run-up to exams?). Regardless it is about choosing a tool well-matched with the thing you want to survey and the context in which you want to survey it.

Use in research: A quick look at an overview of education research shows that survey is a regularly used technique; however once the questionnaires have been eliminated there is wide variety in the approaches used. As you are aiming to survey across a group then pragmatics means that there is a tendency to simplify data, a quantification, to enable the capture across the population. This means measures that ask for a single or simple range of data that can be easily analysed across the sample – you can see why the link with questionnaires is apparent. Apart from this simplification then what you measure is completely up to you; it could be:

- Attitudes and beliefs can be surveyed, for example, developing the idea of a Likert scale (completely agree,

agree, disagree, completely disagree). This could be included in written form, i.e. a questionnaire, or it could be done physically, stand behind the category that reflects how you feel. Alternatively, you could be more creative and use voting systems (electronic or physical), feeling fans or thumbs up/thumbs down–type indications.

- Behaviour can be explored by logging how many times individuals do a certain thing (return homework, attend clubs, get a detention) or exploring how often they act in a particular way (think in a certain way, show a type of learning behaviour). This could be the number of times the behaviour is observed by someone or how regularly the individual perceives they do that thing of interest.
- Learning characteristic or competence: tests are a form of survey; they assess learning across a population, but PVTs would also work to assess metacognition. In addition, you could use a survey of work samples (e.g. systematically graded pieces of free writing) or regular selection of achievement.

Survey is possible qualitatively, but it is likely to be on a smaller scale or require a sampling technique to reduce the number of participants to make the data manageable. So, when you get below a certain size it will be important to ask whether what you are undertaking is really a survey (capturing data across a population) or if you are really undertaking something more akin to a case-study approach (focusing on individual cases within the wider population). Large-scale qualitative survey is possible with visual data, for example, with photographs, pictures or drawings. This qualitative data is relatively easy to collect on a big scale representing the diversity of the population (Wall et al., 2012). If this is what you intend, then we recommend you think carefully about the analysis stage (Wall et al., 2013).

Exemplars:

Mark Rathie, Business studies, Preston Lodge High School: An awareness that students were struggling to be resilient, led the teacher to undertake some practitioner enquiry to explore how he could teach in such a way to develop this skill. As part of this enquiry he wanted to explore how the S3 students of administration's resilience developed over time. Rather than use a pre-existing questionnaire, which although reliable would have been time-consuming to use and analyse regularly, a more creative technique was used that would support the students' engagement with the topic. Two life-size students were drawn onto sheets of paper. As part of a lesson, one was annotated with the characteristics, skills and dispositions of a resilient learner (this one was called Bella) and the other was filled with the characteristics, skills and dispositions of a non-resilient learner (called Bee). These images with their associated prompts were put on the wall of the classroom and after every lesson for the next two months the students would rate, using post-it notes, whether they had been more like Bella or Bee. This meant the teacher could survey their attitudes, explore whether particular types of lessons made resilience particularly problematic and also look at change in the class or specific individual's attitudes over time thus informing student expectations as they enter national qualifications in the subsequent school year.

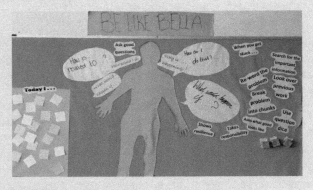

Vicky Lewis and Helen Barwick, High Street Primary, Cheshire: As part of an enquiry exploring how children developed an understanding of the process of learning, staff at High Street Primary introduced children to self-assessment in small steps so that they would be able to fully understand the process and so that they could become more adept at thinking about their own progression. By ensuring that this dialogue occurred daily, children began to improve their ability to summarise their achievements. There were some members of staff who also introduced children to ways in which they could state or record whether they felt they have achieved the lesson objectives or not. Some staff did this in the form of a 'thumbs up' vote, others used 'feelings fans' and some staff members asked children to record happy or sad faces in their books. This engaged the child in regular thought about what they have achieved, while also providing data that surveyed understanding of the class at the end of each lesson. A photo was taken taking care to make sure all children and their fans were visible, and this was used to review how the class progressed.

Quality Criteria

Recognisability	To survey is a common research intent. It is easily recognised by others and read about in the research textbooks with regards different techniques for data collection and analysis, although be careful of the assumption that survey is a questionnaire. In addition, survey links well with the normal practices of school life where we regularly want to explore trends and outcomes across school populations.
Metacognitive	As an output of enquiry, survey has a distinct accessibility advantage as it is recognisable and understandable as a research process to most, including relatively young children. As such it can allow a communication of research to a wide audience and potentially a collaborative approach to understanding what the outcomes mean to different individuals – for example, sharing a survey of observed behaviours in a nursery class to parents can lead to some very interesting learning conversations.
Multiple Voices	The fact that everyone in a population is represented is not the same as them all having a voice; however, to use a survey does maintain a lens across the whole population and therefore a view that is inclusive of everyone. In communicating the data then ensuring that we don't rely solely on means but also show the range of data means that the diversity of the population can start to be captured.
Pragmatic	The wide definition of survey that we are encouraging is inherently pragmatic in facilitating a view supportive of using a range of tools to explore trends across populations. It has close links with normal education practices and as such is easy to incorporate into a busy working day.
Evocative	The good patch with normal education practice means that surveys collected pre and post an intervention, or longitudinally over the period of a term or year, produce findings that chime with professional understanding. In addition, due to surveys' recognisability and common use, survey data can often be compared and contrasted relatively simply to other people's outcomes allowing codification of outcomes. This allows you to see your enquiry in the wider context of research.

Frequently Asked Questions

A survey is a questionnaire, isn't it?	Many individuals use survey and questionnaire interchangeably; however we would argue that survey is a type of research design and questionnaire is just one of many tools that can be used to fulfil that design.
How does this tool give insight for my professional learning?	Survey as a design speaks very closely to normal school practices – surveying children is the basic premise of a lot of assessment, teaching and learning, and democratic process. As such undertaking a survey can be relatively simple and complementary of normal activity. The key is to ensure that you identify clearly what you want to survey and the most accurate way to measure it.

Further reading

Bryman, A. (2008). *Social Research Methods* (3rd Edition). Oxford: Oxford University Press.

Lewis, V. and Barwick, H. (2006). *Developing a Circle Time Model Involving Children in Self-Assessment and Developing Co-operative Learning Strategies for Lifelong Learning.* London: Campaign for Learning.

Wall, K., Higgins, S., Hall, E., and Woolner, P. (2012). 'That's not quite the way we see it': The epistemological challenge of visual data. *International Journal of Research and Methods in Education,* 36(1): 3–22.

Wall, K., Higgins, S., Rafferty, V., Remedios, R., and Tiplady, L. (2013). Comparing analysis frames for visual data sets: Using pupil views templates to explore perspectives of learning. *Journal of Mixed Methods Research,* 7(1): 20–40.

TOOL 13: NARRATIVE INTERVIEWS

Concept: Stories are an important way in which we structure our understanding of the world. A narrative interview differs from a structured interview in which the same questions are asked to all participants or an unstructured interview in which a naturalistic  conversation develops. In asking for a narrative, we are asking people to demonstrate their conceptual understanding and to decide themselves what is a resonant and important story to tell.

Provenance: Narrative interviewing has its roots in anthropology and critical sociologies (race, queer and feminist perspectives) and as such it is based on the belief that respondents can (and should) use their narratives to shape the research project. As a research tool, narratives have the tendency to be divergent in terms of content but relatively convergent in terms of structure as the conventions of stories transcend cultures (Booker, 2004). From an ethical perspective, by asking for a narrative the power is handed back to the interviewee: it's hard to get a story 'wrong' and the questions from the interviewer will be clarifying rather than probing or unexpected.

Use in research: Narrative interviews are widely used in 'giving voice' to vulnerable and marginalised participants and they have a particular value in sensitive interviewing, as both *what* is discussed and *how* remains in the hands of the interviewee/ storyteller. Narratives also have an important place in practitioner research, giving interviewees scope to explore their practice in relation to a rich example. From that narrative patterns of influence ripple outwards into the broader map of practice and the interviewee/storyteller can reflect on why she chose that particular story – is it typical, ideal, worst nightmare?

Exemplars:

***Maria Mroz's PhD commentary – narrative for reflective practice*:** Maria used an analytic autoethnographic interview approach (Anderson, 2006) to reflect on the research papers she was submitting for her PhD by published work. A colleague interviewed her on three occasions over eight months. The transcribed interviews were then analysed using structured coding (Saldana, 2013). By this process, she wrote herself into the story of the research:

- Acknowledging that the research journey for a PhD by publication is a personal one that spans a considerable length of time and in which there are influences on research from an academic context but also, inevitably, from life beyond work.

- Recognising that there were aspects of the self that would be revealed more readily through an interview and storytelling approach.

- Believing that interviews with a trusted colleague would provide a safe place to explore and revise the conceptual framework and the coherence of the research story.

- Taking a snapshot of her thoughts, knowledge and understanding at that particular point in time.

While there was flexibility within the interviews, the overall expectation was that she would ' *"tell the story" of my development as a researcher to a colleague within my changing context; explore the coherence and links between the papers written and reflect on my positionality*'.

Narratives of learning: Mediated fortune line interviews with children aged 4–16: The interviews were designed to be completed on a one-to-one basis with children of all ages and aimed to be narrative in style, asking children to tell the story of their learning as part of the L2L project. The story element was felt to be important and linked to the joint objectives of inclusivity and high levels of reflection, a mediated interview was chosen with a visual prompt providing the mediation. Students were asked how they felt about their learning on the day of the interview to make a distinction between academic self-concept and their general mood. They were then asked to think backwards to gauge their feelings about learning at 'the beginning'. For most students, this was the beginning of the school year, as we were looking at the impact of the particular cycle of inquiry in the school. Students were then asked to track their journey from beginning to end, either as a linear progression or reflecting ups and downs. Whatever kind of line they drew, students were then asked to explain what had either supported an increase in positive affect or contributed to a decline.

The range of shapes allowed students to talk about all aspects of their learning, rather than simple summative evaluations, with the result that the interview data, even from the youngest children, contained subtle and complex ideas.

> Interviewer: Why do you think that you are so happy about your learning at the moment?
>
> L: Because it is really interesting
>
> Int: Can you think back to the beginning of the year when you first came in to this class? How were you feeling then?
>
> L: I was scared because the work had been harder than class 2.
>
> Int: So, if you were to draw yourself on here at the beginning of the year, where would you have put yourself?
>
> L: Here
>
> Int: Right down at the bottom. So, if we think about the journey from here and here, it could be a straight line getting a bit better every day or it could be a really big zig zag or a wiggly line with some ups and downs, what would your line look like?
>
> L: It would probably be down to here and then go a bit further up and get higher and higher and higher.
>
> **(Lucy, Year 4)**

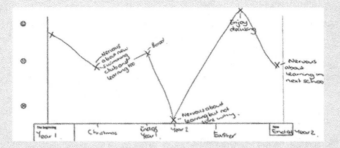

Interviewer: *What about at school, is there anything that makes you happy with your learning?*

A: *Discussing really.*

L: *So you are enjoying the discussing, pop that on. So how do you feel about your learning now at the end of Y2?*

A: *It sucks because I will be leaving so I won't be able to do philosophy.*

L: *So, you are a bit sad because you might be leaving school but how do you feel about you learning? Do you feel confident because you have learnt lots or sad?*

A: *I am happy because I have learnt lots but also scared because I am going to have to learn harder things now. If you talk when you are on the carpet in that school, you go straight to the Head Teacher.*

(Ashleigh, Year 2)

Quality Criteria

Recognisability	The immediate connection to narratives is a particular strength of this tool; everyone involved has some common understanding of what is expected in a story and can feel a degree of control over their involvement.
Metacognitive	While telling a story is a relatively instinctive operation, reflecting upon the story in the moment of telling can be highly illuminating and then critically examining the kind of story chosen and how it is told can lead to deep understanding of the underlying values of practice.
Multiple Voices	By handing the choice of content over to the interviewees, this tool makes sure more likely that different perspectives and ideas can emerge.

Pragmatic	The evolution of the interview process will be in the hands of the participants and narratives chosen will be relevant to practice.
Evocative	The resonance of stories makes this among the most evocative of tools, so much so, that greater control is needed in analysis, so that seductive narratives do not overshadow or crowd out others.

Frequently Asked Questions

Won't the interviews take forever?	Narrative interviews tend to be shorter than semi-structured or unstructured ones, since it is obvious when the story has ended, whereas working through a list of questions can lead to repetition.
By asking for stories, might I get over-idealised tidy versions of real life?	You might. However, the 'true' version is unlikely to emerge from any kind of interview and your reflections on what kind of story is told is also interesting data.

Further reading

Anderson, L. (2006). Analytic autoethnography. *Journal of Contemporary Ethnography*, 35(4): 373–395.

Booker, C. (2004). *The Seven Basic Plots: Why We Tell Stories*. London: Continuum.

Guenette, F. and Marshall, A. (2009). Time line drawings: Enhancing participant voice in narrative interviews on sensitive topics. *International Journal of Qualitative Methods*, 8(1): 85–92.

Mroz, M. (2016). Recognition and support of children with speech, language and communication needs: Knowledge, policy and practice. Available at: https://theses.ncl.ac.uk/dspace/bitstream/10443/3346/1/Mroz%2c%20M.%202016.pdf

Saldana, J. (2013). *The Coding Manual for Qualitative Researchers* (2nd Edition). London: SAGE.

The Learning to Learn in Schools report with a technical appendix on the use of fortune lines can be found here: https://www.researchgate.net/publication/232607647_Learning_to_Learn_in_Schools_Phase_4_and_Learning_to_Learn_in_Further_Education

Thomas, U., Tiplady, L., and Wall, K. (2014). Stories of practitioner enquiry: Using narrative interviews to explore teachers' perspectives of learning to learn. *International Journal of Qualitative Studies in Education*, 27(3): 397–411.

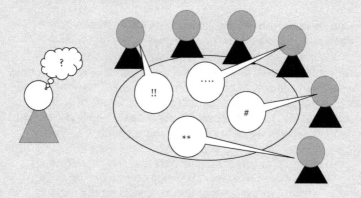

Concept and Provenance: It is actually easier to define focus groups by what they are not. They are not an efficient alternative to one-to-one interviewing and they are not best suited to access individual experience. A group of key informants are gathered together to explore a topic but the process is not the same as "public forums, nominal groups (a formal technique, which has been compared to the Delphi method, for identifying, discussing, and ranking issues in a group setting), hearings, task forces, and committees" (Leung & Savithiri, 2009, 218). Focus groups are a discussion *between* the participants, stimulated and scaffolded by a facilitator; as such they can showcase a range of views but also provide a picture of the shared cultural understanding. The advantages of a focus group include the certainty that participants are interested in the specific topic (provided that this has been made clear by the researcher), removing barriers caused by literacy, allowing concepts to be framed in natural language and that a relatively large amount of qualitative data will be generated in a single session. Disadvantages cluster around issues of scale and balance: how many groups to get a range of views; how many groups for each participant (snapshot or dialogue?); how to ensure relatively equitable participation in a group; how to encourage and manage minority views. Much used in marketing, focus groups can be used in that tradition to assess formatively or summatively the outcomes of research, forming a kind of participant validation technique. However, by drawing on a more ethnographic perspective, focus groups can also be used creatively to define or refine the frame of the enquiry.

Use in research: Focus groups in practitioner research have often been used as a response to problems with the one to one interview, such as the social difficulty of one-to-one conversations with adolescents. They reflect the need to capture a dialogue and also to observe how a group will respond to and frame the question, without the limiting structure of an interview schedule. The range of possible responses is highly dependent upon the way in which the focus group is set up:

- A group of complete strangers may feel more free to speak or alternatively colleagues may feel able to get straight to the meat of the issue without the need for contextual explanation.
- A naturally occurring group is likely to have existing power and personality dynamics in place, a random group will contain participants along the introvert- extrovert range
- A highly structured focus group will provide specific data; any stimuli, artefacts or tasks will give the group cues as to what you want from the session; an unstructured approach may yield surprising new information as well as complicating the analysis.
- A group that is recorded (with audio or video) will produce different kinds of data from one in which summary artefacts are produced by the group
- It is possible to facilitate or to take detailed process note but not to do both adequately, so decisions about help or choosing one role over another also have an impact on the data.

Exemplars:

Northumbria University: Reflecting back on experiences of assessment by graduating degree students.
The four year Law degree programme at Northumbria has a wide range of pedagogic and assessment experiences. There are a number of pathways and options for students to choose and anecdotal evidence to suggest that certain kinds of assessment

act as a disincentive when selecting modules. Module and programme evaluations provide scores of satisfaction about the challenge, support and alignment of assessment, but this data is anonymized and so comparison across modules and years is difficult. Moreover, there is nothing that captures an individual student's assessment journey. Students who had completed all assessments and were awaiting graduation (and who therefore could feel relatively free to speak their minds) were invited to take part in two focus groups on their assessment experiences across the whole degree. The groups were facilitated by a faculty member, new to the department who had never taught them and was not associated with any particular module. The groups were audio recorded. To test the 'disincentive' hypothesis, it was decided that the focus group would be an 'unappreciative enquiry' and would start with the question: "What was the worst assessment for you over the four years?" It was made clear that everyone was free to contribute a narrative and also free to indicate an example without a story. In the event, all but two students told full (and heartfelt, though often very funny) narratives. As the narratives unfolded, the facilitator wrote key ideas onto post-it notes. She then asked the groups to comment on, add, or remove the notes. Many of the 'worst' experiences were on core modules and a hypothesis was offered by the facilitator that the lack of choice was an intensifying factor. The students overwhelmingly rejected this, advancing the idea that these assessments were 'more brutal' because they carried external accreditation from the Solicitors Regulation Authority or Bar Standards Board. Students were then asked "Did that assessment have an impact on your work beyond that module?" Here there were three main schools of thought that emerged in both groups that staff took away to consider for assessment design and to inform personal tutor conversations:

- a 'what doesn't kill you makes you stronger' view that married ideas of resilience with concrete examples of lessons learned or fears faced (reported by just under half);
- a 'never again' view that having endured the awfulness, strategic choices in the future would ensure an easier time, (also reported by just under half) though a subset of

this group reported that they found new, almost as bad experiences and

- a small number of 'Moby Dick' stories in which a similar experience was actively sought out in order to vanquish the failure and create a new story.

The Class Representatives and the New Science Teacher: At 'Firefly Academy', the approaching retirement of a member of staff provided an opportunity for the Science department to involve students in the recruitment of a new teacher in a way that went beyond having a session for candidates with the Student Council and the teaching of 'specimen lessons'. Students were invited to take part in focus groups to help design the job description and interview questions for the new teacher. A series of lunchtime meetings was held in which students were asked to add to mind maps of Qualities of a Good Teacher, Things that have helped me in Science and a third which just had a question mark in the centre and was swiftly marked as RANDOM. Over a two-week period, forty-six students came to a focus group (from a potential pool of over five hundred) and a series of criteria from the meetings were incorporated into the job description. This is a very good example of the efficacy and limitations of focus groups – there was a positive concrete outcome and the assumptions of the staff about what students needed and valued were placed into focus, if not significantly challenged. However, in a team meeting one staff member reported asking a group of students if they were planning to come to the focus group and was told "You don't want to hear from us, sir." He told this anecdote because he was concerned that some student voices were being privileged over others and was disappointed but not surprised when several other members of the team said "No, we DON'T want to hear from them."

Quality Criteria

Recognisability	The group discussion has an apparent set of rules that can potentially de-rail the focus group as a research tool. It's therefore really important that the expectations are clear when the group is recruited and that the talk rules are established at the beginning of the session.

Metacognitive	Focus groups invite participants to consider how much they converge or diverge from the opinions expressed. This is most evident when they are used creatively, as when they are used for validation there is an implicit drive towards a synthesis or compromise and free-floating ideas are discouraged.
Multiple Voices	It is possible, particularly by observing and using non-verbal cues, for the facilitator to increase participation from quieter members of the group. However, it is important to consider what constitutes 'voice' for the group and what an acceptable range of responses will be. Creating artefacts can potentially increase access for some, but not all, participants.
Pragmatic	Focus groups generate a large amount of quite focused data in a short time. It is worth considering that time saved collecting will be transferred to time spent on analysis, so this is a scheduling solution rather than a way to reduce work.
Evocative	In a successful focus group, authentic stories and natural language can provide considerable illumination of key ideas in the research.

Frequently Asked Questions

How many is the right number of participants in a focus group?	'Folk wisdom' in research methods circles is that 5–8 is ideal. This makes sense in that the facilitator can ensure that everyone has been offered the opportunity to participate. However, larger or smaller groups will generate different kinds (not necessarily better or worse) of data.
What if someone doesn't say anything?	That's data in itself, though of course everyone has the right to silence and it isn't a judgement on the topic or the focus group. Depending on the kind of consent you've obtained and your relationship with the participants, you might be able to explore whether this was because the person was uncomfortable or didn't have anything to add to what had already been said.

Further reading:
Breen, R. L. (2006) A Practical Guide to Focus-Group Research, *Journal of Geography in Higher Education*, 30:3, 463–475

Krueger, R., & Casey, M. (2015). *Focus groups: A practical guide for applied research* (5th ed.). Thousand Oaks, California : SAGE

Leung, F.-H., & Savithiri, R. (2009). Spotlight on focus groups. *Canadian Family Physician*, 55(2), 218–219.

Smithson, J. (2000) Using and analyzing focus groups: limitations and possibilities *International Journal of Social Research Methodology* 3, 2, 103–19

TOOL 15: STRUCTURED OBSERVATIONS

Concept: Observations, just like most tools, can be open or closed/convergent or divergent. The design of an observation schedule sets the parameters for what is being looked for. In a structured observation (sometimes called a controlled observation) then the parameters are closed and tightly focused. This produces quantitative data that is useful for answering research questions that are looking to prove (or disprove) relationships, make connections and/or to examine specific behaviours and their occurrence. For practitioners, structured observations are a very useful challenge to the kind of cognitive bias that develops from expertise: we become alert to behaviours that *don't* fit the established pattern and tend to 'over-count' these, which can lead to a false positive finding of a problem. Using structured observations at the beginning of an enquiry can therefore be a very effective (and time-saving) sense-check. If, on the other hand, you are not sure what the parameters of the observation should be, a good first step is to use something like a fixed-view video camera to collect an open observation of what is happening in an environment. This can provide the basis for developing a structured observation tool.

Provenance: Structured observations have a strong tradition, particular in the psychological side of education research. The works of such eminent psychologists as Piaget and Skinner were all based on structured observation. The researcher tries to maintain control of the subject, the context in which they are being observed, the tasks completed and the way the data is recorded and as such removes potential variables that might otherwise impact on the outcomes. The researcher codes the behaviours observed into distinct categories. The end result is usually quantitative data, frequency of behaviours by different actors at different times, which can be analysed statistically to explore trends and relationships. The advantages of this approach are its replicability and ease of administration (it's relatively quick and easy once the schedule has been designed), and quantitative analysis using statistical tools is possible. Disadvantages include the Hawthorne effect (participants know they are being observed) and the idea that the predetermined nature of structures may limit the potential outcomes of an enquiry.

Use in research: Structured observations are useful when looking for certain types of behaviours such as teachers' questioning techniques (Hardman et al., 2005), children's thinking (Whitebread et al., 2009) or on-task/off-task behaviour (see Nicola's research below). The structure provides focus and directs attention to a specific criteria or set of criteria. Therefore, deciding on the specific behaviour that you are looking for (and what you are not), the variation this might include and how you will record it is an important stage of the research process. This usually looks like a set of codes or categories of behaviour and a key aspect is making a decision on what is enough detail to get the information needed to answer the research question but what is too much making the observation process too complicated for a single person to keep track of reliability. The other aspect is deciding who is being observed and why – the sampling strategy – do you want to observe a random, representative or volunteer sample and what are the impacts of these decisions? This is relevant in regards each observation (how many individuals is it possible to keep track of), but also how many individuals/instances will be included in the whole study to ensure findings are reliable and then how many observations are necessary to complete this target number.

The kind of structure required for a structured observation could be seen as limiting in the complexity of the busy classroom, but sometimes having this tight focus is important for being able to target particular outcomes of an enquiry. In particular this kind of emphasis means the production of quantitative data that can be analysed statistically to explore frequency, difference between groups, correlations and significance. If statistical analysis is a target then it is essential to ensure that sample sizes are large enough and robust enough, in regards recruitment and sampling strategy, to ensure the results are reliable (for further information see Van Blerkorm, 2008).

Exemplars:

Pennoweth Primary School, Cornwall: The staff at Pennoweth were exploring formative assessment strategies across the whole school – so all staff in the school were involved. They chose structured observations as one tool in their enquiry, particularly focused on exploring any changes in children's on-task and off-task behaviour. At the same point in the week at the start and end of the school year, the whole school surveyed behaviour using a simple tally chart technique (outlined in Baumfield et al., 2012). The tally chart structured the observation to five children (chosen to represent the ability range in each class). The results, reported in clustered bar charts, showed that in all classes the children were more on task at the end of the year and this was taken as a positive sign that the work on formative assessment had been successful.

SCHOOL		Behaviours	Tally chart of observed behaviours for 5 focus pupils					
			Pupil 1	Pupil 2	Pupil 3	Pupil 4	Pupil 5	TOTAL
CLASS	ON TASK	Talk related to task						
DATE		Answering question						
TIME		Atwork						
LESSON CONTENT		Asking question of teacher/ peer						
TEACHER	OFF TASK	Talk not task related						
OBSERVER		Wandering around room						
		Attempting to draw attention						
		Day dreaming						
		TOTAL						

Jane Morgan, Lewisham College: Jane was responsible for quality assurance in the college and developed a systematic observation schedule, based on Ofsted criteria, with which to engage formatively with their practice. Previous observation processes required the observer to formulate an action plan that was agreed with the observee. The revised process placed the responsibility on the teacher to reflect on their lesson and formulate their own action plan based on their self-assessment and verbal and written feedback. It also required teachers to be resourceful in seeking out strategies, training or support to improve practice. This was based on an assumption that teachers that engage positively and responsibly with the process of observation, that are reflective and take ownership of their professional development are more likely to raise the standard of teaching and learning.

North Yorkshire Nursery: A desire to record and engage with children's activity and learning in the tweenie room (18 months to

3 years old) where some children were pre-verbal and some were developing early language. They used a sheet designed to capture the children's movement around the space and their activity at different points in the day. A staff member took responsibility for observing a child and at regular intervals marked on where they were in the space (on the map of the classroom) and a brief description of what they were doing (in the table). It provided a detailed record of a child's activity that was used to challenge staff understandings of what the children were doing and why. It also gave information to be shared with the child's parents.

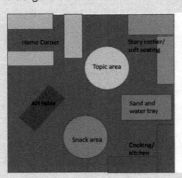 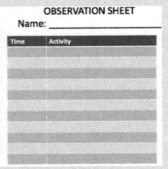

Quality Criteria

Recognisability	Observation is a common tool in the classroom; however outside research, we rarely use the structured form. Yet the tight focus on a set of behaviours is useful in providing specific insight and allowing statistical analysis of relationships between variables.
Metacognitive	As the control for structured observations is largely held by the researcher then the metacognitive potential is held by the teacher and indeed these types of observations can give tight, influential feedback on an enquiry that can shake up an individual's preconceptions. However, if control is given to the student, they take the observer role, or if the findings are fed back in an accessible way, then the relative simplicity of the data is very accessible and supportive of students' active engagement in the teaching and learning process.

Multiple Voices	Voice is not really a characteristic of structured observation; however, the type of data that is produced and its potential to be presented visually, in a histogram, or as a statement of significance, does open doors to new audiences – it can be shared with students and it is definitely the type of data that is listened to by senior leaders and policymakers. This allows the potential for consideration of multiple voices in reaction to the data and therefore to contribute to outcomes.
Pragmatic	Structured observations are relatively quick to administer – an observation of an event, and maybe its repeat later in time – means that impact on teacher time is minimal. Time commitment comes at design stage. One way of negating this is to explore observation schedules such as Whitebread et al.'s (2009) or Hardman et al.'s (2005) as ready-made tools that you can use (credited of course) in your context.
Evocative	Sometimes there is nothing like a graph for showing a relationship in a simple and clear way. The fact that structured observations produce quantitative data means that results can be synthesised clearly and evocatively to speak to multiple audiences. This has to be a strength.

Frequently Asked Questions

What is the best way of deciding on the observation schedule?	To generate an effective schedule, i.e. the number of categories and their characteristics, then consideration of what is too broad a category and what is too detailed will be useful, and it is essential to pilot the schedule as these parameters are explored.
I'm nervous of statistics, does this mean I shoudn't use structured observation?	No, structured observations can elicit data that is appropriate for complex statistical analysis, but if this is not your thing then it is not necessary. The simple production of frequency data such as number of occurrences and visual comparisons between groups or events (using bar charts for example) can still provide powerful insight.

How can structured observations support understanding of professional learning?	Observation is something that most teachers are used to in some shape or form. However, research observations of the type recommended here require the designer of the schedule to have a clear idea of what is being looked for and to target it effectively in the way that it is recorded to the exclusion of other confounding aspects. Structured observation aims to standardise the thing being observed and therefore support comparisons or the search for changes over time.

Further reading

Andrews, E., Delaney, S., Dulwich, H., Farley, P., Furnish, N., Garbutt, S., Horner, A., James, H., Kitto, J., Pedley, J., Sharma, D., and Tonkin, H. (2006). *Developing Formative Assessment Strategies in the Primary School*. London: Campaign for Learning. Available at: http://www.campaign-for-learning.org.uk/cfl/assets/documents/CaseStudies/Pennoweth.pdf

Baumfield, V., Hall, E., and Wall, K. (2012). *Action Research in Education: Learning through Practitioner Enquiry*. London: SAGE.

Hardman, F., Smith, F., and Wall, K. (2005). Teacher-pupil dialogue with pupils with special educational needs in the National Literacy Strategy, *Educational Review*, 57(3): 299–316.

Van Blerkom, M. (2008). *Measurement and Statistics for Teachers* (2nd Edition). London: Routledge.

Whitebread, D., Coltman, P., Pasternak, D. P., Sangster, C., Grau, V., Bingham, S., Almeqdad, Q., and Demetriou, D. (2009). The development of two observational tools for assessing metacognition and self-regulated learning in young children. *Metacognition and Learning*, 4(1): 63–85. doi:10.1007/s11409-008-9033-1

TOOL 16: STANDARDISED QUESTIONNAIRES

Concept: The promise of a standardised questionnaire that it will objectively measure a discrete attribute of a group of learners and provide the teacher with precise information about what they currently know, or can do, or understand about themselves, is compelling. Of course we want to know these things and since a tool exists already, how (relatively) quickly we can find out!

Provenance: Standardised questionnaires come mainly from the discipline of psychology and there is a complex science behind their design (clearly and beautifully explained in the classic book by Oppenheim, 1966), with many technical considerations of construct validity (how well-designed they are to measure what they intend to measure), test-retest reliability (whether individuals get similar results in re-tests) and predictive validity (whether a result can predict future behaviour or performance). It is not necessary to become expert in this language, however as there are a number of ways to find out about the test you are interested in. The Mental Measurements Yearbook website has a page on which they list all the tests reviewed so far (https://buros.org/tests-reviewed-mental-measurements-yearbook-series); if your test is there you will be able to find out how well it holds up. Very helpfully, systematic reviews of tests are often carried out (see, for example, Bradford and Rickford, 2012) in which direct comparisons are made, helping you to make informed choices. If your test hasn't been reviewed anywhere and doesn't provide information about validity and reliability, then we would urge caution. It might be that it is just very new and the work has not been published yet. However, it may be that there is no meticulous science underpinning the test. Oppenheim opens the preface of his book like this:

> The world is full of well-meaning people who believe that anyone who can write plain English and has a modicum of common sense can produce a good questionnaire. This book is not for them.

Use in research: The useful thing about questionnaires like these is that they offer a perspective on aspects of learning that are hard to capture naturalistically in classrooms. However, there's a concept underpinning questionnaire design which has consequences for how they can be used in research that is obvious to the designers but not necessarily obvious to the consumer – trait stability. Some standardised questionnaires are intended to measure relatively stable traits: these are *diagnostic* and therefore provide context and descriptive data for a study ('the people in this study fall into these three categories (Ning, Nong and Nang); we then go on to use that as a variable when looking at behaviour/performance/views'). Other standardised questionnaires are concerned with traits that are highly susceptible to development and therefore focus on *measurement of change*, typically using pre- and post-tests in an experimental design ('the people in this study had scores on the Pooter scale between 15 and 23 (mode 19) before the intervention and scores of 9–14 (mode 10) after'). It's therefore really important to consider what you believe about the trait in question – how fixed or flexible is it? How do you think the trait contributes to or detracts from other things you are looking at? Are you 'testing the test' or using the results of the test as the basis for another research or pedagogic decision? The examples that follow demonstrate a range of uses for questionnaires.

Measures of Thinking Skills: In the systematic review and meta-analysis carried out for the Evidence for Policy and Practice Information (EPPI) Centre, the team found that the research studies mostly assumed the flexibility and development of 'thinking skills ability' and used a range of cognitive measures (such as curriculum tests and/or Ravens Progressive matrices) in experimental studies to judge the effectiveness of particular thinking skills interventions. However, although positive benefits were found on those measures in almost all studies, there were three significant trends: first there appeared to be a greater effect on previously lower-attaining students and secondly there was a much larger impact for metacognitively focused interventions and thirdly there was a noticeable time lag on curriculum scores, with improvements showing up after months or years. This means that a thinking skills intervention might 'bring up the trailing edge' of attainment scores, potentially by increasing metacognitive awareness and then skilfulness but would not show dramatic and instant improvements for all learners in one term. Moreover, the impact on other outcomes (self-concept, attitude, self-efficacy) appeared to be slightly higher, suggesting that for teachers tracking impact in their classrooms, using measures of metacognition and affect might be important in order to capture the *process* of change taking place.

Measures of Self-Concept: A project Learning to Learn in schools and Learning to Learn in Further Education (L2L) used the Self-Description Questionnaire (SDQ) developed by Professor Herb Marsh and his colleagues to measure elements of self-concept. This research method was chosen because of the association reliably found between people's sense of self-efficacy and their performance, although as Marsh describes (2006, pp. 25–30) there is considerable disagreement about the causal relationship between self-concept and performance: on the one hand, an enhanced self-concept seems to produce more success, but performance also appears to impact upon self-concept and there is an emerging model that academic self-concept and academic achievement develop together, reinforcing each other:

> Increases in academic self concept lead to increases in subsequent academic achievement and other desirable educational outcomes. (Marsh, 2006, p. 36)

A number of schools used the SDQ with their students (data from 567 pupils, both boys and girls, who had not been previously involved in L2L). This included a sizeable number of secondary age students, among them a group of Y11 students studying at FE college.

The data shows that the learners have broadly positive self-concepts, although they tend to be more positive about some aspects of themselves than others. Mean responses for the various year groups show self-concept decreasing as age increases for all of the subscales of the SDQ apart from ratings of relationship with parents (PA). This is to be expected given that the self-concepts of children and adolescents generally decline with age. Correlation coefficients between the various scales of the SDQ were all positive, as would be expected, with most of the correlation coefficients lying between 0.3 and 0.6. The correlation of reading and peer relations is the lowest correlation this year, suggesting that learners perceive these as quite different aspects of people, without much overlap. Contrary to expectations based on wider use of the SDQ, however, and our findings in L2L last year, the correlation between mathematics and reading self-concept is bigger than might be expected (0.501). Therefore, there would appear to be less tendency among these learners to identify as either numbers or words people, perhaps suggesting that they hold a less fragmented understanding of learning than is typical.

There are gender-related patterns to the learners' responses, with the primary-aged boys tending to rate themselves more positively in terms of physical appearance and abilities, peer relations and general self, but girls of this age seeing themselves as more successful readers. Strikingly, across the full sample, which includes a considerable number of secondary-aged learners, the boys' responses tended to be significantly higher on all the subscales, apart from reading. This is evidence of self-concept declining faster in girls than in boys as they experience secondary education, despite the nationally noted tendency for girls to achieve more highly at GCSE and our finding of somewhat more evidence of metacognition among girls. This perhaps suggests differing approaches for narrowing the gap between boys' and girls' experiences of education, with more emphasis on learning strategies for the boys but more emphasis on self-concept for the girls.

Some schools administered the SDQ to the same students towards the beginning and towards the end of the school year, allowing quite precise 'before' and 'after' comparisons to be made, which were reported in case studies. In many schools, however, there was only one use of the SDQ, sometimes towards the beginning, sometimes at the end of the year. Some of these students were L2L learners, either at the beginning or towards the end of their experience of L2L, some were from comparison classes in the same school and some were students who had experienced L2L throughout the previous year. From this very mixed data, it is possible to compile a baseline 2009 data set (described above) and a data set of responses from children who had had a distinct L2L approach over at least two terms (and up to a maximum of nearly two years). These 246 students were similar to the baseline group in terms of gender balance and the range of year groups, so it is possible to compare their mean responses with those of the baseline group. This comparison is shown in the graph below.

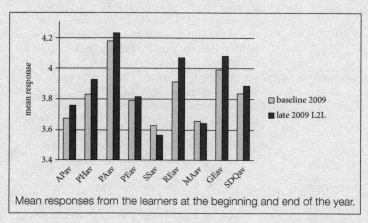

Mean responses from the learners at the beginning and end of the year.

Our understanding is that measures of self-concept all tend to show declines as students get older, so it is gratifying therefore that SDQ responses across the L2L projects tend to be slightly higher at the end of the year. The reading self-concept (RE) has a change in response over the year that is statistically significant ($p < 0.05$). This increase in mean response from 3.912 (standard deviation = 0.951) to 4.071 (standard deviation = 0.852) is not a huge change (representing an effect size of 0.17), but we are more struck by the change in direction of this and some of the other subscales which buck the expected trend. It provides evidence of a consistent tendency for L2L learners to rate themselves as more confident and capable in reading than they and their peers did at the beginning of the school year before the L2L input.

Quality Criteria

Recognisability	Well-designed measurements have been developed with clear language and formatting to be recognisable and accessible for most participants. However, beware of unlabelled or ambiguous Lickert scales (is the difference between tick box four and five clear? Is everyone in agreement about the boundary between 'quite' and 'very'?).

Metacognitive	The use of questionnaires to capture aspects of learning that are not immediately visible is an excellent opportunity to signal the metacognitive element and can potentially start a discussion both of the trait or attribute in question *and* the learners' evaluation of the measurement as a way to capture it.
Multiple Voices	The use of a standardised instrument might not seem on the face of it to be facilitative of multiple voices. However, if the measure is picking up on a feeling, thought or trait that is hard to observe (or difficult for individuals to share) then it may be a very good way to tap into experiences that won't be shared in standard classroom interactions.
Pragmatic	Good questionnaires will have had a number of pilots in which factor analysis has reduced the questions to the best designed and most powerful, with minimum overlap or redundancy, so the time taken to fill them in and analyse them should be as short as possible.
Evocative	Again, the questionnaires themselves and the data they produce might not appear particularly evocative at first glance. However, they are very useful for producing a broader picture against which individuals can locate themselves and their learning narrative ('I'm quite typical/different in this respect').

Frequently Asked Questions

How should I introduce the questionnaire to the learners?	Transparency is really key here, as on top of the ethical considerations, there's a tendency for respondents to second-guess their reactions to unplanned tests, trying to predict what you want and thus skewing the data much more significantly that if they know what's going on. Be really clear about what you're trying to capture and why – this will help to uncover your background thinking about the traits in question.
Should I use a Learning Styles Questionnaire?	No, it's not a good use of your time (Hall, 2016).

Further reading

Bradford, S. and Rickwood, D. (2012). Psychosocial assessments for young people: A systematic review examining acceptability, disclosure and engagement, and predictive utility. *Adolescent Health, Medicine and Therapeutics*, 3: 111–125. Available at: http://doi.org/10.2147/AHMT.S38442

Hall, E. (2016). The tenacity of learning styles: A response to Lodge. *Hansen and Cottrell Learning: Research and Practice*, 2(1): 18–26. doi:10.1080/23735082.2016.1139856

Higgins, S., Hall, E., Baumfield, V., and Moseley, D. (2005). A meta-analysis of the impact of the implementation of thinking skills approaches on pupils. In *Research Evidence in Education Library*. London: EPPI-Centre, Social Science Research Unit, Institute of Education, University of London. Available at: http://eppi.ioe.ac.uk/cms/Default.aspx?tabid=338

Higgins, S., Baumfield, V., Lin, M., Moseley, D., Butterworth, M., Downey, G., Gregson, M., Oberski, I., Rockett, M., and Thacker, D. (2004). Thinking skills approaches to effective teaching and learning: What is the evidence for impact on learners. In *Research Evidence in Education Library*. London: EPPI-Centre, Social Science Research Unit, Institute of Education, University of London. Available at: http://eppi.ioe.ac.uk/cms/Default.aspx?tabid=335

Marsh, H. (2006). Self-concept theory, measurement and research into practice: The role of self-concept in educational psychology (The 25th Vernon-wall Lecture presented at the Annual Meeting of the Education Section of the British Psychological Society). Leicester: The British Psychological Society.

Oppenheim, A. (1966). *Questionnaire Design and Attitude Measurement*. London: Heinemann.

Wall, K., Hall, E., Baumfield, V., Higgins, S., Rafferty, V., Remedios, R., Thomas, U., Tiplady, L., Towler, C., and Woolner, P. (2010). *Learning to Learn in Schools Phase 4 and Learning to Learn in Further Education*. London: Campaign for Learning.

TOOL 17: SMALL-SCALE TRIALS AND EXPERIMENTS

Concept and Provenance:

It is human nature to conduct small-scale experiments: *If I do this, will it have the effect I think it will?* We tend to refer to this as 'trying it out' rather than trials but there is really no significant difference, other than how we  talk about it. The scientific method of hypothesis leading to intervention study with transparent measures and clear reporting of methods and outcomes underpins all intervention research, whether traditionally objectivist, mixed methods or interpretivist. The key thing is that not all questions can be answered at once, for an experiment to be feasible, the elements need to be separated out into a logical progression. *I think x might impact y. I need to know baseline levels of y. X needs to happen (as far as possible) either in isolation or in direct comparison to something else. I need to measure y again afterwards (when the effect might reasonably have taken place/not worn off).* In professional experimentation it's vital to set reasonable scientific standards rather than to aspire to an imagined 'proper science', so we need to acknowledge limits and bias and then be confident about the kind of knowledge claim we make.

Exemplars:

Carterhatch Junior School: Do children show more progression as a result of class organisation which prioritises working independently, in pairs or in larger groups?

Dave Archer carried out this study in three Year 6 classes in a larger-than-average-size junior school: a three-form entry school for 7–11 year olds in the poorer part of Enfield where he taught three identical lessons to the three classes only varying the size of the groups the children were in to complete the task. One class was taught as individuals, a second in pairs and the third in larger groups, in all other respects the lesson content was synchronised.

It was important to ensure that the method to complete this project was as fair as possible. He decided on a lesson that he was comfortable in delivering three times over and also would produce black-and-white result: a numeracy lesson that introduced algebra to the children. It's important to recognise that Dave's belief in group work doesn't invalidate his research – he was conscious of his bias – because of his overwhelming ethical commitment to the students. All of the Year 6 students needed to have 'good enough' teaching of algebra and nobody could be excluded from teaching as a 'no intervention' control, since the comparison was between modes of delivery.

To make the process effective and to produce consistent results he used the three classes in Year 6 where he taught the same lesson over the period of a morning. Class 6A was to work independently, 6T was working in pairs and 6L was working in large groups.

To identify how much progress was made over the lesson it was important for the children to complete a base test. This involved the children answering ten algebra questions of varying difficulties on their own (Appendix 2). The papers were then collected in and the children taught how to answer algebra questions.

It was important at this stage that the teaching part was identical in delivery and he made every effort to do this. He considered taping the first session and then playing it to the other classes, but decided not to in the end because the novelty of watching the tape could have interfered with their understanding of the topic.

Once the lesson had been taught, depending on the class, the children then completed another set of ten algebra questions in one of three conditions:

- independently,
- as a pair *or*
- in a group

The results from the graphs show many interesting findings from the study. One being that the academic levels across the year group are quite varied with 6A having, on average, 19 per cent higher knowledge of algebra.

As expected, all results show an improvement from test A to individual, pair and group tests with an incredible 56.3 per cent rise from working as a group. Class 6A's (independent) results show a steady rise in the results with an average total of 15.50 per cent progression made throughout the lesson.

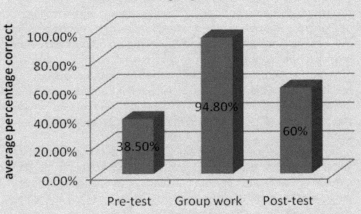

Class 6L: working in groups (8-10 people)

y-axis: average percentage correct (0.00% to 100.00%)
Pre-test: 38.50%; Group work: 94.80%; Post-test: 60%

These results show that children working as a group made the greatest amount of progress in this particular lesson.

Class 6T's (paired) results show an 18 per cent progression made throughout the lesson, whereas 6L's (group) shows that an average 21.50 per cent progress has been made by the pupils. However, this has then uncovered many other questions that could be followed up, such as is group work best for all subjects, classes, lessons, and teachers? He reflects:

> I along with my colleagues in my phase group have concluded that group work creates a noise that needs to be monitored to ensure it is productive. Working as individuals, my colleagues and I noticed that many of the children were not engaged in the lesson at all and lost confidence because they could not ask for help or rely on their peers to guide them.

Aylward High School: Comparing Cognitive Acceleration through Science Education (CASE), Learning to Learn and no intervention conditions on attainment: Stella tracked the impact of two teaching interventions and a control class with baseline and end-of-term standardised science tests. From their CAT scores, the classes appear to be equivalent. A one-way ANOVA also revealed no significant differences between the classes in terms of original CAT scores.

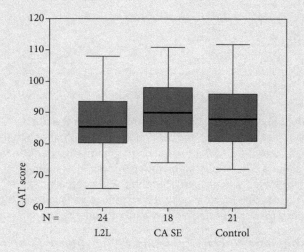

After a year of teaching, the three classes were compared through their members' end-of-year levels, produced by a SAT-type test, and the students' mean levels across three tests. Regressions were also carried out to predict both these outcomes from the CAT scores and the resulting standardised residuals were examined, as measures of gain over the year.

A one-way ANOVA found no statistically significant differences between most of these means. However, the means of the second standardised residual (the end-of-year level gain from the CAT scores) do vary significantly (F = 3.298, p = 0.045) across the classes. The blue box plots show the distributions of this standardised residual in the three classes.

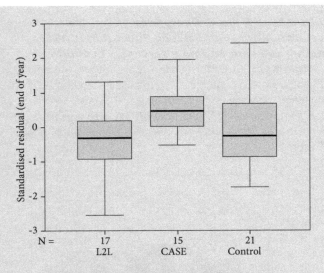

Although the finding of no differences across the other measures of performance should suggest caution, these results do imply that the CASE intervention might improve performance, over either a L2L intervention or no particular intervention. From the box plots, it would seem that the CASE approach might raise the mean performance, but also reduce variation and the tendency for a low-performing tail-end of students.

Northumbria University: Using Philosophical Enquiry to change a group discussion dynamic: Jonny created a design experiment with the intention of disrupting the established conversational patterns in his small group teaching. He was concerned that particular students tended to answer his questions and that he himself was dominating the discussions and perhaps pushing them to specific answers. Using ethical dilemmas, he conducted one session in his normal style and a second using philosophical enquiry techniques (Lipman, 1991). Both were videoed, transcribed and analysed in terms of

- The number of turns taken and length of utterance for each student and the tutor,
- Students speaking unprompted,
- Students developing a point made by another student,
- The kinds of questions (closed/ambiguous/open) asked by the tutor,

- The kind of talk (exploratory/cumulative/disputational) that characterised the session.

This was a very small-scale trial and had mixed results. The differences between the two sessions were not very large, challenging Jonny's original belief that his sessions weren't sufficiently interactive and engaging. However, the students in the philosophy session did engage much more with what each other said, suggesting that using this technique more often might encourage them not to look to the tutor for approval of every idea.

Quality Criteria

Recognisability	Once we set aside the scare associated with scientific language, testing and trialling are easily understood as part of natural professional practice.
Metacognitive	The logical progression of a design experiment requires the researcher to consider the essential versus the desirable aspects of the study and develop a clear theory.
Multiple Voices	The selection of specific measures can be seen as restricting voice, although there is the opportunity to critically evaluate why certain measures are used and whether they do answer the question.
Pragmatic	Experiments have clear parameters and can be carried out in a structured way; it is clear when the data are gathered and the approaches to analysis have been designed into the process.
Evocative	The results of an experiment can provide support and challenge to established beliefs about how things are working and what kinds of impact interventions can have, provoking further cycles of enquiry.

Frequently Asked Questions

Is it a real experiment without a control group?	Yes, it's just not a control experiment. There are some ethical issues to consider when using a control – what if it's a really good intervention and some students miss out?

How do I know that I'm being scientific enough?	Ben Goldacre's work on clinical trials sets out very clearly in lay terms the different kinds of experiments and the strength or nature of the data that they produce. Although his work is in medicine, he's very keen for teachers to get involved and teachers need to be part of that conversation – we know a lot about what needs to be measured and how!
What if the whole thing fails?	Experiments don't fail; they either support or don't support the original idea (hypothesis). This could be because the idea is wrong or because the experiment wasn't designed to get the data needed. In many ways 'failures' are more interesting and provoke more interesting follow-ups.

Further reading

Brown, A. (1992). Design experiments: Theoretical and methodological challenges in creating complex interventions in classroom settings. *Journal of the Learning Sciences* 2(2): 141–178.

Goldacre, B. (2009). *Bad Science*. London: Fourth Estate.

Goldacre, B. (2015). *I Think You'll Find It's a Bit More Complicated Than That*. London: Fourth Estate. More resources on trials and experiments from Ben are available at: http://www.badscience.net/

Hall, J. (in press, 2019). Marginal Gains?: Challenging the structures of interaction in clinical supervision. *The Law Teacher*.

Lipman, M. (1991). *Thinking in Education*. Cambridge: Cambridge University Press.

O'Donnell, A. M. (2004). A commentary on design research. *Educational Psychologist*, 39(4): 255–260.

Palincsar, A. S., Magnusson, S. J., Collins, K. M., and Cutter, J. (2001). Making science accessible to all: Results of a design experiment in inclusive classrooms. *Learning Disability Quarterly*, 24(1): 15–32.

TOOL 18: PRODUCING EFFECT SIZES

Concept: Effect sizes are a useful way to look at measurement data. Something has changed, things have got better (or worse) and you may also know (or be told) that this 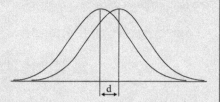 difference is 'significant'. Significance in statistical terms isn't the same as the everyday meaning ('important'), and effect size calculations help us to put that significance into context.

As the name implies, the calculation shows the *size* of the effect claimed by the study. However, it is not a certificate of causation: a large effect size from a study does not 'prove' that homework clubs increase test scores but if you compare two studies of different interventions that both have robust methods, the intervention with the larger effect size might be considered a better bet.

The effect size calculation compares the mean scores of the experimental and control group. In order to calculate an effect size you will need three numbers for each group

- *n* (number of people)
- mean (mathematical average score)
- standard deviation

Robert Coe from the University of Durham has done a great deal to extend the possibilities of bringing effect sizes to research projects by making the effect size calculator freely available on the CEM centre website.

Provenance: John Hattie has done a great deal to promote the use of effect sizes to look back in educational research in order to make sense of the mass of data we have already. The analyses are available on his website www.visiblelearning.org. However, it is equally important that new studies produce effect sizes in order that we have up-to-date information about what is going on, which is why practitioner enquiry studies can be part of the picture if we are transparent about our methods. Hattie's analysis of influence provides us with a sense of scale: interventions that have an effect size of less than 0.4 are not demonstrably better than 'business as usual' and this calculation can help us to consider where to direct scarce resources. Practices that are clearly detrimental, such as holding children back a year, can be discontinued.

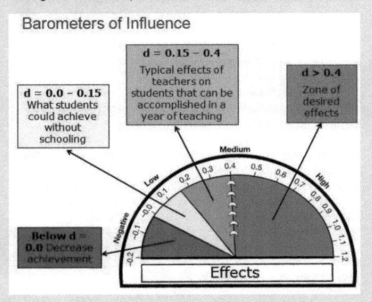

Use in research: The goal of effect size syntheses and meta-analysis has been to provide practitioners with a body of knowledge similar to that used in medicine and there is a repository of these managed by the EPPI centre. Another really good example of this is the work of Steve Higgins for the Sutton Trust and the Education Endowment Foundation. Their website summarises the evidence, cost and impact of different interventions. The research synthesis enables busy practitioners to make informed decisions.

However, a key strength of this resource is the authors' recognition of limits of this method and the need for practitioners to engage critically with the data:

There are examples within each area where interventions have been successful in improving attainment and have been unsuccessful. The most successful approaches have had their failures and the least successful their triumphs. This summarisation, which aims only to provide an overall 'best bet', therefore masks these differences. What we are saying is that the existing evidence so far suggests that some areas are likely to be more productive of success than others and that meta-analysis provides the best evidence for this. What we are not saying is that unsuccessful approaches can never work nor that approaches like feedback and metacognitive approaches will always work in a new context, with different pupils, a different curriculum and undertaken by different teachers.

There aren't a great many studies that use effect sizes, so this example is intended to show how manageable it can be.

Exemplars:

Wilbury Primary School, Enfield: Ann and Elaine wanted to explore the role of assessment in developing a learning environment. By implementing formative assessment strategies they hoped that standards of writing would improve. Wilbury is a very large primary school in an area which is among the highest 10 per cent of deprivation, within the project cohort of six- to seven-year-old children, 43 per cent were on the special needs register and 40 per cent had reading ages below their chronological ages, with similarly low levels of attainment in writing. The assessment intervention scaffolded children's understanding of teacher assessment criteria and gradually built up their ability to give and receive peer feedback. The type of evidence collected was obviously strongly linked to the primary objective – that of improving writing standards. So, teacher assessments of the children's writing levels at the end of Year 1 were collected to act as a baseline comparator to the writing levels obtained in the Key Stage 1 SATs at the end of Year 2. Similarly, samples of children's writing were taken at intervals, to show the progress throughout the year.

The hard data collected, that is the national curriculum writing levels at the start and end of the year, definitely seemed to show the benefits of the project. The sixty 'project' children improved their writing point scores from an average of 7.9 to 14.9 in the writing standardised tests. This was well above the average increase in point scores in the other two 'comparison' classes.

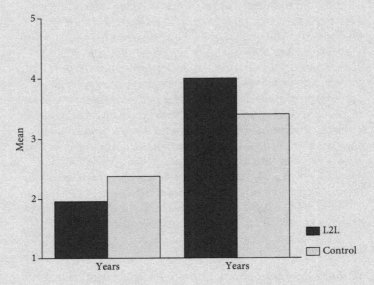

Graph showing differences in writing level achieved
by learning to learn and control classes

An analysis was undertaken using standardised residuals, which for each child looked at the predicted Year 2 level based on the teacher assessments in Year 1 and then calculated the difference between this prediction and what was actually achieved. The difference between standardised gain scores was statistically significant at the 0.001 level, with the project classes making greater gains. This difference is equivalent to an effect size of 0.76; in other words an average class using this approach would move up from 50th to 23rd in a ranked list of 100 classes.

Quality Criteria

Recognisability This is one of the issues for effect sizes. The maths seems scary and many practitioners are reluctant to get involved in case their study is not 'rigorous' enough. This is something we experienced ourselves. We can only say that it really is ok once you are in.

Metacognitive	The metacognitive benefit of effect sizes is twofold: first assumptions about 'what is working' are challenged and practitioners have to deal with this dissonance. (Surely, aspiration is a good thing? Why is there no evidence of impact?). Secondly, the nature of the evidence that exists can be questioned: is it adequate to give a picture of how the impact might work? From these experiences, practitioners can develop more articulated Theories of Change, which will then generate better evidence.
Multiple Voices	Small-scale projects can be part of a much larger research conversation; interventions (such as homework) can be assessed within focused boundaries (secondary geography) or across populations (all secondary subjects).
Pragmatic	All sites of learning collect measures of student performance as a matter of routine. This data can be re-purposed to calculate effect sizes and can allow meaningful comparisons between groups.
Evocative	Again, the d score lacks the evocative qualities of a story. Stories – however powerful and resonant – carry more weight when you can locate them in the Zone of Desired Effects. If Billy's success is part of a broader story that applies to more of the children who experienced the intervention, perhaps particularly the most in need, your case for support and funding is that much stronger.

Frequently Asked Questions

What kind of measurements can be used?	The more standardised the measurement, the more robust the calculation that can be made. However, standardisation does not just mean the use of numerical texts; moderated teacher assessments have a different but still powerful validity. The most important thing is to be comparing like with like.
Do I have to have baseline data to calculate an effect size?	This depends on the kind of study you are doing. Lots of practitioner enquiry projects are focused on the researcher's own students and it's quite unusual to have a control or comparison group. If you are looking at within-group effects, a baseline is helpful.

Further reading

In addition to the effect size calculator (http://www.cem.org/effect-size-calculator), the CEM centre provides a brief introduction and a downloadable pdf guide at http://www.cem.org/effect-size-resources

Schagen, I. and Elliot, K. (eds.). (2004). *But what does it* **mean?** *The use of effect sizes in educational research*. Slough: NFER. Available at: https://www.nfer.ac.uk/publications/SEF01/SEF01.pdf

The annotated image 'Barometers of Influence' is from John Hattie's original graphic (2007). Available at: www.visiblelearning.org

The Evidence for Policy and Practice Institute. The website https://eppi.ioe.ac.uk/cms/ contains reviews of crime, health and social policy as well as education.

The Teacher Toolkit is available at: https://educationendowmentfoundation.org.uk/evidence-summaries/teaching-learning-toolkit

5 UNDERSTANDING

What do we mean when we talk about understanding?

In exploring the understanding of research, we return to principles of learning: who is learning what, by which means and for what purpose? When we consider the production and consumption of research, it is useful to consciously position ourselves as learners and to consider 'what has it been like for me to learn something?' It is through this lens that we can examine our experience of knowledge construction, to track the connections between theoretical 'knowledge about' and experiential 'knowledge of', to note threshold moments and liminal spaces as these knowledges come together into our lived and embodied expertise, our *praxis*. In reflecting on this journey we note the gateways to understanding and ask 'who or what stood guard over those gates?' This chapter therefore is going to be about the standards – universal, local and personal – by which knowledge is judged. In our discussion of quality and warrant we are going to consider a number of dimensions:

- the ipsative standard, where we essentially ask 'is that a good one of those?';
- the relational standard, asking 'does that count with my audience?'; and
- the pragmatic standard, assessing 'does this help me to move forward?'

However, we cannot underestimate the power of contextual differences to cause problems of communication. Sharing expertise across boundaries or knowledge brokerage is a process of translation:

To translate is to connect, to displace, to move, to shift from one place, one modality, one form to another while retaining something. Only something. Not everything. While therefore losing something. Betraying whatever is not carried over. (Meyer, 2010, p. 121; quoting Law, 2002, p. 99)

When assessing quality in practitioner enquiry we are encouraging everyone to consider whether the data and evidence provide 'good enough' warrant for action. We are concerned with establishing a concept of evidence that takes account of the intent of the producers and consumers of evidence (Biesta, 2012), the nature of the public dialogue about evidence, choice, policy and outcomes, and the role of the public in democratic decision-making. The meta-awareness of evaluative criteria – the play of context, purpose and form of outcome – is, for us, the core of the concept of warrant. Foregrounding warrant in our discussion of knowledge about evidence provides a space in which to engage with the juxtaposition of at least three perspectives:

- contemporary demands that educational research concurs with the emphases on 'what works' impact' and 'evidence-informed policy' (Kasipataki and Higgins, 2016; Kvernbekk, 2011) in which evidence has implicit authoritarian power;

- 'fallibility' and 'knowledge in the long run' (Peirce, 1877/1958) that provide an authoritative view of evidence which encourages deliberation and dialogue about quality in relation to evidence; and

- ethical and identity debates about the role of educational research as force for public good and democracy (Dewey, 1927) in which concerns about who gets to participate and whose views are treated as 'expert' can be explored.

Quality – What's 'good', what's 'good enough', what 'counts'?

This 'good thing' – how do we know that it is 'good'? Are we absolutely sure that we know what 'good' means? This is not an invitation to philosophical dead ends but instead a challenge to all of us to be more precise – what do we mean by good right now, in this context – so that our intent and the criteria we are using to judge ourselves are clear. Wittek and Kvernbekk remind us that 'even in the absence of an agreed-upon, unified definition of quality, we all (think we) recognise quality when we see it' (2011, p. 675) and helpfully synthesise a number of philosophical studies to offer the five kinds of quality summarised in Table 5.1 and previously discussed.

As Table 5.1 makes clear, exception and perfection are theoretically and practically polar opposites, yet our everyday reading of quality often conflates them, thereby frustrating our attempts to reflect on, evaluate and change practice. While fitness for purpose and value for money appear to be servants of the perfection category, they are also in competition with one another, with differing perspectives on who the outcomes are for and therefore how the system works.

TABLE 5.1 *Summary of the Forms of Quality*

Quality as	Description	Paradoxical qualities and questions
exception	*Distinctiveness* [possessors, e.g. Oxford or Harvard] *simply embody quality and thus have no need to prove themselves*	Self-evident and holistic/ unattainable, inimitable
perfection	Based on *specifications for how quality is to be strived for in every part of a process,* emphasising the responsibility of individual actors for their contribution	Processual and atomised/reliant upon perfect knowledge of system
fitness for purpose	*Functional* meeting the needs of an external 'client', e.g. *the education received by students should match the requirements of work life*	Who is the client? Imagining the future/ Concrete or simple outcome measures
value for money	Similar to fitness but the emphasis is on *profit and/ or accountability to the funders (tax payers) and the consumers (the students)*	Is there a good enough overlap between efficiency and effectiveness?
transformation	*Cognitive and personal growth ... enhancing the student and empowering the students*	Phenomenological and individualistic/are all transformations equal?

From Wittek and Kvernbekk (2011, pp. 673–674).

Similarly, the idealistic and holistic aspirations of transformation seem to place it alongside exception; although it is hard to know whether the 'distinctiveness' required to become a Harvard student means that the transformation has already occurred at some earlier stage and if so, what has changed and how? Indeed, contemporary critiques of elites suggest that social, cultural and economic replication rather than transformation is taking place (Ball, 2002). Transformation is the aspect of quality with which most educators identify, since it is a personal agency: 'I offer you something, [a specific] you take it up in your own way, we dance with it together and it becomes something that changes us both' (Winnicott, 1960). Transformation, experienced in the relationships, the micro-interactions and the sense of a particular narrative unfolding, seems to stand in opposition to systems and standardisation, in competition with discourses of perfection, fitness and value.

Thus, to explore a project, an intervention or a research tool and to assess its quality, it is necessary to consider what kinds of quality we (think we) mean (Wittek and Kvernbekk, 2011) and which of the multiple frames for quality we are choosing to focus upon. In this book we have made frequent use of Heikkinen et al.'s (2012) quality criteria, so what sort of questions do we need to ask when we place the Heikkinen principles in relation to Wittek and Kvernbekk's types of quality? (Table 5.2). Let's return to Sandview Primary School and their complex mapping of how students fare and what messages about learning the children and adults give and receive (Appendix 3). Given that the initial stimulus for this research was a sense that external evaluations of the school's performance were only 'satisfactory', it seems likely that the research was framed – at least at the beginning – by 'quality as fitness' and by a desire to understand the historical context.

By locating their first question '1. What are the patterns of achievement in the school?' (represented as 1 in Table 5.2) in the overlap between historical continuity and fitness, the quality criteria for this part of the investigation become

- complete data sets of student achievement
  - analysed by year group to locate patterns of development
  - analysed across cohorts to locate patterns of difference
  - analysed by time at Sandview to locate patterns of individual trajectory

TABLE 5.2 *Questions arising from Heikkinen alongside Wittek and Kvernbekk*

Sandview	Exception	Perfection	Fitness	Value	Transformation
Historical continuity			1		
Reflexivity			4		2
Dialectics		3	4c		
Ethics and Workability		3a	4a		2b
Evocativeness			4b		2a

Ray and Sue from Sandview are able to feel confident that their data analysis has attempted to meet these criteria and that the findings from this phase provide a reasonable basis for further investigation: the 'what was going on' question has been partly addressed, with an emerging hypothesis that

Children make greater progress in the earlier years and
    Children who have been at Sandview since the early years tend to do better than those who join us later

leading to the development of the second question '2. What do we do well with our youngest pupils?' (represented as **2** in Table 5.2), which sits in the overlap between reflexivity and transformation, requiring from a 'quality' perspective

- narratives of good practice
  - from all staff
  - from a range of contexts
    - to be discussed and explored collaboratively.

This is where difficulties emerged, since there was a desire for the sharing to be simultaneously reflexive for the staff as a whole (**2**), evocative to any audience (**2a**) and manageable pragmatically (**2b**). As the narrative in Appendix 3 demonstrates, it was not possible to achieve all of these things, particularly communicating the theory of change to parents and governors. When the problem of communication was partly resolved by the development of the model of communication and agency, the research shifted into an implementation phase – 'what happens if we ... ?'. Implementation, however loosely framed, tends to fall under quality as perfection, in this case in the overlap with dialectics (3) since the emphasis of the intervention was on talk. The implicit quality criteria are:

- Performance of the intervention (fidelity of implementation)
  - Accurate monitoring of teacher behaviour and
  - Student response
    - Developing some criteria for measuring change

It now becomes clear why staff were so concerned to 'get it right', with the paradoxical result that their authentic talk with children became less effective. Only by considering the ethical dimension (3a) and acknowledging the position of staff as learners with a need for support and permission to experiment and fail were Ray and Sue able to maintain enthusiasm and commitment to the project. The staff were re-positioned as the clients as well as the producers of the data (moving from perfection to fitness), with more exploratory quality criteria:

- Performance of more self-aware talk (4)
  - Recognition and acceptance of variation as useful data (4a)
  - Student responses as part of a broader narrative (4b)
    - Deferring change criteria with a plan to involve others (4c)

Through this example, we have made the apparently common-sense concept of 'quality' more fluid and ambiguous but also hopefully made the assessment of 'qualities' a reasonable and achievable aim. From here we move to the evaluation of evidence.

The weight of evidence: Heavy enough for what?

Tone Kvernbekk (2011, 2013) again provides the foundation for our discussion of evidence and warrant. In her 2011 paper, she incorporates Achinstein's categories of evidence (2001), which allow us to un-pack what kind of evidence we might be dealing with in a particular inquiry and to make the links between these types of evidence and the types of inquiry that privilege or accommodate them (Table 5.3). We have borrowed Kvernbekk's notation, so that E= evidence, H= hypothesis. These are complex philosophical ideas and it is important – as with Fixation of Belief explored in Chapter 2 – not to assume too much about ideal

TABLE 5.3 *Forms of evidence from Achinstein and Kvernbekk*

	Subjective evidence	Epistemic situation evidence	Veridical evidence	Potential evidence
Description	*Evidence that is part of an individual or group belief structure*	*Evidence that is understood within a particular cultural, historical or knowledge context*	*Evidence that transcends situations and beliefs*	*Evidence that is strongly related to experience, present and future*
Requirement	*That the links between E and H are held to be true and consistent by the inquirer(s)*	*That the enquirer could construct or maintain H based on the E within the limitations of their context*	*The data supporting E needs to be objective, although not necessarily complete (conclusive)*	*The data supporting E must be objective and rigorous and is understood not to be conclusive*
Limitation	*It is not necessary for any empirical elements to come into this inquiry*	*This belief is not challenged by ideas from beyond the epistemic context*	*Both E and H need to be true (very hard to establish)*	*H may be false even where there is good E to support it*
Link to beliefs	*The inquirer(s) believe that E is evidence for H, that H is true, E does not have to be empirically true, provided that it is believed*	*The inquirer was justified in believing this H on this E, in context*	*E is evidence for H and provides a good reason to believe H, since both E and H are true*	*E is evidence for H and provides a good reason to believe H until other E emerges to challenge*

types and also not to dismiss the usefulness of the 'less than ideal' types. As with the methods of tenacity and authority, the use of subjective or epistemic situation evidence is part of human behaviour: it has meaning and value and is deserving of our interest in order to better understand how we construct our own knowledges. Subjective evidence is defined by the strength of the belief in the hypothesis and tends to result in a certain circularity of argument and a criticism that 'proxy indicators' are being used, such as school uniforms as a marker for effective discipline. However, just as with methods of fixing belief, the act of laying out the argument creates the space for any inconsistencies to emerge. This is why it is perfectly valid for practitioner-researchers to focus on something that others consider 'junk science', such as learning styles (Hall, 2016) if it makes sense to them. The activities of enquiry require some engagement with quality criteria but nobody is going to place their work in the 'subjective' category if that's where the useless, stupid people are. Some of everyone's frame of reference is formed of subjective evidence and we are all vulnerable to *post hoc ergo propter hoc* (after it, therefore because of it) errors in logical thinking. Permission to label some part of the landscape 'potentially subjective – maybe come back to this later' – is more likely to encourage bravery in research.

Epistemic system evidence, sometimes referred to as 'lost world' evidence, appears to require both levels of authority within the community and relatively little contradictory 'news from outside'. However, even connected communities can get locked into 'this is how things are because this is how things are and have always been'. The familiar structures of institutions and practice are particularly good at blinding us to the presence of an epistemic system. For example, the prevalence of one-hour teaching sessions – research into passive listening suggests that there is significant tail-off after 20–30 minutes with a general flat-lining at 45, while for more active learning, after a typically slow start engagement is peaking just as the session comes to a close. Lots of education research therefore focuses on what to put in the hour, rather than standing back from the structure.

When we talk about 'hard evidence' in an everyday conversation, we are often using the ideas described in the veridical definition. However, some philosophers of science do not believe in the existence of veridical evidence, seeing it as an idealised goal: useful in terms of being something to strive for ('in the long run'; Pierce, 1877), problematic in terms of setting standards that put people off conducting research since they can never achieve it. It seems therefore that potential evidence might be a realistic goal for practitioner research. However, although the emphasis on the temporary and falsifiable nature of the hypothesis is an excellent basis for enquiry, we still have to grapple with the language(s) of quality when considering how the evidence meets the criteria for *objective and rigorous*. This takes us back to the need for an explicit quality framework described in the previous section that looks in detail at the intent of each phase of the research. Potential evidence requires the researcher to know more or less what she intends to do, what a 'good enough one of those' might look like and how close she has come on this occasion: this is a rigorous demand but not an unreasonable one. Once we have this evidence in our possession, warrant speaks to how we are able to make use of it within our system of thought.

Where's your warrant?: Justification for your actions

Warrant is an important concept in pragmatism which allows us to focus on the immediate needs of the situation rather than the production of ultimate (or veridical) truths. It is a product of evidence that builds on an assessment of quality criteria that are both explicit and considered relevant to the situation and the framing of the problem (as discussed in the previous two sections); and thirdly, warrant looks outwards to the audience by considering the justification for action. To make the nature of warrant more transparent, we have followed Kvernbekk in using Toulmin's model of argumentation (1958/2003), which shows that evidence is used pragmatically to provide backing (Figure 5.1) for the warrant.

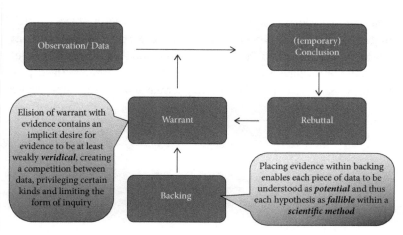

FIGURE 5.1 The place of evidence in Toulmin's argumentation and the impact on inquiry (from Kvernbekk, 2013).

We offer the example of one of our own projects – Learning to Learn in Schools and Colleges – to work through the use(s) of warrant: since warrant is about justification for action or inaction, it is therefore about 'winning the argument' and so inevitably bound up in the power relations between researchers, between researchers and audiences.

Learning to Learn was a collaborative practitioner enquiry project that produced evidence mainly in the form of case studies, so our focus was to convert these cases into warrant. Our overt intent was to privilege the teachers' voice in case studies, to give equal respect to teachers' praxis and prioritise joint publications (e.g. Hall et al., 2010; Wall et al., 2009). We have described this way of working as a move away from the traditional model of central control by the university of topic, research questions and with two key benefits: teachers keep engaged in cycles of enquiry because they have some ownership of the process and the relevance of the enquiry questions to practice are ensured by teachers' intimate knowledge of their own context (Lieberman and Pointer-Mace, 2009). We rationalised this in terms of our self-identity as teachers, our comfort with overtly democratic practice and to undercut (to us) the artificial distinctions between Mode 1 and Mode 2 knowledge (Hessels and van Lente, 2008) in educational practice. There was a division of responsibility and ownership: teachers had complete control over the focus of their research, the conduct of the enquiry was negotiated with the university team and the structure of reporting was common to all the projects (Figure 5.2).

It was, of course, more complicated than that. There are three areas of difficulty: one which relates to the outward facing aspect of the research project, one which is nested in the developing relationships and trust between the teachers and the university team and a third which is about the modes of learning permitted and promoted in the project. The degree of control that we set up in the reporting format and the ways in which we

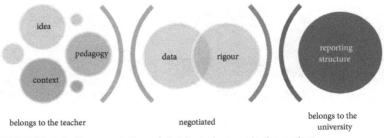

FIGURE 5.2 Representation of distributed power in the project.

lobbied the teachers to accept a particular view of rigour in their research was bound up with our sense that we were the 'public face' of Learning to Learn, that we would write, speak and represent to colleagues and to government. It was necessary for us that the project had the accoutrements of academic respectability and that the outputs from the teachers, the case studies, functioned not just as outcomes in their own right but as data for us. The degree of structure in the writing reflects this: we used a tight format to aid our analysis and arguably in doing so, we lost the opportunity for the voices of the teachers to come through unmediated. In this, we privileged our traditions and our convenience over the potential for our teachers to develop their own style and indeed for us to interact with their communications in a more hermeneutic fashion. We struggled throughout the project with the tensions between quality, rigour, ownership and audience as realities in the relationships. Our relationships with teachers were initially mediated through others, in particular the local authority co-ordinators, who acted initially as linking agents (Thompson, Estabrooks and Degner, 2006) and whose main role was to recruit and retain schools through existing regional networks (which needed to be seen to be flourishing to keep the goodwill of local management). In their interpretation of this role, some of these charismatic individuals used subtle and not-so-subtle power plays, so that we found that our early recruits included many conscripts as well as volunteers. What this meant for us as a team is best expressed in highly emotional language: we had to manage the teacher's resentment, our own disappointment and the fear that we all felt that the ambitions of the funders would not or could not be met. We set up a model of managing the partnership that we jokingly referred to as 'killing with kindness': so as to recruit the teachers to our endeavour, we offered much more than we had been contracted for in terms of active support in research design and data analysis (see, for example, Baumfield et al., 2008 for a discussion of the workload implications). This was very successful in that the teachers became more confident in their social relationships with us, and we became more comfortable in offering challenge (e.g. persuading teachers to publish ambiguous or negative findings; Wall et al., 2009). It had a further, unintended effect on the university team: since we were spending so much extra time on this project, we became more and more interested in it, indeed invested in it. We became connected not just to facilitation (for teachers and funders) but more intimately connected to our personal professional desires. The effort expended led us first to want and then to expect that Learning to Learn would produce not just interesting data about teachers and their enquiries but that the project would act as a testing ground for our methodological enthusiasms and as a crucible for our theoretical development. Of course, this range of desires and purposes required a range of warrants, none of which was completely satisfied. Knorr-Cetina makes the point that the process of understanding the knowledge object can only be experienced at a remove

> mediated by representations – through signifiers, which identify the object and render it significant. But these representations never quite catch up with the empirical object; they always in some aspects fail (misrepresent) the thing they articulate. They thereby reiterate the lack rather than eliminate it. (2001, p. 185)

This idea brings into focus the tension between the desire to frame the structure and outcomes (Bernstein, 1996) of the project through choosing activities and inputs and the aversion we have felt to arriving at too tight a representation of what Learning to Learn is, was or might be. We have claimed that it has been a model which emphasises partnership, trust and complementary roles in research undertaken collaboratively by HE researchers, local authorities, schools and colleges; thus it represents part of a developing trajectory of a dispersed research-informed practice community (McLaughlin et al., 2007). This is one way of framing it but each time we try, another possible frame emerges and we are drawn to the possibility of another way of knowing what we have been engaged in.

The engagement with intent, ideas of quality and outcomes is also not a static process; it is part of professional and personal development, dependent on the position of the individual within her own learning journey, her work context and her current motivation. In this respect, thinking about warrant takes us back to enquiry as professional learning.

Given the problems with the data, one might expect the verdict on CPD (continuing professional development) to be overly rosy. However, a key finding from these studies is that there is a discord between what we (think we) know about effective professional learning and the actual practice taking place (Cordingley, 2015a and b): the syntheses suggest that CPD is not particularly well-tailored to local need, tends to be structured around homogenous groups and single events and rarely focuses on long-term growth and integration. If the data was of higher quality, it seems likely that the picture would be even more gloomy. Nevertheless, it is a part of all our professional learning and lives, so how can we understand it as a stimulus for enquiry?

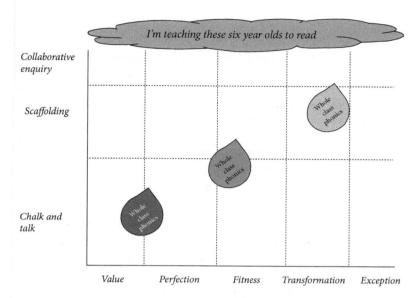

FIGURE 5.3 Ways in which Dora might formulate her enquiry.

Dora has been sent on a day's training course to improve her understanding of whole class phonics. She has no input to the course content, so it is a bit like a weather event for her, she encounters it and tries to make sense of it from her perspective, using her existing values and experience. In Figure 5.3, we have tried to map out some of the ways in which Dora could meet and engage with the training and incorporate it into her practice and what would be a reasonable way to assess the quality of that approach.

Drop 1: I've got a lesson plan and I've **been told how** to use it. Phonic awareness is linked to reading (not quite sure how but apparently it is) so on we go…These children are going to experience how to make these sounds, they are going to repeat them back to me, possibly with fancy actions and there will be a worksheet.

Drop 2: I've got a lesson plan and I **know how** to use it. Children's phonic awareness is being developed in conjunction with their pattern-recognition, semantic and pragmatic skills and enables them to problem solve new or irregular words. We'll explore phonics in relation to current decoding needs – topic words, words for today's story- and reflect back on the work already covered. We're building up procedural knowledge but not in isolation.

Drop 3: We are a group of sense makers and phonics is one of our tools. There is an open and fluid discussion between the children's questions, the ongoing work of the classroom and the phonics curriculum – coverage, relevance and ownership are all important, none more than the others.

If Dora is a new practitioner, or someone new to phonics, it is reasonable that in drop 1 she would take what she's been given in training relatively uncritically and use outcome measures aligned to value and perfection (did they all experience the sound and complete the worksheet?) to evaluate her practice. Her tools are convergent (all the worksheets should have the same correct answer on them) and give her immediate and useful feedback on the effectiveness of her delivery. Dora might be relatively experienced and integrating phonics into her practice, so in drop 2 her outcome measures will be pragmatically aligned with students' ongoing activities (she may be tracking worksheet completion but it's more likely she's also noting decoding errors in paired reading and topic work and relating that back both to students' performance and whether phonics is helping). Fitness for purpose requires an evaluation of both the outcome and the intervention, so while the tools might still be – mostly – convergent, they are set alongside one another to allow that criticality to emerge. The Dora working in drop 3, however, is working from a divergent position, focusing on individual journeys towards literacy (she is probably using individual portfolios which track the children's mastery of phonic and other skills and the need to complete individual worksheets on specific dates will be subsumed to a longer-term plan). We claimed earlier that our values are pluralist and democratic (Dewey, 1916): none of the Doras are right or wrong, they are being authentic to their position, beliefs and intent.

Each of the Doras can be seen to be conducting a practitioner enquiry but it is likely that they would resist such a label. Their work is not 'proper' research, it is too small, too home-made. It has nothing to say to the wider world. Who would be interested? Above all, it is not 'generalisable'.

Dealing with evidence and generalisability

This looks like it is going to be a problem, since generalisability is seen as the epitome of research quality, the riposte to 'so what?'. It is possible to devise practitioner enquiry projects that conform to objectivist standards for generalisability, with stratified samples of sufficient size and power and accepted, reliable measures. It is also not necessary, unless you are asking that kind of question. Larsson (2009, p. 28) sets it out with admirable clarity:

Five lines of reasoning on generalisation
Five possible lines of reasoning are sketched. The first two argue that there is no need for generalisation, i.e. certain kinds of empirical research are meaningful without any claims of generalisation. The other three argue in different ways in favour of possible ways of generalising. My point of departure is very pragmatic insofar as I try to think of the practice of qualitative research with all its diversity and pose the question: What are the possible answers to a question about generalisation in different cases? I am looking for the fundamental logic in ways of answering such a question in the social practice that we call qualitative research. I am not looking for philosophical justifications but, rather, for how people use interpretations that emanate from research. The first two lines of reasoning concern cases when generalisation claims are redundant or not appropriate:

(1) The ideographic study;
(2) Studies that undermine established universal 'truths'.
The next three can be useful when generalisation is called for:
(3) Enhancing generalisation potential by maximising variation;
(4) Generalisation through context similarity; and
(5) Generalisation through recognition of patterns. (Larsson, 2009, p. 28)

The Doras may achieve the 'respectability of generalisability' for their small studies through their

1 Novelty – telling a story not heard before
2 Originality – telling a counter-cultural story

3   Contribution – adding to the fund of stories

4   Resonance – enabling others to recognise their experience

5   Theory building – showing narrative structure.

This contribution, so often lost, is dependent on the willingness to share the messy, partial knowledge that each enquiry produces. All studies have limitations and have the potential to be disproved as we discussed back in Chapter 2 and all researchers suffer from 'imposter syndrome'. Therefore, practitioner enquiry is not just for novices, for frontline staff, for those with a problem to solve, but can be part of all practice at all levels of the system – it can be both a personal and an organisational imperative. There is considerable value from all enquirers, including head teachers and senior leaders, policymakers and academics being transparent about their intent, questions, tools, whether they succeed or fail and how they know it. We will deal with this in detail in Chapter 6 but finish with Samuel Beckett, who sums up the imperfect nature of enquiry as entwined with its necessity and rewards:

All of old. Nothing else ever. Ever tried. Ever failed. No matter. Try again. Fail again. Fail better. (1983)

6 EMBEDDING

Throughout this book, in our exploration of learning, asking questions, recommending tools and strategies, we have been positioning Practitioner Enquiry as a *Good Thing*; however, up to this point we have largely been talking about the practitioner enquirer in isolation. It has been about the conception of an enquiry, the individual choices that facilitate the carrying out of that enquiry process and the sharing of findings. Across all this discussion there have been hints of the importance with which we view a supportive community within which this process of enquiry process might be embedded and therefore codified. So, if we do not believe effective practitioner enquiry occurs in isolation, we need to be explicit about what that community might look like. Therefore, in this final chapter we want to focus on the embedding of practitioner enquiry in a professional community, exploring how the process and dispositions inherent in engaging with other enquirers should be supportive of effective professional learning for all. For this 'good thing' to work then we need to think about the community setting for those individual practitioner enquirers.

Our starting point is this fairly consistent observation of successful practitioner enquiry organisations: they are often led by an individual or team of individuals who are openly engaging in the process of enquiry themselves. In this way they are using their own experience to facilitate others in doing the same. There have been exceptions, where critical numbers of keen individuals have come together despite the dominant discourse set by the leadership team, but this is certainly a harder route and runs the risk of becoming an elite 'cult' for the few rather than something that is supportive of others' involvement.

Let us think for a moment about what it signals if the leadership of any organisation is actively engaged in practitioner enquiry. It makes explicit that they have questions and, of course, don't have all the answers. It shows the importance placed on the practitioner enquiry process as part of normal professional practice and says something very important about the nature of career-long professional learning. To lead a community of practitioner enquirers means modelling the practices and thinking that underpin a fundamental commitment to professional learning and this can only happen through dialogue. Through leaders undertaking enquiry, and particularly the making public element, then it makes explicit the real-life experience of (professional) learning through success and failure (as the latter is inevitable at some point) as something that is career-long rather than just for the novice.

For school leaders, the 'class' they are investigating might not be made up of children or young people, but rather comprise the staff of the school, but we don't think this makes a difference and in fact can be an advantage. What a powerful message for a head teacher to state they are doing an enquiry into how to make staff meetings more inclusive, for example, or to explore the impact of practitioner enquiries undertaken across the school in improving school outcomes. In the same way as opening up a dialogue with children about classroom practice brings an investment that might otherwise be missing, we have seen staff more likely to engage and support a development process because they are involved and consulted. This therefore increases the likelihood that the enquiry might be useful. Not only does this do all of the above, but it also opens a useful dialogue about how to improve the school community – and we are sure there are not many schools around the world that would be confident they have this sorted!

This willingness to share learning in action, to enter into a dialogue of improvement where all might have a contribution to make and to model the dispositions and skills needed, if done authentically and transparently, means these leaders are 'practicing what they preach'. As such they will be acting as practitioner enquiry and metacognitive role models to their staff in the same way as we have observed teachers doing with their classes (Wall and Hall, 2016). Therefore, for practitioner enquiry to be embedded system wide, we need enquirers visible at all levels of the professional community from senior school and local authority leaders, to CEOs of education organisations, to policymakers and academics as well as to children and young people all exemplifying a commitment to systematic enquiry made public (Figure 6.1). This leads to mutually reinforcing behaviours and dispositions that make practitioner enquiry more doable when it is competing against all the other things that take up the day. It makes the successes and failures of the process, of real-life learning, easier to cope with and reconcile with all the other professional pressures under which we work. Until we have levelled out these variations in commitment, hierarchical assumptions around who should be engaged in practitioner enquiry, what is 'good' research, who should control professional learning and where expertise lies will remain entrenched. Without a more systemic operationalisation of practitioner enquiry it will remain as pockets of engagement or as tokenistic, on/off, activity that is more about accountability than authentic engagement with improvement of learning outcomes.

Within this model of community engagement with practitioner enquiry then issues of power, voice, partnership and professional courage are all exemplified and can be seen as challenging. We understand that what we are suggesting is fraught with dilemmas with many hurdles to overcome; but do believe that these very dilemmas should prompt the enquiries of leaders in such a way that they are seen as shared problems rather than insurmountable blockages.

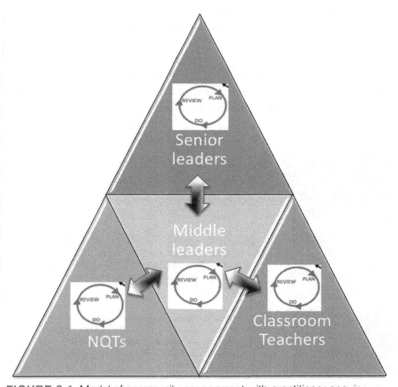

FIGURE 6.1 Model of community engagement with practitioner enquiry.

Developing enquiry networks

Working over the years with practitioner enquiry networks attempting to relate that work to 'traditional' university research and struggling with some of the contradictions of action research models (e.g. Baumfield et al., 2008, 2012), we have gradually realised:

- Research projects don't need to be designed in advance of forming partnerships with schools, in fact *the teacher knows which question to ask*

- Teachers and researchers tend to want to hide the failed and ambivalent results in a drawer but *ethical and robust research is communicated*, that's how we can ensure that what we do becomes more ethical and robust over time

- While research projects often set out to address (or even naively, solve) a particular problem, *good questions cause extra thinking* and researchers are drawn into repeated cycles of enquiry.

This thinking has crystallised into a series of principles (Figure 6.2) which prompt certain kinds of critical question and encourage a framing that we consider to be pluralist and democratic.

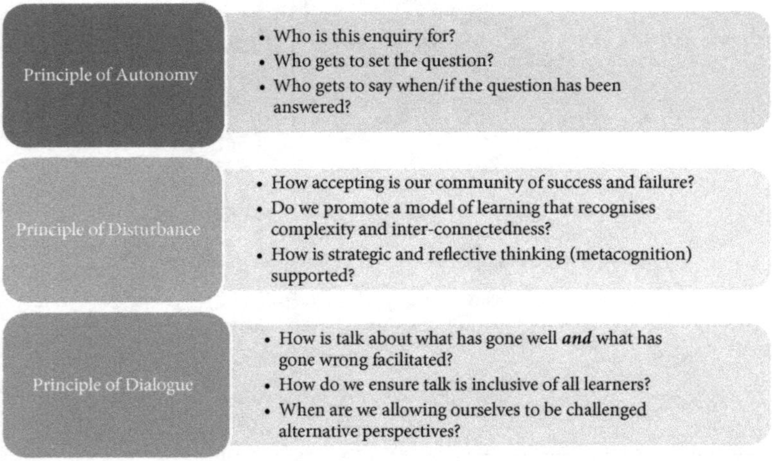

| Principle of Autonomy | • Who is this enquiry for?
• Who gets to set the question?
• Who gets to say when/if the question has been answered? |

| Principle of Disturbance | • How accepting is our community of success and failure?
• Do we promote a model of learning that recognises complexity and inter-connectedness?
• How is strategic and reflective thinking (metacognition) supported? |

| Principle of Dialogue | • How is talk about what has gone well *and* what has gone wrong facilitated?
• How do we ensure talk is inclusive of all learners?
• When are we allowing ourselves to be challenged alternative perspectives? |

FIGURE 6.2 Principles of practitioner enquiry (adapted from Wall and Hall, 2017).

These principles are discussed in detail elsewhere (Wall and Hall, 2017); here we want to focus on a particular perspective relating to research for understanding professional learning: the development of metacognitive thinking. For us this is linked to a fundamental question about the extent to which these principles can be applied merely to practitioner enquiry or to all kinds of learning? In real-life application these principles are mutually reinforcing, but we will discuss them in turn using examples and providing links to the themes of power, voice, partnership and professional courage. Of course we also, at the same time, encourage the reader to make his or her own judgement.

Principle of autonomy

The principle of autonomy suggests that practitioners are experts, however little they may feel that they deserve that title. Expertise about their context and the students with which they work every day is probably easier to admit: although it amazes us how many practitioners don't see or value this knowledge and skill. Practitioners therefore have an insight into which questions to ask that is denied to the outsider.

As Timperley (2008) notes, effective professional learning has to be connected to perceived student need and this expertise, the ability to recognise it and to identify your own questions about what is going on, is paramount in the success of practitioner enquiry. It is paramount that the questions asked as the impetus for practitioner enquiry are the teacher's own and that they are asking about real problems faced within their practice. If they are decided by someone else or are not authentic in terms of asking about something that the individual truly does not know all about, then they will be ineffectual in producing learning. That is not to say that there might not be some guidance or some expectation of an answer, but rather there has to be a level of challenge that will facilitate the momentum of the enquiry process. This is especially important when it gets difficult.

The expertise related to the process of undertaking research is harder for the practitioner to see and embrace. Research for most is something that maybe formed as part of their university career, and as such is largely seen as the domain of the academic, of the full-time researcher. The distance perceived between what teachers do all day and the research world is vast, and if anything, in universities, we are guilty of increasing this gap. As Kilburn et al. (2014) note, we tend to teach research methods as something that is highly theoretical and distanced from application and practice. This widens the expertise gap and makes ownership of the practitioner enquiry element even harder. The challenge is that for practitioner enquiry to be successful it is essential that the enquirer has ownership of the inception of the project *and* the process of enquiry: only the question poser can decide what evidence will answer it satisfactorily.

We would of course argue that the expertise of the practitioner and the expertise of the academic are not necessarily in competition, indeed we would favour what Berliner (2001) describes as 'fluid expertise': substantive knowledge that is alive with reflexivity, criticality and

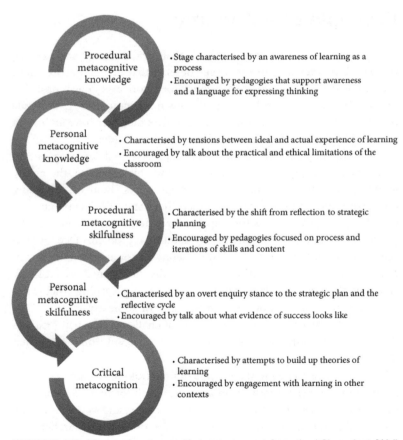

Procedural metacognitive knowledge
- Stage characterised by an awareness of learning as a process
- Encouraged by pedagogies that support awareness and a language for expressing thinking

Personal metacognitive knowledge
- Characterised by tensions between ideal and actual experience of learning
- Encouraged by talk about the practical and ethical limitations of the classroom

Procedural metacognitive skilfulness
- Characterised by the shift from reflection to strategic planning
- Encouraged by pedagogies focused on process and iterations of skills and content

Personal metacognitive skilfulness
- Characterised by an overt enquiry stance to the strategic plan and the reflective cycle
- Encouraged by talk about what evidence of success looks like

Critical metacognition
- Characterised by attempts to build up theories of learning
- Encouraged by engagement with learning in other contexts

FIGURE 6.3 Model of metacognitive engagement from the L2L project (Wall and Hall, 2016, p. 7).

curiosity is hallmark of an expert learner or researcher from any context. We consider that the enquiry process privileges the metacognitive knowledge, awareness and skilfulness that underpin fluid expertise. Figure 6.3 shows a model of development drawn from the learning that teachers in the Learning to Learn (L2L) enquiry project, where the focus shifted from 'problem-solving' difficult pupils/boring bits of curriculum to collaborative enquiry about the nature and purpose of learning *with* problem-solving (Wall and Hall, 2016).

The research process can produce a natural 'modelling' of metacognition from teacher to student and then from student to teacher.

> Amongst the many interesting aspects of the process has been the growth in confidence and levels of metacognition of the student steering group. This has led to the unexpectedly prominent involvement of the student group in designing, criticising and analysing the questionnaire results and in some very frank discussions about the state of teaching in learning in certain subject areas. Clearly, this engagement has benefited the students involved in the research group, who are now able to stand aside and observe the processes of teaching and learning as they are applied to themselves in school. In turn, these discussions have enabled the teacher leading the project to gain valuable and otherwise unavailable insights into the students' daily experiences in school. (John Welham, Camborne Science and Community College)

Here the development and ownership of expertise take place largely within a social space (Hall, 2009; McLaughlin and Black-Hawkins, 2004). In this space a language and structure for 'being a practitioner-researcher' are developed, a process of identification with others coupled with a recognition of difference leading to an acceptance of messiness in the reality of practice.

> The process of critical review and evaluation has allowed us to reflect upon our practice in a much more thorough, methodical and analytical manner than would typically be the case. (Senior leader Fallibroome High School)
>
> It made me think I am not alone here, it was a tremendous experience and it seems to have grown to include people who aren't so eccentric in their thinking and is still going strong. (Deborah Currans, Wooler First School)

This means that the principle of autonomy is characterised by an increased sophistication of thought about an individual's own learning trajectory and the different perspectives that it reflects. It is interwoven with their students' learning because they will always be the impetus for enquiry, but over time and through dialogue with the students and with other enquirers it becomes an increasingly informed stance that is reflective and strategic about metacognition, pedagogy and methodology. At first it can feel a big step to trust the individual teacher to engage with their own questions, but overtime with increasing confidence to articulate the rationale, the process and outcome to different audiences it becomes more of a risk not to.

Principle of disturbance

If you are asking questions to which you genuinely don't know the answer, then you have to be prepared to find out something new. This something might confirm your existing beliefs and practices, but it may also be partly, or wholly, challenging to your fundamental core thinking. The practitioner enquirer has to be ready for this. New knowledge might come from the pedagogical implications, the methodology or the metacognition. In all likelihood it will be a mixture of all three. How this is managed in relation to current practices and understandings is really important especially when tied to the 'making public' part of our model. Sharing a negative finding or challenging outcome is hard.

It should be slightly reassuring to think about this challenge in relation to what we know about learning in regards our students and how we set up our classes every day. We know tasks that support effective learning tend to be loosely bound and allow for concept generation with an inherent amount of challenge that facilitates the learners in operating out of their zone of proximal development (Vygotsky, 1978). This is what we are asking of practitioner enquiry with the aim being teacher learning. The big question is whether we are ready for this in the context of our own professional learning.

By achieving these aims, we aim to increase the Readiness, Resilience and Resourcefulness for learning of both pupils and staff. We hope a whole school approach to developing ... an active repertoire of approaches to learning, will enable pupils, staff and parents to engage more fully with their learning, thus improving attainment and motivation in school and in life.

We need to consider the metacognitive competencies, dispositions and skills that we require of our students and the extent to which we, truthfully, model those same behaviours when it comes to our own learning, especially our professional learning. Many of us work hard to teach and develop this metacognitive awareness in our students across a wide range of learning experiences; however often the same cannot be said about our professional learning. It is presumed to be part of our learning repertoire garnered up to this point in our lives honed by Initial Teacher Education (ITE) experience; however, the traditional continuing professional learning experiences don't tend to promote this way of learning and in our observation it tends to get supressed. There is quite a lot of research that shows that students' metacognition tends to develop in a domain-specific manner (Borkowski et al., 2000; Pressley et al., 1989), and although the direction of travel is not uncontested (Veenman and Elshout, 1999) there is a tendency for skills to become compartmentalised in areas of our lives and experience. We think you can see this in teacher's learning too and a high level of thinking is just not the norm in relation to professional learning.

Undertaking practitioner enquiry promotes an inherently active stance (Stephenson and Ennion, 2012). Where the questions are an enquirer's own, encompassing a genuine dilemma from practice, then there is likely to be an investment in undertaking a process to find a satisfying answer. However, to undertake research in real life is to embrace a level of complexity and unpredictability which will lead to confounds and genuinely destabilising ups and downs in the learning. This is all normal and leads to the challenge that we have already argued is so important, but largely missing from most professional learning provision. It is what ensures a usefulness to the learning that ensues, however it also makes it hard.

> L2L has enabled teachers to be creative and ambitious in their practice. As a school it gave us the opportunity to look more closely at how to develop the skills of reflectiveness with our children … L2L has now become embedded in our whole school ethos.

Therefore, a crucial part of the enquiry community is to support the individual enquirer in coping with a healthy amount of challenge. Not only to cope when things go wrong or not as expected, although this is important, but being supportive when the challenge gets too much, coping with feelings of being 'stuck' or slightly 'out of control'. But also to maintain a level of healthy challenge from outside of the enquiry to keep the learning moving forwards. This is a level of critical friendship that we would see having good fit with coaching dimensions (Lofthouse and Hall, 2014).

The community therefore should provide a space where individuals can talk through their own personal challenge and be metacognitive about the underpinning thinking, their own and their students. While simultaneously providing an outside questioning of process and thinking, prompting a codification of process, that in itself will be of challenge to the individual, helps to ensure a 'thoughtful, explicit examination of practices and their consequences' (Little, 1990, p. 520). By focusing on the reasons 'why' (you did that thing) rather than the detail of what you did, then the discourse around these dilemmas will be metacognitive in its character.

> The [community] altered the lead teachers' views on teaching and a considerable change in classroom practice has been initiated. Fundamentally, the change in viewpoint encompasses the realisation that teaching is not something that is simply delivered in the form of a series of lessons but that it encompasses a journey of discovery that the teacher and child undertake together in order to understand not just the context of the subject, but the principles and processes of learning.

The practitioner enquiry process arguably enables increasingly tight associations to be made between the student's and teacher's learning pathways and for them to be foregrounded in community thinking. A virtuous cycle can be evident between the practitioner enquiry process tightly focused on student learning and the teachers understanding of their own learning and thinking processes (professionally and personally). If we conceive of practitioner enquiry as more than process but as a stance (Cochran-Smith and Lytle, 2009), then this can be seen to underpin all aspects of the teachers' practice, their pedagogy, research, and personal and professional learning, and the implications for the parallel pathways increase. The epistemological basis of the manifestation of enquiry means the teachers take on not only a critical and often political and socially motivated engagement with research and practice, but also a transformative role (Menter, 2010) with responsibility for moving learning (their own and their students) forwards, lifelong and lifewide. Inherent in this stance is the extent to which they will take risks, personally and professionally, and the confidence with which they can articulate the extent of those risks (in light of their own and other's research and practice): they start to embrace challenge and self-moderate the level of disturbance implicit in their learning at any stage, turning it up and down depending on the other commitments and personal well-being. The process of practitioner enquiry as manifest in this book therefore facilitates the teacher's alignment with this enquiry stance by suggesting a community structure that is perceived simultaneously as reassuring and consistent, flexible and free to encompass the teacher's interests and perceptions of need in their context as well as questioning and challenging of the thinking processes behind professional decision-making.

Principle of dialogue

For the principles of autonomy and disturbance to be manifest in a community, dialogue is necessary. It is not a simple conversation that we are suggesting but something that is productive of learning. As Little (2003) noted, change occurs as teachers learn to describe, discuss and adjust their practices according to a collectively held standard of teaching quality. But this is not something that happens easily. It is therefore essential to spend some time thinking about the characteristics of this dialogue and the characteristics of the community in which it is encouraged. An important question to ask is 'how is a culture of enquiry with all the inherent challenge described above developed that encourages dialogue in an authentic manner?'

Dunne et al. (2000) in their studies of teachers learning with colleagues concluded that the underpinning skills were something to be learned, insinuating that they were either something the teachers did not have already or, as we have previously argued, skills they are not used to using within the professional learning context. We need to think more about the nature of the practitioner enquiry community that we are trying to develop and as a result what skills we need to develop.

We have seen useful parallels between what we know from the student voice field about creating democratic spaces for students and in the same way as we have suggested parallels between student's learning and teacher's, we would suggest that some of these understandings transfer to how we think teachers should be encouraged to engage in metacognitive dialogue. In the Look Who's Talking Project (Wall et al., 2017a and b) we generated eight principles for eliciting voice with children aged from birth to seven (Wall et al., 2018), an age group chosen for its particular characteristics and the resulting challenges for voice work. However, what we have found since is that these principles transfer to older children easily. We now propose to go one step further and think about them in relation to teachers and what we know about the learning in practitioner enquiry community. In particular in the discussion below we will think about how this teacher voice can be related to professional learning:

1. *Define: It is essential to address the question what is voice.*

Bringing a group of autonomous professionals together is challenging especially when they are all undertaking their own enquiry that they care deeply about. It is important to ask what does voice look like in this context. There may be a tendency towards spoken dialogue, but it is worth being aware of other methods of expression including behaviours, expressions, silences and body language – teachers are all experienced at using different ways to express themselves and in reading those signs in others. Therefore, it is important to think about what is appropriate voice in this context (without the presumption that appropriate is about fluffy agreement, but also how disagreement and critique are managed) and what tools might be useful to support dialogue that supports learning. In addition, it is worth remembering that as the community becomes established then understandings and use of voice will change with experience and confidence. The definition will need to be constantly revisited with the group to adapt to these developments while also accommodating new joiners.

2. *Power: Voice is about power; it is relational.*

School staff rooms are loaded with power dynamics and so the extent to which they can be suspended within an enquiry network is challenging. We would argue, however, this is no more so than those existing between adult and child or teacher and student, so we should try. For a start we should be honest about where the power is and then use techniques and tools to play with that power or turn it around, for example, supporting a newly qualified colleague in leading sessions on their own enquiry outcomes or openly learning from students within an enquiry frame. Our point about leaders showing their learning is central to this – leading by example and showing the ups and downs of real professional learning will support an authentic enquiry process is helpful in this as it promotes a shared expertise. Just as influential as actual power is how power and hierarchy are perceived and how this changes under different circumstances. Therefore, spending some time thinking about different voices can be facilitated and how approaches and tools might privilege or inhibit them is important. Reliance on the same methods that promote the same perspectives/voices should be avoided.

3. *Inclusivity: Everyone has an equal voice.*

Encouraging a range of individuals to be involved in your enquiry network is helpful. It particularly supports the principle of disturbance outlined above as talking to someone with a different experience or context to you will automatically introduce challenge to the dialogue. However, it is also important to recognise there will be a lot of personalities, a range of experience and different perspectives to be accommodated. Mixing up the groupings and who speaks to who will be useful to prevent cliques. Inclusion is also about allowing different viewpoints. Teaching and learning are inherently personal and while there will be rules to follow (either house rules from the host organisation, professional codes etc.), there will be disagreements. Indeed, it is important that there is disagreement. So, it is useful to think about how your community encourages and supports expression of a range of views and what it looks like if there is a dispute. How would you feel to share an enquiry outcome that challenges the status quo in your school?

4. *Listening: Voices should not have to be loud to be heard.*

Creating a culture where the contributions of different individuals are heard is essential as voice is nothing without a listener. In our networks, the teachers have often described a process of active listening. The need is to come to the community prepared to hear a diverse range of thinking, processes and ideas, some of which will fit in their context, some of which won't. However, the need to be open to hearing with the potential of tinkering with the core idea gives it better fit to their context, to the needs of their students. This active stance and this propensity to tinkering mean that the listener will automatically be asking questions about the different aspects of what they have heard and this supports a different type of dialogue with the person sharing. This goes directly against the traditional continuing professional development model of the passive receiver of information.

5. *Time and space: There is always time for voice.*

We all work under a huge amount of pressure; the culture of 'busy' is rife in schools. So, finding formal and informal space and time for dialogue about enquiry is important. Arguably the formal spaces come first and then the informal spaces will emerge from that base. Spaces that complement the enquiry cycle, that provide time to come together and talk about specific aspects of research – data collection, analysis, sharing outcomes – are a useful starting point. We would also encourage the (partial) use of existing training days to focus on enquiry, thus raising the profile and perceived importance of this activity within the professional development culture of the school. However, thinking about how these times might be organised in such a way to support dialogue: 'Novel: a conference where we have to confer!' (Head teacher, Learning to Learn in Schools project). Thinking about the organisation of physical spaces to support peer-to-peer conversation as well as activities and tools that allow genuine sharing of ideas and thinking is important.

6. *Approaches: Open dispositions support voice.*

Once you have created the spaces then thinking about how people enter them is important – the dispositions, competencies and expectations they bring. This is relevant to the participants, but also the facilitator. Just as with student voice work, nothing is as damaging as a facilitator who proposes voice, but actually dominates and doesn't listen. There needs to be movement towards partnership working and a genuine interest in the thinking and learning others bring to the table. Contemplating how you can change expectations and encourage flexibility promoting the active stance we have talked about above is helpful – take the meeting outside the school grounds (to the woods or to a posh hotel) or give out preparatory tasks (not too onerous, but enough to get people thinking and always relevant to their practice/students' learning). Remember not participating is just as valid a form of voice, so be realistic in your expectations and remain inclusive to different forms of voice – how would you feel doing what you have asked of others?

7. Processes: Processes should enable voice.

The structures and conditions should provide opportunity for consultation, collaboration and dialogue in order to support reflective and strategic thinking (metacognition). Remember that for most of us this is hard work and so allowing time for individuals to gather their thoughts is important. It is really important to think critically about who is talking and when – too much time with the facilitator dominating does not make for effective dialogue. Processes should be dynamic and have a forward momentum – take your clues from what works in supporting productive talk and thinking in the classroom and use these techniques with staff. Remember that processes often require innovation and this is risky with an audience of colleagues – so be brave and be open about what you are doing and why; make it an enquiry that others can share in.

8. Purposes: Shared goals will advance voice.

Enquiry is for the long haul and so having shared clarity about the goals of the enquiry activity is important. These goals are likely to be multiple; some will be shared by the community, others will be more individual. It is not just about at project level, individual cycles of enquiry, but it is also about how practitioner enquiry contributes to the culture of professional learning for all. Talking about this and sharing understanding of the teacher and community learning arising are helpful in maintaining momentum and a commitment to new learning over time. How new members of the community are inducted into this 'hive mind' is a significant challenge, as is how people depart especially if they are staying within the wider organisation.

An addition: Principle of connectivity

Our communities of practices (we deliberately use the plural here) have helped us to crystallise a final principle that practitioner enquiry is characterised by: connectivity (see Figure 6.4). We see two key aspects to this principle. First, the connections that undertaking enquiry facilitates for the professional learner, to the context and learners as an ethical basis, through dialogue to other practitioners in similar and different contexts who will be both supportive and critical friends and returning again to the individual for a sense-check. Secondly, it is the parallels of the enquiry process to other aspects of education, such as metacognition, voice, pedagogy and methodology and teaching and learning, which facilitate the process. Both types of connections support practice, helping enquiry to be doable in fitting with all the other competing demands that dominate school life.

We would suggest that practitioner enquiry becomes more doable when we see the productive connections it has with teaching and learning. When it is not something else to fit onto the long list of things to do and when it is being useful in advancing practice forwards. This means we have to look for bridges and associations that enable a more pragmatic, manageable outlook. For example, making the most of the fact that the enquiry cycle fits on to the plan-do-review cycle, and, while we are not recommending research on every lesson, it is relatively simple to see how a lesson might be scaled-up to include a research element. Similarly, by seeing the ways of thinking encouraged by the practitioner enquiry

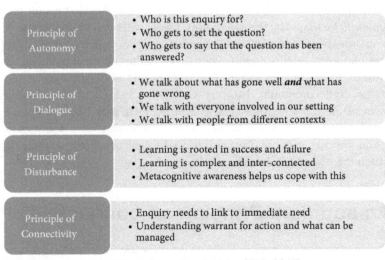

Principle of Autonomy	• Who is this enquiry for? • Who gets to set the question? • Who gets to say that the question has been answered?
Principle of Dialogue	• We talk about what has gone well **and** what has gone wrong • We talk with everyone involved in our setting • We talk with people from different contexts
Principle of Disturbance	• Learning is rooted in success and failure • Learning is complex and inter-connected • Metacognitive awareness helps us cope with this
Principle of Connectivity	• Enquiry needs to link to immediate need • Understanding warrant for action and what can be managed

FIGURE 6.4 Amended list of enquiry principles (Wall, 2017).

process, to reflect back and make strategic decisions about moving forwards, to understandings of metacognitive knowledge and skilfulness (Veenman and Spaans, 2005) represented in Figure 6.5. We think there a useful space is created by seeing metacognition as a methodology for professional learning (Porthilo and Medina, 2016) and how practitioner enquiry embeds this way of thinking in the context and on student need (Timperley et al., 2009).

A major tenet of this book has been to support the 'doability' of practitioner enquiry by seeing greater connections between the understandings of evidence that we use in teaching and learning and those in research. It is important that one of our principles underpins this fundamental belief. Schools are evidence-rich and as teachers we use a wide range of evidence all the time to assess student's progress and outcomes. Why can't we use that evidence within our enquiry projects? In addition, when thinking about quality, we need to be more confident in translating how we think about the effective pedagogic tools that we know work (in capturing children and young peoples' learning and perspectives) to thinking about tools for engaging in research (Baumfield et al., 2012). Teachers set themselves high standards of 'warrant' (Dewey, 1938/1991) – they know what evidence is good enough to support next steps for themselves and their students, but are shy at translating this thinking about what works and why to the world of research, and yet from my perspective it is too similar not to be a productive synergy.

Similar connections should be considered between how teachers learn and how students learn (it is not coincidence that enquiry-based approaches are also useful in classrooms), how we support student voice and teacher voice (the spaces, tools, dispositions and cultures) and how

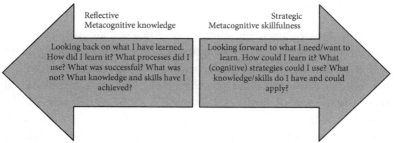

FIGURE 6.5 Making connections between practitioner enquiry and metacognition.

we support teacher's and student's metacognition. These different aspects should be interconnected and complementary. A practitioner enquiry frame can help bring them together (Wall and Hall, 2016), but also by seeing them as connected it makes a practitioner enquiry feel more doable.

Final thoughts: Brave spaces

There's a lot of time, money and effort spent on professional development in all sectors of education. As one might hope, considerable effort has also gone into trying to understand and evaluate professional development experiences (e.g. Timperley, 2008; Cordingley et al., 2015): these studies bring together the outcome measures of CPD (uptake of courses, feedback on the quality of the immediate experience, extent to which learning is incorporated into practice) and from this build up a picture of more and less successful approaches to ongoing professional learning. Of course, as the authors acknowledge, there are a number of problems with the data that these syntheses rely upon, in terms of both its innate quality and the complexity of the environment that produces it. A naïve perspective on uptake of courses suggests that good ones will be fully subscribed, so can be identified by this popularity and this may well be true. However, using the lens of the principle of autonomy, we have to ask:

- Who decided this was the training needed?
- Who goes on this training and how voluntary is it?
- How flexible is the content of the training to the needs of the specific people who show up on the day? (See, for example, Timperley et al., 2009.)

A first-level reading of provision suggests that specific groups are well-catered for: there are plenty of curriculum-focused (maths, geography) and stage-specific (early years, secondary) courses. Everyone who has ever been on one of these and indeed everyone who has ever run one will recognise the generic feedback sheet: it asks about the relevance of the material and the quality of the presentation, often with a linguistic steer towards a positive/neutral response. Almost all of the free-text comments are about the temperature of the room and the quality of the catering. If feedback sheets had to engage with the principle of dialogue, we might have to include questions such as

- How much time did the presenter/facilitator spend delivering content compared to how much time participants spent thinking and talking about it?
- Were there different perspectives and experiences in the room?
- Were fundamental ideas about curriculum, pedagogy and assessment open to debate? (See, for example, Opfer and Pedder, 2011.)

Long-term, in-depth follow-up studies of CPD are relatively rare, since for those who provide them and those who, at an administrative level, fund them are naturally concerned in the first instance to demonstrate provision and immediate satisfaction. Finding out how we 'make the knowledge stick' is seen as important but not urgent (Cordingley, 2015b). Follow-up studies are expensive, complex and tend to yield unsatisfactory, messy data: Is the change in Bob's practice due to the course or the new Head of Department or the very challenging Year 10 girls?; Is the lack of change in Sara's practice due to the course, her new role as Special Needs Co-ordinator or the budget cuts? The principle of disturbance might prompt an ecological (Priestley et al., 2015) research design that looked at

- the teacher's learning environment, his/her priorities and passions;
- the non-linear progress of changing practice through triumph, disaster and boring bits;
- the way in which the teacher makes sense of his/her own learning. (See, for example, Reeves and Drew, 2013.)

Enquiry is enriching and it is also difficult, time-consuming and painful – as Peirce (1877) reminds us, we will only resort to it if all other methods of fixing our beliefs fail. Engaging in an enquiry and sustaining it to a conclusion require us to be realistic about what we can undertake. They also take the support of a community and the use of brave spaces (Cook-Sather, 2016) in which individuals can speak out, be tentative and play with different thinking about the practice that they experience. Throughout this book we have highlighted curiosity as a key aspect of fluid expertise, arguably it is also what keeps practitioners in a profession. Practitioner enquiry enables us to harness our curiosity, to reflect on its fruits and share them with others. We will not always be fully engaged in an enquiry project; learning takes time to be absorbed and motivation and energy fluctuate (Day et al., 2006) but the potential to be involved is always there, whenever we want it.

REFERENCES

Achinstein, P. (2001). *The Book of Evidence*. Oxford: Oxford University Press.

AERA (American Educational Research Association). (2011). 'Code of Ethics'. Available at: http://www.aera.net/Portals/38/docs/About_AERA/CodeOfEthics(1).pdf (accessed 28 September 2015).

Alexander, R. J. (ed.). (2010). *Children, Their World, Their Education: Final Report and Recommendations from the Cambridge Primary Review*. Abingdon: Routledge.

Allen, L. (2009). 'Snapped': Researching the sexual cultures of schools using visual methods. *International Journal of Qualitative Methods in Education*, 22(5): 549–561. doi:10.1080/09518390903051523.

Amini, F., Lannon, R., and Lewis, T. B. (2000). *A General Theory of Love*. London: Vintage.

Ananiadou, K. and Claro, M. (2009). '21st Century Skills and Competences for New Millennium Learners in OECD Countries', OECD Education Working Papers, No. 41, OECD Publishing. Available at: http://dx.doi.org/10.1787/218525261154

Anderson, L. (2006). Analytic autoethnography. *Journal of Contemporary Ethnography*, 35(4): 373–395.

Andrews, E., Delaney, S., Dulwich, H., Farley, P., Furnish, N., Garbutt, S., Horner, A., James, H., Kitto, J., Pedley, J., Sharma, D., and Tonkin, H. (2006). *Developing formative assessment strategies in the primary school*. London: Campaign for Learning. Available at: http://www.campaign-for-learning.org.uk/cfl/assets/documents/CaseStudies/Pennoweth.pdf

Aristotle. (1987). The Politics. In J. L. Ackrill (ed.), *A New Aristotle Reader*. Princeton, NJ: Princeton University Press.

Arter, J. A. and Spandel, V. (1992). Using portfolios of student work in instruction and assessment. *Educational Measurement: Issues and Practice*, 11(1): 36–44.

Bailey, C. (2016). Free the sheep: Improvised song and performance in and around a Minecraft community. *Literacy*, 50(2): 62–71.

Ball, S. J. (2002). *Class Strategies and the Education Market: The Middle Classes and Social Advantage*. Hoboken: Taylor and Francis.

Ball, S. J. (2003). The teacher's soul and the terrors of performativity. *Journal of Education Policy*, 18(2): 215–228.

Barnes, J. (2003). *The Pedant in the Kitchen*. London: Guardian/Atlantic Books.

Baumfield, V. and Butterworth, M. (2007). Creating and translating knowledge about teaching and learning in collaborative school-university research partnership. *Teachers and Teaching*, 13(4): 411–427.

Baumfield, V., Hall, E., and Wall, K. (2008). *Action Research in the Classroom.* London: SAGE.

Baumfield, V., Hall, E., and Wall, K. (2012). *Action Research in the Education: Learning through Practitioner Enquiry*, 2nd Edition. London: SAGE.

Baumfield, V., Hall, E., Higgins, S., and Wall, K. (2009). Catalytic tools: Understanding the interaction of enquiry and feedback in teachers' learning. *European Journal of Teacher Education*, 32(4): 423–436.

Baumfield, V., Hall, E., Wall, K., and Higgins, S. (2008). Forming a Community of Inquiry: The practice of questioning in a school/university partnership. Paper presented at the American Educational Research Association Conference, New York, March 2008. Published at http://www.aera.net/Default.aspx?menu_id=362&id=4696

Baumfield, V. M. (2016). Democratic pedagogy: Thinking together. In F. Coffield and S. E. Higgins (eds.), *Dewey Centenary of Democracy and Education.* London: Institute of Education Press.

Beckett, S. (1983). *Worstward Ho!* London: Calder Publications Ltd.

Beere, J. (2013). The Perfect Teacher, Independent Thinking Press, an Imprint of Crown House Publishing.

BERA (British Education Research Association) (2011) 'Ethical Guidelines for Educational Research.' Available at: https://www.bera.ac.uk/researchers-resources/publications/ethical-guidelines-for-educational-research-2011 (accessed 18 September 2015).

Berliner, D. (2001). Learning about and learning from expert teachers. *International Journal of Educational Research*, 35: 463–482.

Bernstein, B. (1996). *Pedagogy, Symbolic Control and Identity, Theory, Research, Critique.* London: Taylor and Francis.

Biesta, G. (2012). Philosophy of education for the public good: Five challenges and an agenda. *Educational Philosophy and Theory*, 44(6): 581–593.

Biesta, G. J. (2010). Why 'what works' still won't work: From evidence-based education to value-based education. *Studies in Philosophy and Education*, 29(5): 491–503.

Billett, S. (2011). Workplace curriculum: Practice and propositions. In F. Dorchy and D. Gijbels (eds.), *Theories of Learning for the Workplace.* London: Routledge, 17–36.

Black, P. (2001). Dreams, strategies and systems: Portraits of assessment past, present and future. *Assessment in Education: Principles, Policy & Practice*, 8: 65–85.

Black, P. and Wiliam, D. (1990). *Inside the Black Box: Raising Standards Through Classroom Assessment.* Swindon: GL Assessment Limited.

Blackmore, S. (2005). *Consciousness: A Very Short Introduction.* Oxford: Oxford University Press.

Blades, M. and Spencer, C. (1987a). The use of maps by 4–6-year-old children in a large-scale maze. *British Journal of Developmental Psychology*, 5(1): 19–24.

Blades, M., and Spencer, C. (1987b). Young children's recognition of environmental features from aerial photographs and maps. *Environmental Education and Information*, 6(3): 189–198.

Booker, C. (2004). *The Seven Basic Plots: Why We Tell Stories.* London: Continuum.

Borkowski, J. G., Chan, L. K., and Muthukrishna, N. (2000). 1. A process-oriented model of metacognition: Links between motivation and executive functioning. In G. Schraw and J. C. Impara (eds.), *Issues in the Measurement of Metacognition.* Lincoln: Buros Institute of Mental Measurements, 1–42.

Boston, M. D. (2014). Assessing instructional quality in mathematics classrooms through collections of students' work. In *Transforming Mathematics Instruction.* Rotterdam: Springer International Publishing, 501–523.

Bowker, R. and Tearle, P. (2007). Gardening as a learning environment: A study of children's perceptions and understanding of school gardens as part of an international project. *Learning Environment Research,* 10: 83–100.

Bradford, S. and Rickwood, D. (2012). Psychosocial assessments for young people: A systematic review examining acceptability, disclosure and engagement, and predictive utility. *Adolescent Health, Medicine and Therapeutics,* 3: 111–125. http://doi.org/10.2147/AHMT.S38442

Bragg, S. (2007). 'But I listen to children anyway!'—Teacher perspectives on pupil voice. *Educational Action Research,* 15(4): 505–518.

Bragg, S. and Buckingham, D. (2008). 'Scrapbooks' as a resource in media research with young people. In P. Thomson (ed.), *Doing Visual Research with Children and Young People.* London: Routledge.

Breen, R. L. (2006). A practical guide to focus-group research. *Journal of Geography in Higher Education,* 30(3): 463–475.

Brown, A. (1992). Design experiments: Theoretical and methodological challenges in creating complex interventions in classroom settings. *Journal of the Learning Sciences,* 2(2): 141–178.

Brown, L. and Hunter, L. (2008). *Developing a Language for Learning to Support Assessment for Learning.* Available at: http://www.campaign-for-learning.org.uk/cfl/index.asp

Bruner, J. (1960). *The Process of Education.* Cambridge, MA: Harvard University Press, 97 + xxvi.

Bryman, A. (2008). *Social Research Methods,* 3rd Edition. Oxford: Oxford University Press.

Burke, C. and Grosvenor, I. (2003). *The School I'd Like.* London: RoutledgeFalmer.

Burns, H. (in press). Imagining better learning: A theoretical exploration of our understanding of imagination, its role in cognition and metacognition, its relationship with visual-art and what is implied for visual-arts-pedagogies, EdD thesis, Newcastle University.

Byrnes, L. J. and Rickards, F. W. (2011). Listening to the voices of students with disabilities: Can such voices inform practice? *Australasian Journal of Special Education,* 35(01): 25–34.

Cahnmann-Taylor, M. and Siegesmund, R. (2008). *Arts-based Research in Education: Foundations for Practice.* New York: Routledge.

Cameron, C. A. and Theron, L. (2011). With pictures and words I can show you: Cartoons portray resilient migrant teenagers' journeys. In L. Theron et al. (eds.), *Picturing Research: Drawing as Visual Methodology*. Rotterdam: Sense Publishers, 205–217.

Campbell, A. and Groundwater-Smith, S. (2007). *An Ethical Approach to Practitioner Research: Dealing with Issues and Dilemmas in Action Research*. Abingdon: Routledge.

Carr, W. (2007). Educational research as a practical science. *International Journal of Research & Method in Education*, 30(3): 271–286.

Charlton, D., McArthur, J., Douglas, S., and Smith, A. (2008). *How Will Cooperative Learning Strategies Impact on Social Interaction?* (Learning to Learn in Schools Phase 4 Year 1 Case Study). London: Campaign for Learning.

Clark, A. and Moss, P. (2011). *Listening to Young Children: The Mosaic Approach*. London: Jessica Kingsley Publishers.

Clark, J. (2012). Using diamond ranking as visual cues to engage young people in the research process. *Qualitative Research Journal*, 12(2): 222–37.

Claxton, G. (2002). *Building Learning Power: Helping Young People Become Better Learners*. Bristol: TLO Ltd.

Cochran-Smith, M. and Lytle, S. L. (1999). Relationships of knowledge and practice: Teacher learning in communities. *Review of Research in Education*, 24: 249–305.

Cochran-Smith, M. and Lytle, S. L. (2009). *Inquiry as Stance: Practitioner Research for the Next Generation*. London: Teachers College Press.

Cook-Sather, A. (2014). The trajectory of student voice in educational research. *New Zealand Journal of Educational Studies*, 49(2): 131–148.

Cook-Sather, A. (2016). Creating brave spaces within and through student-faculty pedagogical partnerships. *Teaching and Learning Together in Higher Education*, 1(18): 1.

Cordingley, P. (2013). *The Contribution of Research to Teachers' Professional Learning and Development. Research and Teacher Education: The BERA-RSA Inquiry*. London: British Educational Research Association.

Cordingley, P. (2015a). Evidence about teachers' professional learning and continuing professional development. In C. McLaughlin, P. Cordingley, R. McLellan, and V. Baumfield (eds.), *Making a Difference: Turning Teacher Learning Inside-out*. Cambridge: Cambridge University Press: 53–75.

Cordingley, P. (2015b). The contribution of research to teachers' professional learning and development. *Oxford Review of Education*, 41(2): 234–252.

Cordingley, P., Higgins, S., Greany, T., Buckler, N., Coles-Jordan, D., Crisp, B., Saunder, L., and Coe, R. (2015). Developing great teaching: Lessons from the international reviews into effective professional development. Project Report. Teacher Development Trust, London.

Creswell, J. W. (2003). *Research Design: Qualitative, Quantitative and Mixed Methods Approaches*, 2nd edition. London: SAGE.

Dagenais, C., Lysenko, L., Abrami, P. C., Bernard, R. M., Ramde, J., and Janosz, M. (2012). Use of research-based information by school practitioners and determinants of use: A review of empirical research. *Evidence & Policy: A Journal of Research, Debate and Practice*, 8(3): 285–309.

Day, C., Kington, A., Stobart, G., and Sammons, P. (2006). The personal and professional selves of teachers: Stable and unstable identities. *British Educational Research Journal*, 32(4): 601–616.

Dean, J. (2017). *Doing Reflexivity: An Introduction*. Bristol: Policy Press.

De Waal, C. (2013). *Peirce: A Guide for the Perplexed*. London: Bloomsbury.

Dewey, J. (1916). *Democracy and Education*. Carbondale: Southern Illinois University.

Dewey, J. (1927). *The Public and Its Problems: An Essay in Political Inquiry*. London: G. Allen & Unwin.

Dewey, J. (1938/1991). *Logic, the Theory of Enquiry*. Carbondale: Southern Illinois University Press.

Dewey, J. (1999). *The Essential Dewey*, edited by L. Hickman and T. Alexander. Bloomington: Indiana University Press.

Dillon, J. T. (1994). *Using Discussion in Classrooms*. Milton Keynes: Open University Press.

Downton, A. and Wright, V. (2016). A Rich Assessment Task as a Window into Students' Multiplicative Reasoning. Paper presented at the Annual Meeting of the Mathematics Education Research Group of Australasia (MERGA) (39th, Adelaide, South Australia).

Dunne, F., Nave, B., and Lewis, A. (2000). Critical friends groups: Teachers helping teachers to improve student learning. *Phi Delta Kappan*, 28(4): 31–37.

Dweck, C. (2017). *Mindset: Changing the Way You Think to Fulfil Your Potential*. London: Hachette UK.

Efklides, A. (2008). Metacognition: Defining its facets and levels of functioning in relation to self-regulation and co-regulation. *European Psychologist*, 13(4): 277–287.

Eisner, E. (1997). The promise and perils of alternative forms of data representation. *Educational Researcher*, 26(6): 4–11.

Eraut, M. (1994). *Developing Professional Knowledge and Competence*. London: Falmer.

Ericsson, K. A., Krampe, R. T., and Tesch-Römer, C. (1993). The Role of Deliberate Practice in the Acquisition of Expert Performance. *Psychological Review*, 100(3): 363.

Fielding, M. (2001). Students as radical agents of change. *Journal of Educational Change*, 2(2): 123–141.

Flavell, J. H. (1977). *Cognitive Development*. Upper Saddle River, NJ: Prentice Hall.

Flavell, J. H. (1979). Metacognition and cognitive monitoring: A new area of cognitive developmental inquiry. *Cognitive Development*, 34(10): 906–911.

Flyvbjerg, B. (2006). Five Misunderstandings about Case Study Research. *Quailitative Inquiry*, 12(2): 219–245.

Gallas, K. (1994). *The Languages of Learning: How Children Talk, Write, Dance, Draw, and Sing Their Understanding of the World*. New York: Teachers College Press.

Galman, S. A. C. (2009). The truthful messenger: Visual methods and representation in qualitative research in education. *Qualitative Research*, 9(2): 197–217. doi:10.1177/1468794108099321

Gascoine, L., Higgins, S., and Wall, K. (2016). The Assessment of Metacognition in Children Aged 4–16 Years: A Systematic Review. Review of Education. Available in first access.

Goldacre, B. (2009). *Bad Science*. London: Fourth Estate.

Goldacre, B. (2015). *I Think You'll Find It's a Bit More Complicated Than That*. London: Fourth Estate.

Groundwater-Smith, S. and Mockler, N. (2007). Ethics in practitioner research: An issue of quality. *Research Papers in Education*, 22(2): 199–211.

Guba, E. G., and Lincoln, Y. S. (1994). Competing Paradigms in Qualitative Research. *Handbook of Qualitative Research*, 2(163–194): 105.

Guenette, F. and Marshall, A. (2009). Time line drawings: Enhancing participant voice in narrative interviews on sensitive topics. *International Journal of Qualitative Methods*, 8(1): 85–92.

Hall, E. (2009). Engaging in and engaging with research: Teacher inquiry and development. *Teachers and Teaching: Theory and Practice*, 15(6): 669–682.

Hall, E. (2011). 'Enacting Change in Classrooms' PhD, Newcastle University. Available at: https://theses.ncl.ac.uk/dspace/handle/10443/1203

Hall, E. (2016). The tenacity of learning styles: A response to Lodge, Hansen and Cottrell Learning. *Research and Practice*, 2(1): 18–26. doi:10.1080/23735082.2016.1139856

Hall, E., Wall, K., Higgins, S., Stephens, L., Pooley, I., and Welham, J. (2010). Learning to Learn with Parents: Lessons from two research projects. In A. Campbell and S. Groundwater-Smith (eds.), *Action Research in Education: Volume 3: Key Examples of Action Research in Schools Within Different National Settings* (Fundamentals of Applied Research Series). London: SAGE Publications, 121–135.

Hall, J. (in press, 2019). Marginal gains?: Challenging the structures of interaction in clinical supervision. *The Law Teacher*.

Hammersley, M. (2004). Action research: A contradiction in terms? *Oxford Review of Education*, 30(2): 165–181.

Hammersley, M. (2006). Are ethics committees ethical?. *Qualitative Researcher*, 2(Spring): 4–8.

Hammersley, M. (2007). The issue of quality in qualitative research. *International Journal of Research & Method in Education*, 30(3): 287–305. doi:10.1080/17437270701614782

Hammersley, M. and Traianou, A. (2012). *Ethics in Qualitative Research: Controversies and Contexts*. London: SAGE.

Hardman, F., Smith, F., and Wall, K. (2003). Interactive whole class teaching in the national literacy strategy. *Cambridge Journal of Education*, 33(2): 197–215.

Hardman, F., Smith, F., and Wall, K. (2005). Teacher-pupil dialogue with pupils with special educational needs in the National Literacy Strategy. *Educational Review*, 57(3): 299–316.

Hargreaves, A., Earl, L., Moore, S., and Manning, S. (2001). *Learning to Change. Teaching Beyond Subjects and Standards*. San Francisco, CA: Jossey-Bass.

Harper, D. (2002). Talking about pictures: A case for photo elicitation. *Visual Studies*, 17(1): 13–26. doi:10.1080/14725860220137345

Hart, R. A. (1992). *Children's Participation: From Tokenism to Citizenship. Innocenti essays No.4*. Florence: UNICEF International Child Development Centre.

Hatt, L. (2016). What's Distinctive about Entrepreneurship and Entrepreneurship Education? Threshold Concepts and Expertise. Practitioner Development Workshop at 3E (ESCB Enterprise Educators Conference), Leeds. Available at: https://www.ee.ucl.ac.uk/~mflanaga/L%20 Hatt%20ECSB%20Paper.pdf

Hattie, J. (2008). *Visible Learning: A Synthesis of Over 800 Meta-analyses Relating to Achievement*. Abingdon: Routledge.

Hattie, J. and Yates, G. C. (2013). *Visible Learning and the Science of How We Learn*. London: Routledge.

Heikkinen, H. L. T., Huttunen, R., Syrjala, L., and Pesonen, J. (2012). Action research and narrative enquiry: Five principles for validation revisited. *Education Action Research*, 20(1): 5–21.

Hessels, L. K. and Van Lente, H. (2008). Re-thinking new knowledge production: A literature review and a research agenda. *Research Policy*, 37: 740–760.

Higgins, C. (2010). Human Conditions for Teaching: The Place of Pedagogy in Arendt's 'Vita Activa'. *Teachers College Record*, 112(2): 407–445.

Higgins, S., Baumfield, V., and Leat, D. (2001). *Thinking Through Primary Teaching*. Cambridge: Chris Kington Publishing.

Higgins, S., Hall, E., Baumfield, V., Moseley, D. (2005). A meta-analysis of the impact of the implementation of thinking skills approaches on pupils. In *Research Evidence in Education Library*. London: EPPI-Centre, Social Science Research Unit, Institute of Education, University of London. Available at: http://eppi.ioe.ac.uk/cms/Default.aspx?tabid=338

Higgins, S., Katsipataki, M., Kokotsaki, D., Coleman, R., Major, L. E., and Coe, R. (2013). *The Sutton Trust - Education Endowment Foundation Teaching and Learning Toolkit*. London: Education Endowment Foundation.

Higgins, S., Wall, K., Baumfield, V., Hall, E., Leat, D., Moseley, D., and Woolner, P. (2007). *Learning to Learn in Schools Phase 3 Evaluation: Final Report*. London: Campaign for Learning.

Higgins, S., Katsipataki, M., Villanueva-Aguilera, A. B., Coleman, R., Henderson, P., Major, L. E., Coe, R., and Mason, D. (2016). *The Sutton Trust-Education Endowment Foundation Teaching and Learning Toolkit*. London: Education Endowment Foundation.

Higgins, S., Baumfield, V., Lin, M., Moseley, D., Butterworth, M., Downey, G., Gregson, M., Oberski, I., Rockett, M., and Thacker, D. (2004). Thinking skills approaches to effective teaching and learning: What is the evidence for impact on learners. In *Research Evidence in Education Library*. London: EPPI-Centre, Social Science Research Unit, Institute of Education, University of London. Available at: http://eppi.ioe.ac.uk/cms/Default.aspx?tabid=335

Hopkins, E. (2008). Classroom conditions to secure enjoyment and achievement: The pupils' voice. Listening to the voice of Every Child Matters. *Education 3–13*, 36(4): 393–401.

James, M. and Pedder, D. (2006). Beyond method: Assessment and learning practices and values. *Curriculum Journal*, 17: 109–138.

Johnson, R. B. and Onwuegbuzie, A. J. (2004). Mixed methods research: A research paradigm whose time has come. *Educational Researcher*, 33(7): 14–26.

Jones, H. (2008). Thoughts on teaching thinking: Perceptions of practitioners with a shared culture of thinking skills education. *Curriculum Journal*, 19(4): 309–324.

Jones, S. R. (2015). *Intersectionality in Educational Research*. Sterling, VA: Stylus Publishing, LLC.

Katsipataki, M. and Higgins, S. (2016). What works or what's worked? Evidence from education in the United Kingdom. *Procedia, Social and Behavioral Sciences*, 217: 903–909.

Kellett, M. (2005). *How to Develop Children as Researchers: A Step by Step Guide to Teaching the Research Process*. London: SAGE.

Kellett, M. (2010). Small shoes, big steps! Empowering children as active researchers. *American Journal of Community Psychology*, 46(1–2): 195–203.

Kellett, M. (2011). Empowering children and young people as researchers: Overcoming barriers and building capacity. *Child Indicators Research*, 4(2): 205–219.

Keogh, B. and Naylor, S. (1999). Concept cartoons, teaching and learning in science: An evaluation. *International Journal of Science Education*, 21(4): 431–446. doi:10.1080/095006999290642

Kilburn, D., Nind, M., and Wiles, R. (2014). Learning as researchers and teachers: The development of a pedagogical culture for social science research methods?. *British Journal of Educational Studies*, 62(2): 191–207.

Kirova, A. and Emme, M. (2008). Fotonovela as a research tool in image-based participatory research with immigrant children. *International Journal of Qualitative Methods*, 7(2): 35–57.

Knorr-Cetina, K. (2001). Objectual practice. In T. Schatzki, K. Knorr-Cetina, and E. Von Savigny (eds.), *The Practice Turn in Contemporary Theory*. London: Routledge.

Krueger, R. and Casey, M. (2015). *Focus Groups: A Practical Guide for Applied Research*, 5th edition. Thousand Oaks, CA: SAGE.

Kvernbekk, T. (2011). The concept of evidence in evidence based practice. *Educational Theory*, 61(5): 515–532.

Kvernbekk, T. (2013). Evidence-based practice: On the function of evidence in practical reasoning. *Studier i Pædagogisk Filosofi*, 2(2): 19–33.

Lampert, M. (2010). Learning teaching in, from, and for practice: What do we mean? *Journal of Teacher Education*, 61(1–2): 21–34.

Larsson, S. (2009). A pluralist view of generalization in qualitative research. *International Journal of Research & Method in Education*, 32(1): 25–38.

Lash, S. (2003). Reflexivity as non-linearity. *Theory, Culture and Society*, 20(2): 49–57.

Law, J. (2002). *Aircraft stories: Decentring the object in technoscience*. Durham, NC: Duke University Press.

Leat, D. and Reid, A. (2012). Exploring the role of student researchers in the process of curriculum development. *Curriculum Journal*, 23(2): 189–205.

Leat, D., Reid, A., and Lofthouse, R. (2015). Teachers' experiences of engagement with and in educational research: What can be learned from teachers' views?. *Oxford Review of Education*, 41(2): 270–286.

Leat D. J. K. and Higgins, S. E. (2002). The role of powerful pedagogical strategies in curriculum development. *Curriculum Journal*, 13(1): 71–85.

Leavy, P. (2008). *Method meets art: Arts-based research practice*. New York: Guilford Press.

Leung, F.-H. and Savithiri, R. (2009). Spotlight on focus groups. *Canadian Family Physician*, 55(2): 218–219.

Lewis, A. N. N., Newton, H., and Vials, S. (2008). Realising child voice: The development of Cue Cards. *Support for Learning*, 23(1): 26–31.

Lewis, V. and Barwick, H. (2006). *Developing a Circle Time Model Involving Children in Self-Assessment and Developing Co-operative Learning Strategies for Lifelong Learning*. London: Campaign for Learning.

Lieberman, A. and Pointer-Mace, D. H. (2009). The role of 'accomplished teachers' in professional learning communities: Uncovering practice and enabling leadership. *Teachers and Teaching: Theory and Practice*, 15(4): 459–470.

Lincoln, Y. S. and Guba, E. G. (1985). *Naturalistic Inquiry*. Beverly Hills, CA: SAGE.

Lipman, M. (1991). *Thinking in Education*, Cambridge: Cambridge University Press.

Little, J. W. (1990). The persistence of privacy: Autonomy and initiative in teachers' professional relations. *Teachers College Record*, 91(4): 509–536.

Little, J. W. (2003). Inside teacher community: Representations of classroom practice. *Teachers College Record*, 105(6): 913–945.

Lodge, C. (2005). From hearing voices to engaging in dialogue: Problematising student participation in school improvement. *Journal of Educational Change*, 6(2): 125–146. doi:10.1007/s10833-005-1299-3

Lofthouse, R. (2015). Metamorphosis, model-making and meaning; developing exemplary knowledge for teacher education, PhD, Newcastle University.

Lofthouse, R. and Hall, E. (2014). Developing practices in teachers' professional dialogue in England: Using coaching dimensions as an epistemic tool. *Professional Development in Education*, 40(5): 758–778.

Long, L., McPhillips, T., Shevlin, M., and Smith, R. (2012). Utilising creative methodologies to elicit the views of young learners with additional needs in literacy. *Support for Learning*, 27(1): 20–28.

Maitland, G. and Murphy, D. (2008). *How Can Cooperative Learning Strategies Support A4L, Group Work & Social Interaction?* London: Campaign for Learning.

Mannion, J. and Mercer, N. (2016). Learning to learn: Improving attainment, closing the gap at Key Stage 3. *The Curriculum Journal.* doi:10.1080/0958517 6.2015.1137778

Marsh, H. (2006). Self-concept theory, measurement and research into practice: The role of self-concept in educational psychology (The 25th Vernon-wall Lecture presented at the Annual Meeting of the Education Section of the British Psychological Society). Leicester: The British Psychological Society.

Mavers, D., Somekh, B., and Restorick, J. (2002). Interpreting the externalised images of pupils' conceptions of ICT: Methods for the analysis of concept maps. *Computers & Education,* 38(1): 187–207.

McCloud, S. (1993). *Understanding Comics: The Invisible Art.* New York: HarperCollins.

McConney, A. A., Schalock, M. D., and Del Schalock, H. (1998). Focusing improvement and quality assurance: Work samples as authentic performance measures of prospective teachers' effectiveness. *Journal of Personnel Evaluation in Education,* 11(4): 343–336.

McLaughlin, C. and Black-Hawkins, K. (2004). A Schools-University Research partnership: Understandings, models and complexities. *Journal of In-Service Education,* 30(2): 265–284.

McLaughlin, C., Black-Hawkins, K., and McIntyre, D. (2007). *Networking Practitioner Research.* Hoboken, NJ: Taylor and Francis.

McNiff, S. (2008). *Art-based Research.* London: Jessica Kingsley Publishers.

Menter, I. (2010). *Teachers: Formation, Training and Identity.* Newcastle upon Tyne: Culture, Creativity and Education.

Menter, I., Elliott, D., Hulme, M., and Lewin, J. (2010). *Literature Review on Teacher Education in the Twenty-first Century.* Edinburgh: The Scottish Government.

Menter, I., Elliot, D., Hulme, M., Lewin, J., and Lowden, K. (2011). *A Guide to Practitioner Research in Education.* SAGE.

Mercer, N. and Hodgkinson, S. (eds.). (2008). *Exploring Talk in School: Inspired by the Work of Douglas Barnes.* London: SAGE Publications Ltd.

Mercer, N. and Sams, C. (2006). Teaching children how to use language to solve maths problems. *Language and Education,* 20(6): 507–528.

Meyer, M. (2010). The rise of the knowledge broker. *Science Communication* 32(1): 118–127.

Miholic, V. (1994). An inventory to pique students' metacognitive awareness of reading strategies. *Journal of Reading,* 38(2): 84–86.

Moos, R. H. (1979). *Evaluating Educational Environments.* San Francisco, CA: Jossey-Bass.

Morrison, K. (2001). Randomised controlled trials for evidence-based education: Some problems in judging 'what works'. *Evaluation & Research in Education,* 15(2): 69–83.

Moseley, D., Elliott, J., Higgins, S., and Gregson, M. (2005b). Thinking skills frameworks for use in education and training. *British Educational Research Journal,* 31(3): 367–390.

Moseley, D., Baumfield, V., Elliott, J., Higgins, S., Miller, J., and Gregson, M. (2005a). *Frameworks for Thinking: A Handbook for Teaching and Learning.* Cambridge: Cambridge University Press.

Mroz, M. (2016). Recognition and support of children with speech, language and communication needs: Knowledge, policy and practice. Available at: https://theses.ncl.ac.uk/dspace/bitstream/10443/3346/1/Mroz%2c%20M.%202016.pdf

Mulholland, K. (2016). 'I think when I work with other people I can let go of all of my ideas and tell them out loud': The impact of a Thinking Skills approach upon pupils' experiences of Maths, e-Thesis, Newcastle University.

Nassaji, H., & Wells, G. (2000). What's the use of 'triadic dialogue'?: An investigation of teacher-student interaction. *Applied Linguistics*, 21(3): 376–406.

Nias, J. and Groundwater-Smith, S. (eds.). (1988). *The Enquiring Teacher: Supporting and Sustaining Teacher Research.* London: Routledge.

Niemi, R., Kumpulainen, K., and Lipponen, L. (2015). Pupil as active participants: Diamond ranking as a tool to investigate pupils' experiences of classroom practices. *European Educational Research Journal*, 14(2): 138–150.

Nystrand, M., Gamoran, A., Kachur, R., and Prendergast, C. (1997). *Opening Dialogue: Understanding the Dynamics of Language and Learning in the English Classroom.* New York: Teachers College Press.

O'Donnell, A. M. (2004). A commentary on design research. *Educational Psychologist*, 39(4): 255–260.

O'Kane, C. (2010). The development of participatory techniques: Facilitating children's views about decisions which affect them. In P. Christensen and A. James (eds.), *Research with Children: Perspectives and Practice.* London: RoutledgeFalmer, 136–159.

O'Mara, A. J., Marsh, H. W., Craven, R. G., and Debus, R. L. (2006). Do self-concept interventions make a difference? A synergistic blend of construct validation and meta-analysis. *Educational Psychologist*, 41(3): 181–206.

Opfer, V. D. and Pedder, D. (2011). Conceptualizing teacher professional learning. *Review of Educational Research*, 81(3): 376–407.

Oppenheim, A. (1966). *Questionnaire Design and Attitude Measurement*, London: Heinemann.

Palincsar, A. S., Magnusson, S. J., Collins, K. M., and Cutter, J. (2001). Making science accessible to all: Results of a design experiment in inclusive classrooms. *Learning Disability Quarterly*, 24(1): 15–32.

Passini, R. (1984). Spatial representations, a wayfinding perspective. *Journal of Environmental Psychology*, 4(2): 153–164.

Pearson, M. and Somekh, B. (2003). Concept-mapping as a research tool: A study of primary children's representations of information and communication technologies (ICT). *Education and Information Technologies*, 8(1): 5–22.

Peirce, C. S. (1877). The Fixation of Belief. *Popular Science Monthly*, 12 November: 1–15.

Peirce, C. S. (1878). How to make our ideas clear. *Popular Science Monthly*, 12: 286–302.

Pope, C. C., De Luca, R., and Tolich, M. (2010). How an exchange of perspectives led to tentative ethical guidelines for visual ethnography. *International Journal of Research and Method in Education*, 41(3): 311–325.

Portilho, E. M. L. and Medina, G. B. K. (2016). Metacognition as methodology for continuing education of teachers. *Creative Education*, 7(01): 1.

Pressley, M., Borkowski, J. G., and Schneider, W. (1989). Good information processing: What it is and how education can promote it. *International Journal of Educational Research*, 13: 857–866.

Priego, E. (2016). Comics as research, comics for impact: The case of higher fees, higher debts. *The Comics Grid: Journal of Comics Scholarship*, 6(1): 1–15. doi:10.16995/cg.101

Priestley, M., Biesta, G., and Robinson, S. (2015). *Teacher Agency: An Ecological Approach*. London: Bloomsbury.

Prosser, J. (2007). Visual methods and the visual culture of schools. *Visual Studies*, 22(1): 13–30. doi:10.1080/14725860601167143

Reed, H. (1942/1991). 'Naming of Parts; Lessons of the War' in *Collected Poems*. Manchester: Carcanet Press.

Reeves, J. and Drew, V. (2013). A productive relationship? Testing the connections between professional learning and practitioner research. *Scottish Educational Review*, 45(2): 36–49.

Robinson, C. and Taylor, C. (2007). Theorising student participation: Values and perspectives. *Improving Schools*, 10(5): 5–17. doi:10.1177/1365480207073702

Rockett, M. and Percival, S. (2002). *Thinking for Learning*. Stafford: Network Educational Press.

Rogers, C. (1961/2012). *On Becoming a Person: A Therapist's View of Psychotherapy*. New York: Houghton Mifflin Harcourt.

Ruddock, J., Chaplin, R., and Wallace, G. (eds.). (1996). *School Improvement: What Can Pupils Tell Us?* London: Fulton.

Sachs, J. (2001). Teacher professional identity: Competing discourses, competing outcomes. *Journal of Education Policy*, 16(2): 149–161.

Saldana, J. (2013). *The Coding Manual for Qualitative Researchers*, 2nd edition. London: SAGE.

Salzberg-Ludwig, K. (2008). Scholarly research on mind maps in learning by mentally retarded children. In *A paper presented at the European Conference on Educational Research, University of Goteborg*. Available at: http://www. leeds.ac.uk/educol/documents/174867.pdf

Schagen, I. and Elliot, K. (eds.). (2004). *But what does it **mean?** The use of effect sizes in educational research*. Slough: NFER. Available at: https://www.nfer. ac.uk/publications/SEF01/SEF01.pdf

Schön, D. (1987). *Educating the Reflective Practitioner: Towards a New Design for Teaching Learning in the Professions*. San Francisco, CA: Jossey Bass.

Schön, D. A. (1991). *The Reflective Turn: Case Studies in and on Educational Practice*. New York: Teachers Press, Columbia University.

Sendak, M. (1963). *Where the Wild Things Are*. New York: Harper and Rowe.

Sinclair, J. and Coulthard, M. (1975). *Towards an Analysis of Discourse: The English Used by Teachers and Pupils*. London: Oxford University Press.

Smithbell, P. (2010). Arts-based research in education: A review. *The Qualitative Report*, 15(6): 1597–1601.

Smithson, J. (2000). Using and analyzing focus groups: Limitations and possibilities. *International Journal of Social Research Methodology*, 3(2): 103–119.

Spybrook, J., Shi, R., and Kelcey, B. (2016). Progress in the past decade: An examination of the precision of cluster randomized trials funded by the US Institute of Education Sciences. *International Journal of Research & Method in Education*, 39(3): 255–267.

Stenhouse, L. (1983). Research as a basis for teaching. Inaugural lecture from University of East Anglia. In L. Stenhouse (ed.), *Authority, Education and Emancipation*. London: Heinemann, 178.

Stephenson, E. and Ennion, T. (2012). Promoting independent learning through an enquiry-based approach. *Learning & Teaching Update*, 53: 9–11.

Sullivan, G. (2010). *Art Practice as Research: Inquiry in Visual Arts*. London: SAGE Publishing.

Symonds, J. E. and Gorard, S. (2010). Death of mixed methods? Or the rebirth of research as a craft. *Evaluation & Research in Education*, 23(2): 121–136.

Symons, V. and Currans, D. (2008). *Using Marking Ladders to Support Children's Self-Assessment in Writing*. London: Campaign for Learning.

Thomas, G. (2011). The case: Generalisation, theory and phronesis in case study. *Oxford Review of Education*, 37(1): 21–35.

Thomas, G. (2016). After the gold rush: Questioning the 'gold standard' and reappraising the status of experiment and randomized controlled trials in education. *Harvard Educational Review*, 86(3): 390–411.

Thomas, U., Tiplady, L., and Wall, K. (2014). Stories of practitioner enquiry: Using narrative interviews to explore teachers' perspectives of learning to learn. *International Journal of Qualitative Studies in Education*, 27(3): 397–411.

Thompson, G. N., Estabrooks, C. A., and Degner, L. F. (2006). Clarifying the concepts in knowledge transfer: A literature review. *Journal of Advanced Nursing*, 53(6): 691–701.

Thomson, D. (2017). *Getting Older Quicker*. Education DataLab Blogpost. Available at: http://educationdatalab.org.uk/2017/03/getting-older-quicker/

Thomson, P. and Gunter, H. (2006). From 'consulting pupils' to 'pupils as researchers': A situated case narrative. *British Educational Research Journal*, 32(6): 839–856.

Timperley, H. S. (2008). *Teacher Professional Learning and Development*. Geneva: The International Bureau of Education.

Timperley, H. S., Parr, J. M., and Bartanees, C. (2009). Promoting professional enquiry for improved outcomes for students in New Zealand. *Professional Development in Education*, 35(2), 227–245.

Toulmin, S. E. (1958/2003). *The Uses of Argument*. Cambridge: Cambridge University Press.

Towler, C., Wooler, P., and Wall, K. (2011) 'In college it's more explicit. Outside college it's just your life': Exploring Teachers' and Students' Conceptions of Learning in Two Further Education Colleges. *Journal of Further and Higher Education*, 35(4): 501–520.

UNCRC (United Nations Convention on the Rights of the Child). (1989). UN General Assembly Resolution 44/25. Available at: http://www.un.org/documents/ga/res/44/a44r025.htm (accessed 1 October 2015).

Van Blerkom. (2008). *Measurement and Statistics for Teachers*, 2nd edition. London: Routledge.

Varga-Atkins, T. and O'Brien, M. (2009). From drawings to diagrams: Maintaining researcher control during graphic elicitation in qualitative interviews. *International Journal of Research & Method in Education*, 32(1): 53–67.

Veenman, M. V. J. and Elshout, J. J. (1999). Changes in the relation between cognitive and metacognitive skills during the acquisition of expertise. *European Journal of Psychology of Education*, 14(4): 509–523.

Veenman, M. V. J. and Spaans, M. A. (2005). Relation between intellectual and metacognitive skills: Age and task difference. *Learning and Individual Differences*, 15(2): 159–176.

Vermunt, J. D. (2014). Teacher learning and professional development. In S. Krolak-Schwerdt, S. Glock, and M. Böhmer (eds.), *Teachers' Professional Development: Assessment, Training, and Learning*. Rotterdam, The Netherlands: Sense, 79–95.

Vermunt, J. D. and Endedijk, M. (2011). Patterns in teacher learning in different phases of the professional career. *Learning and Individual Differences*, 21: 294–302.

Vigurs, K., Jones, S., and Harris, D. (2016a). *Greater Expectations of Graduate Futures? A Comparative Analysis of the Views of the Last Generation of Lower-Fees Undergraduates and the First Generation of Higher-Fees Undergraduates at Two English Universities, Research report for SRHE* (Society for Research in Higher Education). Available at: http://eprints.staffs.ac.uk/2502/

Vigurs, K., Jones, S., and Harris, D. (2016b). *Higher Fees, Higher Debts: Greater Expectations of Graduate Futures? – A Research-Informed Comic*. Stoke-on-Trent: Staffordshire University. Available at: http://eprints.staffs.ac.uk/2503/

Vygotsky, L. S. (1978). *Mind in Society: The Development of Higher Psychological Processes*. Cambridge, MA: Harvard University Press.

Wall, K. (2008). Understanding metacognition through the use of pupil views templates: Pupil views of Learning to Learn. *Thinking Skills and Creativity*, 3(1): 23–33.

Wall, K. (2017). Exploring the ethical issues related to visual methodology when including young children in wider research samples. *International Journal of Inclusive Education (Special Issue: Researching ethically with children and young people in inclusive educational contexts)*, 21(3): 316–331.

Wall, K. (2012). 'It wasn't too easy, which is good if you want to learn': An exploration of pupil participation and Learning to Learn. *The Curriculum Journal*, 23(3): 283–305.

Wall, K. (2018). Building a bridge between pedagogy and methodology: Emergent thinking on notions of quality in practitioner enquiry. *Scottish Education Review*, 49(2): 3–24.

Wall, K. and Hall, E. (2016). Teachers as metacognitive role models. *European Journal of Teacher Education*, 39(4): 403–418.

Wall, K. and Hall, E. (2017). The teacher in teacher-practitioner research: Three principles of inquiry. In P. Boyd and A. Szplit, *International Perspectives: Teachers and Teacher Educators Learning Through Enquiry*. Kielce-Krakow: The Jan Kochanowski University, 35–62.

Wall, K. and Higgins, S. (2006). Facilitating and supporting talk with pupils about metacognition: A research and learning tool. *International Journal of Research and Methods in Education*, 29(1): 39–53.

Wall, K. Higgins, S., and Burns, H. (2017a). The role of research in learning and teaching: Practitioner enquiry as a catalyst for both teachers' and students' metacognitive development. Paper presented at ECER, Copenhagen, Denmark.

Wall, K., Hall, E., Higgins, S., and Gascoine, L. (2016). What does learning look like? Using cartoon story boards to investigate student perceptions (from 4 to 15) of learning something new. In M. Emme and A. Kirova (eds.), *Good Questions: Creative Collaborations with Kids*. Thunder Bay, ON: National Art Education Association.

Wall, K., Higgins, S., Hall, E., and Woolner, P. (2013a). 'That's not quite the way we see it': The epistemological challenge of visual data. *International Journal of Research and Methods in Education*, 36(1): 3–22.

Wall, K., Higgins, S., Glasner, E., Mahmout, U., and Gormally, J. (2009). Teacher enquiry as a tool for professional development: Investigating pupils' effective talk while learning. *Australian Educational Researcher*, 36(2): 93–117.

Wall, K., Higgins, S., Rafferty, V., Remedios, R., and Tiplady, L. (2013b). Comparing analysis frames for visual data sets: Using pupil views templates to explore perspectives of learning. *Journal of Mixed Methods Research*, 7(1): 20–40.

Wall, K., Arnott, L., Cassidy, C., Beaton, M., Christensen, P., Dockett, S., Robinson, C. (2017b). Look who's talking: Eliciting the voices of children from birth to seven. *International Journal of Student Voice*, 2(1): 3.

Wall, K., Hall, E., Baumfield, V., Higgins, S., Rafferty, V., Remedios, R., Thomas, U., Tiplady, L., Towler, C., and Woolner, P. (2010). *Learning to Learn in Schools Phase 4 and Learning to Learn in Further Education*. London: Campaign for Learning.

Wall, K., Cassidy, C., Arnott, L., Beaton M., Blaisdell, C., Hall, E., Kanyal, M., McKernan, G., Mitra, D., Pramling, I., and Robinson, C. (2018). Look who's talking: Factors for considering the facilitation of very young children's voices, Paper presented at AERA 2018, New York.

Walsh, S. and Mann, S. (2015). Doing reflective practice: A data-led way forward. *ELT Journal*, 69(4): 351–362.

Watson, J. (2008). Autographic disclosure and genealogies of desire in Alison Bechdel's Fun Home. *Biography*, 31(1): 27–58. doi:10.1353/bio.0.0006

Welham, J. (2010). *Why do some student engage more fully with L2L than others?* Available at: http://www.campaign-for-learning.org.uk/cfl/index.asp

Wells, G. (1993). Re-evaluating the IRF Sequence: A proposal for the articulation of theories of activity and discourse for the analysis of teaching and learning in the classroom. *Linguistics and Education*, 5: 1–37.

Wheeldon, J. (2011). Is a picture worth a thousand words? Using mind maps to facilitate participant recall in qualitative research. *The Qualitative Report*, 16(2): 509.

Wheeldon, J. and Faubert, J. (2009). Framing experience: Concept maps, mind maps, and data collection in qualitative research. *International Journal of Qualitative Methods*, 8(3): 68–83.

Whitebread, D., Coltman, P., Pasternak, D. P., Sangster, C., Grau, V., Bingham, S., Almeqdad, Q., and Demetriou, D. (2009). The development of two observational tools for assessing metacognition and self-regulated learning in young children. *Metacognition and Learning*, 4(1): 63–85. doi:10.1007/s11409-008-9033-1

Williamson, B. (2005). What is metacognition? Available at: http://www2.futurelab.org.uk/resources/publications-reports-articles/web-articles/Web-Article520 (accessed 2 June 2012).

Wilson, N. S., and Bai, H. (2010). The Relationships and Impact of Teachers' Metacognitive Knowledge and Pedagogical Understandings of Metacognition. *Metacognition and Learning*, 5(3): 269–288.

Winnicott, D. W. (1960). The theory of the parent-child relationship. *International Journal of Psychoanalysis*, 41: 585–595.

Wittek, L. and Kvernbekk, T. (2011). On the problems of asking for a definition of quality in education. *Scandinavian Journal of Education Research*, 55(6): 671–684.

Wittrock, M. C. (1987). Teaching and Student Thinking. *Journal of Teacher Education*, 38(6): 30–33.

Wood, D. (1992). Teaching talk. In K. Norman (ed.), *Thinking Voices: The Work of the National Oracy Project*. London: Hodder & Stoughton.

Woolner, P. (ed.). (2014). *School Design Together*. Abingdon: Routledge.

Woolner, P., McCarter, S., Wall, K., and Higgins, S. (2012). Changed learning through changed space: When can a participatory approach to the learning environment challenge preconceptions and alter practice? *Improving Schools*, 15(1): 45–60.

Woolner, P., Hall, E., Higgins, S., McCaughey, C., and Wall, K. (2007). A sound foundation? What we know about the impact of environments on learning and the implications for building schools for the future. *Oxford Review of Education*, 33: 47–70.

Woolner, P., Clark, J., Hall, E., Tiplady, L., Thomas, U., and Wall, K. (2010). Pictures are necessary but not sufficient: Using a range of visual methods to engage users about school design. *Learning Environments Research*, 13(1): 1–22.

Yardley, L. (2000). Dilemmas in qualitative health research. *Psychology and Health*, 15: 215–228.

Zeichner, K., Payne, K. A., and Brayko, K. (2015). Democratizing teacher education. *Journal of Teacher Education*, 66(2): 122–135.

Zohar, A. (1999). Teachers' Metacognitive Knowledge and the Instruction of Higher Order Thinking. *Teaching and Teacher Education*, 15(4), 413–429.

APPENDIX I:
CASE EXAMPLES OF
RESEARCH DESIGN

a) Class 9G: Is performance linked to particular characteristics?

Table A.1 overleaf introduces us to class 9G and to a range of things that are known about them. For the purposes of this worked example we have simplified reality – our genders are limited to male and female, our ethnicity categories to the aggregates used by the UK statistics office rather than more diverse groups and our indicators of deprivation by free school meals (FSM) and additional needs by School Action, School Action Plus and Special Education Needs (SA/SAP/SEN) are very broad. Even so, we have small numbers in an individual class – only two people with identified additional needs, only four with Asian heritage, six eligible for FSM. This emphasises the underlying problems of apparently simple categorisation. Individuals experience their lives intersectionally; meanings are constructed locally (Jones, 2015). This does not mean that this information is useless but nor is it definitive. We may be able to identify patterns and then try to test them out.

Nevertheless, looking at this group you might begin to create narratives for particular individuals: Ian is young for the year, from a white working-class background and has some identified support need; Lara has English as an Additional Language (EAL). Each of us will draw from our own experience **as a** learner and **with** learners and it is difficult, if not impossible, to approach without some expectations. So, we note them alongside the hypotheses generated by other scholars from their experience and remain curious about whether this group of learners will show patterns that conform to these ideas.

Jo is new to the school and to the class. She scans the class data, prioritises a conversation with the Special Needs Co-ordinator about what

TABLE A.1 *Characteristics of class 9G*

Class 9G	Gender	Month born	Ethnicity	FSM	EAL	SEN/SA/SAP
Adam	M	January	W	yes		
Abby	F	September	W			
Bobby	M	November	M			yes
Bella	F	July	W			
Colin	M	October	W			
Carrie	F	August	W			
Donald	M	March	W			
Debbie	F	December	B	yes		
Euan	M	July	W			
Ellie	F	December	W			
Fred	M	September	A			
Flora	F	May	W			
Grant	M	July	B			
Georgia	F	March	W	yes		
Harry	M	February	W			
Helen	F	November	A			
Ian	M	August	W	yes		yes
India	F	October	W			
Jordan	M	June	B			
Juliet	F	January	W	yes		
Karim	M	June	A			
Kelly	F	April	M			
Louis	M	September	M			
Lara	F	February	W		Polish	
Mohamed	M	October	A			
Maria	F	March	W			
Niall	M	February	W	yes		
Natalie	F	May	W			

Categories for ethnicity
W – White (all groups)
M – Mixed multiple ethnicity (all groups)
A – Asian (all groups)
B – Black (all groups)
O – Other
EAL – English as an additional language
SEN – Statement of Special Educational Needs

she needs to consider to support Bobby and Ian and wonders how different the dynamics in the class will be from her last post, a small suburban school with a middle-class catchment and mainly white British students.

Although year 9 might be considered a relatively low-stress cohort to teach as they are still two years away from their public exams, Jo feels that she has something to prove as a new member of staff. It is important to demonstrate that she is competent and one of the key indicators of this is her students' performance in assessment. Therefore, although she is also interested in classroom interaction and whether gender and culture have an impact on participation, her focus in this first year is on understanding her students' performance and her own. In other words, she is choosing to engage with two elements – the 'good enough' teacher and students – of the hypothesis explored in Chapter 2, and in order to do this she needs to engage with the naturally occurring assessment data.

Class 9G are studying geography and have undertaken a mid-module assessment using a past exam paper with a mixture of multiple-choice questions designed to test recall of facts, short answer questions designed to test basic understanding of concepts and extended answer questions designed to test the ability to link concepts in an argument. This assessment is repeated at the end of the module with another past exam paper. Table shows the grades and Figures A.1 and A.2 reveal that there are relative normal distributions of grades across the class, with some indication of general improvement.

She has demographic data about these students (A.1 and A.2) and attainment data that seemed to suggest a broadly successful module: ten students improved, sixteen held steady. Jo now has a number of key reflexive questions to consider:

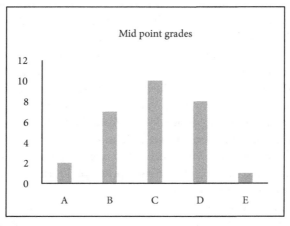

FIGURE A.1

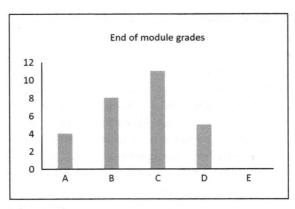

FIGURE A.2

1 Does this improvement satisfy her; does it chime with her sense of 'good enough'?

2 Will it have weight with her Head of Department and other authority figures?

3 If the answer to both of these questions is yes, is the enquiry complete?

4 If the answer to one or more of these is no (or ambiguous), what additional analysis of the existing data could be done to remedy this?

Jo, being fairly typical of teachers in general, is not completely satisfied by the outcome. Her initial broad performance questions about herself and the students become more focused. 'Am I "good enough" for every student?' and 'Is each student performing to their individual potential?' are still addressing the core elements of the hypothesis but with more detail and nuance. She realises that there are a number of things she can do, beginning with a survey of the data to look for patterns: this reveals variations in rate of progress across the class. Again, this might satisfy Jo as fitting in with her view of the world or she might be moved to ask if there are ways to understand the patterns – explanations from authority (more experienced teachers, policy or research literature) or from a priori reasoning – and then to test these explanations for fit on her class.

Table A.2 now includes a trajectory column to clarify this and to indicate that although prior performance does predict future

TABLE A.2

Class 9G	Mid-module grade	End-of-module grade
Adam	D	C
Abby	A	A
Bobby	D	D
Bella	C	C
Colin	D	C
Carrie	B	B
Donald	C	C
Debbie	D	C
Euan	C	C
Ellie	B	B
Fred	D	D
Flora	C	B
Grant	A	B
Georgia	C	C
Harry	B	B
Helen	C	C
Ian	B	A
India	C	D
Jordan	D	C
Juliet	C	C
Karim	B	A
Kelly	E	C
Louis	C	B
Lara	B	B
Mohamed	D	D
Maria	B	B
Niall	C	A
Natalie	D	D

performance there are two students whose attainment has dipped – Grant and India. Potential new question: What's happening in these two cases? Are there any demographic factors that other scholars have claimed might predict this?

Grades going up are obvious successes but with the goal of 'all children being above average' moving from satire to policy discourse we tend to look suspiciously at (some) stable grades. The perspective depends on whether we are looking at an individual's performance based on an assessment of

TABLE A.3 *Class 9G Progression trajectory*

Class 9G	Mid-module grade	End-of-module grade	Trajectory
Adam	D	C	Up
Abby	A	A	Same
Bobby	D	D	Same
Bella	C	C	Same
Colin	D	C	Up
Carrie	B	B	Same
Donald	C	C	Same
Debbie	D	C	Up
Euan	C	C	Same
Ellie	B	B	Same
Fred	D	D	Same
Flora	C	B	Up
Grant	A	B	Down
Georgia	C	C	Same
Harry	B	B	Same
Helen	C	C	Same
Ian	B	A	Up
India	C	D	Down
Jordan	D	C	Up
Juliet	C	C	Same
Karim	B	A	Up
Kelly	E	C	Up
Louis	C	B	Up
Lara	B	B	Same
Mohamed	D	D	Same
Maria	B	B	Same
Niall	C	A	Up
Natalie	D	D	Same

their potential and current capacity (an ipsative assessment) or whether we are judging the performance against externally mandated targets (e.g. increased percentage of grades A–C for all secondary school learners). If Jo just looks at the first eight of the sixteen with the same grade at both assessment points, it becomes clear that she will 'catch' different students, depending on which filter she uses: Bobby will be the focus of an intervention driven by cohort targets, even though he performed as well as expected, whereas Bella and Ellie would be the focus if personal targets are used. Neither of these is definitely 'better' than the other; for

TABLE A.4 *Class 9G progression and targets*

Class 9G	Mid-module grade	End-of-module grade	Ipsative target	Cohort target
Abby	A	A	Met	Met
Bobby	D	D	Met	Not Met
Bella	C	C	Not Met	Met
Carrie	B	B	Met	Met
Donald	C	C	Met	Met
Euan	C	C	Met	Met
Ellie	B	B	Not Met	Met

TABLE A.5 *A and B Students/C and D students (final grade), gender and ethnicity*

	Gender	Ethnicity	End-of-module grade		Gender	Ethnicity	End-of-module grade
Abby	F	W	A	Bella	F	W	C
Ian	M	W	A	Georgia	F	W	C
Niall	M	W	A	Juliet	F	W	C
Karim	M	A	A	Kelly	F	M	C
Carrie	F	W	B	Debbie	F	B	C
Ellie	F	W	B	Helen	F	A	C
Flora	F	W	B	Adam	M	W	C
Lara	F	W	B	Colin	M	W	C
Maria	F	W	B	Donald	M	W	C
Harry	M	W	B	Euan	M	W	C
Louis	M	M	B	Jordan	M	B	C
Grant	M	B	B	India	F	W	D
				Natalie	F	W	D
				Bobby	M	M	D
				Fred	M	A	D
				Mohamed	M	A	D

example, cohort targets challenge 'normal for round here' low ambitions for learners but do not provide positive feedback for improvements that do not meet external standards; ipsative targets encourage learner metacognition and autonomy but generate considerably more work.

At this stage Jo is still assessing the data by eye, still looking for patterns and simply re-sorting the data in tables. Jo had wondered about

TABLE A.6 *Analysis of progress focusing on date of birth*

	Month	Mid	End		Month	Mid	End
Abby	September	A	A	Maria	March	B	B
Louis	September	C	B	Georgia	March	C	C
Fred	September	D	D	Donald	March	C	C
India	October	C	D	Kelly	April	E	C
Colin	October	D	C	Flora	May	C	B
Mohamed	October	D	D	Natalie	May	D	D
Helen	November	C	C	Karim	June	B	A
Bobby	November	D	D	Jordan	June	D	C
Ellie	December	B	B	Grant	July	A	B
Debbie	December	D	C	Bella	July	C	C
Juliet	January	C	C	Euan	July	C	C
Adam	January	D	C	Ian	August	B	A
Lara	February	B	B	Carrie	August	B	B
Harry	February	B	B				
Niall	February	C	A				

TABLE A.7 *Summary of Class 9G*

Summary Table: Class 9G			
What claims can be made?	**What kind of evidence is this?**	**Questions answered?**	**New questions**
Prior attainment is a pretty good predictor of future attainment	Quantitative measurement, widely recognised measures **(transparency, evocativeness)**	Do some characteristics correlate with attainment?	*Does the standard measure tell us everything we want to know about 9G's progress?*
Birth month is not a good predictor for this cohort	Limited to this cohort, challenges large data studies **(criticalness, empowerment)**		*If birth month is not a key indicator for this cohort, what might be? Can we dig deeper into intersectional experiences?* **(polyphony)**
The picture on gender and ethnicity is fuzzy			
Overall attainment is good and most learners make progress. However, it is unclear which stable grades indicate the need to intervene	Variable depending on the view of progress and norms **(ontological assumptions)**	Where should we focus our attention to raise attainment?	*Are cohort and ipsative approaches mutually exclusive? What might we gain/lose from choosing one or trying to do both?* **(pragmatic quality)**

gender and ethnicity as factors in classroom interaction and this was an opportunity to examine those ideas. In Table A.4 and A.5, ordering the students by their end-of-module grade and using gender and ethnicity as factors suggest that students getting As and Bs are broadly similar to the cohort as a whole, although she did notice that boys dominate the A grades, girls the Bs and students of Asian heritage are overrepresented in the Ds.

Jo has read the recent analysis of the data on birth month and achievement of just under 500,000 students at 7, 11 and 16 years old in England that suggests that there is a significant gap at the beginning, with close to 70 per cent of September born and less than 45 per cent of August born 7-year-olds meeting expected standards. The gap narrows to just over 65 per cent and 50 per cent at 11 and just under 65 per cent and 57 per cent at 16. (Thomson, 2017). Her cohort of Year 9s falls between the latter two – does their performance fit the big data, at either the first or the second assessment? Abby fits the profile of 'older, higher achieving' and Kelly's trajectory seems to reflect the pattern of younger students catching up over time, particularly as she makes up more than one grade by the final assessment. However, Fred doesn't and overall, more of the students who do less well in the first assessment have birthdays earlier in the year.

The summary table below indicates both the limits of and the potential for this enquiry. In this round, Jo has partially addressed her questions and can be clear about the kind of evidence she has, while simultaneously recognising that she is generating more questions at every turn. Overall, her quantitative analysis has given her more information about her students than about her interaction with them, suggesting that she could make use of a mixed or qualitative design in the next cycle.

b) City College: How do the learners understand their performance?

At City College, students in the first semester of their Business degree study three rather diverse modules:

- Introduction to Financial Management Systems, taught through lectures and practical workshops and assessed by a multiple-choice and short answer exam paper;

- Business Models and Economics, taught through lectures and seminars and assessed by a piece of written coursework; and

- Introduction to Entrepreneurship, taught through collaborative group projects and assessed by portfolio.

All of the modules result in a percentage which is then interpreted against grade boundaries (Table A.8).

Staff acting as personal tutors have regular meetings with students to discuss their results and get together beforehand for an informal briefing as a team. Over coffee and biscuits, the theme of performance emerged as they recalled from previous years that students appear to be interpreting their grades very differently, some see a mark in the fifties as indicative of 'not being up to it', others see the same mark as 'good – better than I thought I'd do'.

In theory, a 2:2 represents equivalent performance regardless of the module (or discipline) being studied. Studying the learning outcomes documents across subjects and institutions reveals that the descriptors used indicate that these performances being 'ok': not too many errors or omissions; a basic grasp of the key ideas; no flashes of brilliance or originality. On that basis, students' perceptions of a mark in the fifties as either triumph or disaster are incorrectly calibrated. However, the staff discussion reveals that students are not alone in this: the grading profile of each module is quite different (with the curve of portfolio marks being higher than coursework, for example) depending on the allocation of marks to tasks and the convergence of the assessment. Moreover, it emerges that staff have different ideas about what constitutes 'good enough' performance in the first semester: some are pinning their marks to expectations of what a first year might be able to do, others are looking at mastery of a subject that the students won't be taught again and will need for future modules.

TABLE A.8 *Percentages and grade boundaries*

Raw score	Grade
Below 40%	Fail
40–49%	Third Class
50–59%	Lower Second Class (2:2)
60–69%	Upper Second Class (2:1)
70% and above	First Class

One response to this might be for the staff to attempt to amend their practice into something more consistent and, indeed, this is what Greg suggested, arguing that it is not fair to students that assessment is so variable. Alex agreed about the lack of fairness but said she thought it unlikely that being more prescriptive about marking and feedback would help, instead it might make offering diverse learning experiences more difficult and how would that be fair to the student body? At this stage, Mohammed pointed out that even if the staff were all in agreement, they still didn't know enough about what the students were experiencing: 'We need more detail!'.

With very little time before the meetings were due to happen, Greg and Mohammed designed a mediated interview (Figure A.3 shows the artefact shared in advance of the interview) to reveal experience naturalistically without too many pre-conceptions of what that experience might be or how it might be framed. Keeping it simple and structured, so that the focus of the research – the grades – would form the basis for a free-ranging conversation between the student and the interviewer about how they understood the learning experience, the assessment and their own performance. Only the opening gambit 'What do you think about these?'

Student	Intro to Finance Management	Business Models and Economics	Intro to Entrepreneurship	Semester Average
Bob Jones	65	52	58	58
We're going to ask	What do you think about these?			
The interview could cover	You will decide how the conversation goes and it is most helpful if you bring your own ideas. If you're not sure how to begin, you could use the topics below and say as much or as little as you like.			

- Your experience on the modules
- Your experience of the assessments
- What you think the grades tell us about
  - what you can do
  - how you have done and
  - how you will do
- Your thoughts and/or feelings about
  - developing business knowledge and skills
  - developing graduate knowledge and skills
- Are the grades fair?

FIGURE A.3 City College: Example of grade summary artefact for the mediated interview.

is fixed and the interviewee then directs the course of the conversation. There is a thirty-minute time limit agreed in advance to make the experience less daunting for the student and the quantity of data less daunting for the staff.

All 200 students are invited to take part in the project, which is presented to them as an opportunity within the tutorial to understand their performance better. They are also offered the option to take part in focus groups after the interviews. Staff find that student engagement with the artefact varies considerably: some are apparently seeing it for the first time in the tutorial, some have clearly given it some thought and a small number have produced written responses to each question. Staff use of the artefact is also idiosyncratic, some 'forget' to use it, others refer to it briefly, some make it the centrepiece of the tutorial, a subset of these insist that students respond to all of the questions. This provides Greg and Mohammed with some problems when considering the data: should the written response of Student A be directly compared with the direct quote from Student B and the scribbled note referring to the conversation with Student C? In conversation with Alex, they recalled that staff were interested in generating really rich data about individual experiences and that the variation in the kinds of data was perhaps less important than looking across the types to find themes. It seemed to make sense to the three researchers to start with the direct quotes from students in tutorials, as these were the closest to what they had intended to collect and then to use the written answers from students and the less detailed notes from staff as a check to the emerging themes. After all, some things might be difficult to express in person and come out from the written pieces, while the larger number of instances of moderate emotion in brief notes might balance out the impact of 'headline-grabbing' quotes.

What was immediately apparent in this first analysis was the level of distress generated by what the student perceived to be a 'bad mark'.

The tutors conducted a basic content analysis, underlining the parts of the interviews that struck them as important or interesting (fig A.5).

This is a profoundly subjective process; each of us might choose different aspects to highlight. However, this does not make it meaningless or unreliable if – as the City College researchers did – the meaning attributed to the underlining is made transparent. This enabled the research team and any reader to understand what is being claimed and to make a judgement for themselves about the strength of the evidence.

Once the categories are clear and agreed, it becomes possible to group responses from different interviewees under these headings (Fig A.7), both to build up a picture and, simultaneously, to test whether the categories are good enough (Saldana, 2013), to merge or split them as needed. Alex, Mohammed and Greg did this with a mixture of coding in word documents, highlighting print-outs and sticking pieces of paper and post-its to the wall.

The City College researchers chose to focus on particular data and it was sometimes difficult to maintain that focus: negative emotion and worries about the impact on grades were prioritised because they wanted to understand and work quickly with students' distress. However, they

	Intro to Finance Management	Business Models and Economics	Intro to Entrepreneurship	Semester Average
Participant #1	45	58	62	55

I was really upset when I saw the mark for Finance, I felt it had dragged down my average although I still got a 2.2. Actually what really upset me is that I really thought I had understood what was required of me on this degree, I got the theory on Models and our firm in the Entrepreneur module came up with some really cool ideas. The 45 makes me feel like I can't do the basics, that perhaps I'm not suited to this at all.

FIGURE A.4 Example of a students' experience.

	Intro to Finance Management	Business Models and Economics	Intro to Entrepreneurship	Semester Average
Participant #1	45	58	62	55

I was really upset when I saw the mark for Finance, I felt it had dragged down my average although I still got a 2.2. Actually what really upset me is that I really thought I had understood what was required of me on this degree, I got the theory on Models and our firm in the Entrepreneur module came up with some really cool ideas. The 45 makes me feel like I can't do the basics, that perhaps I'm not suited to this at all.

FIGURE A.5 Basic content analysis of interview.

	Intro to Finance Management	Business Models and Economics	Intro to Entrepreneurship	Semester Average	Labels
Participant #1	45	58	62	55	
	I was <u>really upset</u> when I saw the mark for Finance, I felt it had				Emotion, negative
	<u>dragged down my average although I still got a 2.2.</u> Actually what				Impact on overall grade
		<u>really upset</u> me is that I really <u>thought I had understood</u> what was			Emotion, negative
		<u>required of me on this degree,</u> <u>I got the theory on</u> <u>Models</u> and our			Learning, mastery
			firm in the Entrepreneur module came up with some really cool		
			ideas. The 45 <u>makes me feel like I can't do the basics,</u> that perhaps		Motivation, confidence
	I'm not suited to this at all.				

FIGURE A.6 Content analysis with meaning attributed.

also had an eye on their overall programme outcomes and consciously sought evidence of learning and mastery (or awareness of its absence).

Even with this reflexivity and analysis, the researchers still weren't sure whether the themes they'd identified were a good representation of the students' experiences as a whole or, more crucially, what the students found most important.

A pool of thirty volunteers are available for the focus groups but as time is tight, twelve are selected on the basis of their performance from the pool of volunteers:

- three with high scores across all three modules,
- three with two high scores and one lower,
- three with two lower scores and one higher and
- three with lower scores across all three modules.

A diamond hierarchy tool is used to rank statements from the interviews (stripped of identifying details, figure A.7 and A.8) with the binary 'reflects my experience/does not reflect my experience'. Preliminary findings from the focus groups are then shared with all 200

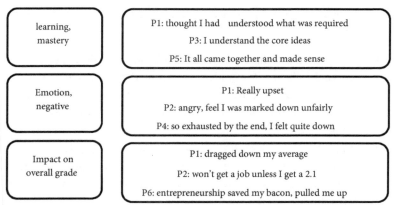

FIGURE A.7 Grouping examples of interview exerts to key themes.

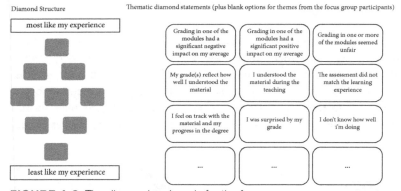

FIGURE A.8 The diamond and cards for the focus groups.

students via a document on the Virtual Learning Environment (VLE) for comment.

Nine statements drawn from (but not copied from) the interviews were given to the groups to work with as well as three blank cards, so participants could swap out statements that they found less meaningful. This option really depends on the position of the researcher at this stage – are you wanting to validate your ideas or to disrupt them? – and in this case the City College staff want to provide space for new ideas to emerge, in case their original sample's responses are not typical of the whole cohort. The figure A.9 shows two of the diamonds when partially completed. Even at this early stage, there are some clear differences emerging from these two focus groups:

- Group 2 are signalling an overall satisfaction with the assessment process by placing 'My grades reflect how well I understand the material' in the top third of the diamond (whereas Group 1 place it in the bottom third) and by working with the nine cards as offered.

- Group 1 have made their own card 'The whole process is confusing' and placed it at the very top with their sense of negative impact and that the assessment did not match the learning experience.

- Interestingly, Group 2, although happier, also note the disconnect between learning and assessment by placing that card in the middle row.

After the three focus groups, the researchers did a second round of analysis. Since there were only three diamonds, the data didn't lend itself to a more quantitative analysis; however with more groups or smaller groups within groups, it is quite easy to generate enough diamonds to track the relative strength of ideas and their relationship to one another (see Chapter 4). The tutors looked at the images of the

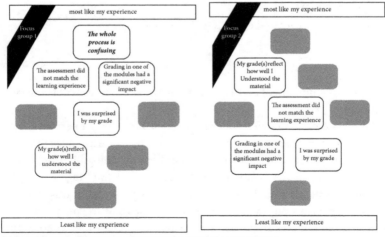

FIGURE A.9 Exemplar diamond 9s partially completed.

diamonds in process and the completed diamonds and noted several key trends (figure A.10): a mismatch between understanding the learning and assessment experiences; a degree of agreement that students could not track or predict their performance; a sense that while grades on individual modules might be critical, the grading was more unclear than unfair. These results were shared with the staff team and with the student cohort, generating many conversations in seminars and informal settings as well as tutorials.

From this, the team were able to evaluate their students' experience and to consider their next steps, detailed in the summary Table.

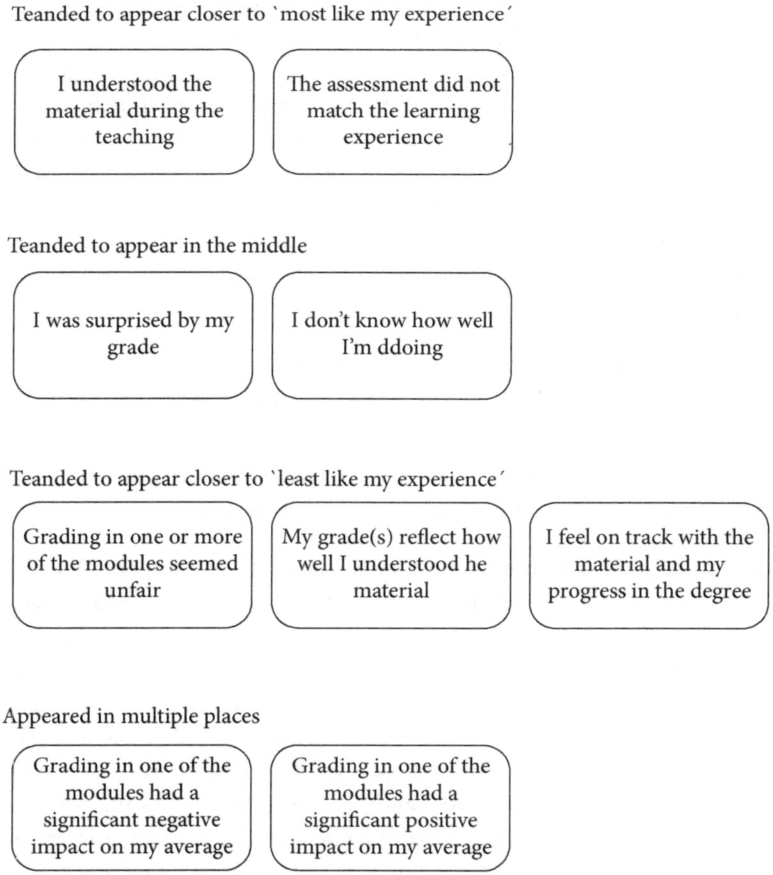

Teanded to appear closer to `most like my experience´

| I understood the material during the teaching | The assessment did not match the learning experience |

Teanded to appear in the middle

| I was surprised by my grade | I don't know how well I'm ddoing |

Teanded to appear closer to `least like my experience´

| Grading in one or more of the modules seemed unfair | My grade(s) reflect how well I understood he material | I feel on track with the material and my progress in the degree |

Appeared in multiple places

| Grading in one of the modules had a significant negative impact on my average | Grading in one of the modules had a significant positive impact on my average |

FIGURE A.10 Key trends in the diamond 9 analysis.

Although staff were troubled and moved by students' distress, they found that their analysis discussions began to coalesce around the problem of mismatch between the learning and assessment experiences. This, they felt, was a practical problem that they could engage with, hoping that this would have the secondary effect of reducing students' confusion and unhappiness.

c) Sandview Primary: Does learner identity impact performance?

Sandview Primary School serves a mainly working-class community in a large city and is deemed to be 'satisfactory' by the inspectorate in terms of the achievements of its learners when they leave to enter secondary school. The head teacher and staff are not satisfied with 'satisfactory': not as part of this 'culture of continuous improvement' and not as a description of their practice. Everyone agrees that they can 'do better', although the students' performance on external tests broadly maps onto national patterns, and it is not clear where this 'better' needs to happen. Staff meetings are devoted to discussions and from these emerge two areas of concern:

- The impression that 'value added' from school entry to age seven is above the average but this levels off between seven and eleven;
- The sense that the confidence and curiosity of the children decline over time and that they are heading into secondary school with rather fixed ideas about their abilities.

This is a difficult conversation, as it appears to be placing responsibility on the teachers who work with the older children and the head teacher, Ray, becomes concerned that his staff may 'split'. As the tone of the staff meeting hardens, he turns to his deputy, Sue. Sue cuts to the heart of the issue: 'We're all afraid that it might be our fault, but we actually don't know exactly what's going on. It might turn out to be one person or a group of us, it might be lots of factors together. We'll never find out if we don't take the risk of looking closely, so can we agree to be kind and supportive?' Ray chips in, 'Nobody will be fired, we'll all learn something.' Whether or not everyone is completely convinced by this, it does alter the frame for the research that follows.

The first phase is to take that close look Sue proposed: retrospectively analysing the school's performance data to check whether the 'levelling off' is happening and if so, where. This requires a more fine-grained analysis than simple cohort results (see Table A.9), since this initial quantitative exploration reveals that only 60 per cent of the children tested at eleven were pupils at Sandview at seven. By looking at the performance of children based on when they entered the school, the patterns beneath '67% performing at the national average' are revealed.

TABLE A.9 *Summary of City College example*

Summary Table: City College Business Students

What claims can be made?	What kind of evidence is this?	Questions answered?	New questions
High levels of distress	Rich qualitative data from a subset of volunteer students **(subjective adequacy, authenticity)**	How do students interpret their grades?	*Is this level of distress tolerable for staff and students?* **(subjective adequacy, ethics)**
Confusion about assessment among lower-attaining students	Qualitative data triangulated with student characteristics **(emplotment, polyphony)**		*Are we doing enough to develop procedural autonomy?* **(history of action, empowerment)**
Global interpretations of self from single assessments	Rich qualitative data from a subset of volunteer students **(evocativeness)**		*Are our students particularly fragile?* **(pragmatic quality)**
Tutor reflection on lack of match between learning experience and assessment		What action can we take to make an impact on the student experience?	*Need for clearer, more personalised and frequent guidance to students – how to achieve this?***And/or** *A critical re-examination of how we teach and what we assess, what is the underlying rationale, pedagogy or convenience?*

Trajectories are clearly worse for pupils who join the school later. The second phase of the research could have been 'what's wrong with our incoming pupils?' but, bearing in mind the commitment to learning rather than assigning blame, instead staff choose to focus on 'what do we do well with our youngest pupils?'. This appreciative action enquiry has an iterative developmental structure:

1   *Collaborative information gathering*: Colleagues who teach the older children take turns to be participant observers in the younger learner's classrooms. All the observation notes are typed up and shared.

2   *First-level analysis – shared meaning making*: At a staff meeting where mind maps of key ideas and themes are created, staff focus on the way in which younger learners (supported by their teachers and independently) spend time setting goals and articulating their awareness of *what, why and how well* they are doing.

3   *Second-level analysis – generating a theory*: From this, the staff develop a Theory of Change based on growth mind sets and mastery orientation (Dweck, 2017) that might explain the impact of the early years culture and the differences between the groups of learners.

4   *Intervention to test the theory*: Staff devise an intervention programme for themselves in which they track the number and content of their metacognitive conversations with older pupils. The focus is on changing culture through staff modelling, so there are no external targets, rather staff become curious about the *what, why and how well* of their conversational practice. The hypothesis is that by directing attention to this area, staff practice will become more explicit and purposeful and that this will encourage mastery orientation in the learners.

5   *Evaluation of the intervention – exploring evidence of impact*: In addition to the staff's observations and day-to-day conversations with children, the staff chose to use the children's pre- and post-scores on the SDQI, a psychometric test of self-concept (O'Mara et al., 2006).

6   *Evaluation of the theory of change – questioning the explanatory power of the theory*: The staff 'loop back' to their first theory-building meeting in the light of the evidence they have generated and add strength and complexity to their working model of how children understand their learning.

TABLE A.10 *Sandview results analysed in more detail (Literacy example)*

Cohort BYear group tracked through school	Literacy (all children)			Literacy (children new to the school)		
	% Below national average	% At national average	% Above national average	% Below national average	% At national average	% Above national average
6 (10–11)	18	67	15	23	67	10
5 (9–10)				20	70	10
4 (8–9)				18	71	11
3 (7–8)				12	72	16
2 (6–7)				8	70	22
1 (5–6)				8	67	25

The Sandview staff had taken a very positive and proactive stance to a perceived problem by focusing on appreciative enquiry and they felt confident that they had a map for this process. As the Table A.10 illustrates, the map doesn't match the journey but this provides an opportunity for the unexpected and for refining ideas.

This iterative development is very recognisable to anyone who has been involved in enquiry, since life is always messier than textbooks. By keeping the ideal narrative and the actual events in their awareness, Sandview staff were able to engage with *the history of action* and *emplotment*, to demonstrate *transparency*. However, the process threw up multiple problems in which *pragmatic* and *critical qualities* seemed at odds with one another, with negative impacts on staff *empowerment*. This is often the point at which enquiry projects wither and die.

Two factors that supported the Sandview project and enabled it to tolerate the awkwardness, confusion and uncertainty were

- the *ontologic and epistemologic assumptions*: the staff knew that they didn't understand, that it wasn't a simple problem and that they were exploring their way towards a new, partial understanding. Testing and proof are a long way off, so it is safer to propose ideas and raise issues.

- the *subjective adequacy*: there was an underlying commitment to individual learner's intrinsic knowledge and potential and to multiple pathways to achievement. As the staff came to see themselves more explicitly in the role of learners, they were able to grant the same permissions to themselves that they offer to the children.

TABLE A.11 *Summary of project map and actual journey*

The map	The journey
Collaborative information gathering: Colleagues who teach the older children take turns to be participant observers in the younger learners' classrooms. All the observation notes are typed up and shared.	First round of observation notes were brief and bland. Rather than repeat the observations, staff were asked to bring 'one bright memory' to the staff meeting.
First-level analysis – shared meaning making: At a staff meeting where mind maps of key ideas and themes are created, staff focus on the way(s) in which younger learners (supported by their teachers and independently) spend time setting goals and articulating their awareness of *what, why and how well* they are doing.	The staff meeting over-runs spectacularly. All the memories are eventually shared but there is no time to analyse the themes. Staff are enthused and confused. One of the more junior teachers has been sketching a mind map, which is quickly photocopied and shared. Staff agree to extend this or make their own and pin them up in the staff room.
	Versions of the mind map proliferate over one wall. Post-its, stickers and connecting threads are added, debated, moved. It starts to resemble the conspiracy theorist's lair in a movie. Staff love the complexity. The Chair of the Board of Governors asks what it means and becomes bamboozled by the responses.
Second-level analysis – generating a theory: From this, the staff develop a Theory of Change based on growth mind sets and mastery orientation that might explain the impact of the early years culture and the differences between the groups of learners.	This stimulates the staff into a process of simplification from which the theory of change begins to emerge. A key element, which had not initially seemed of central importance, is repetition. Although the staff had begun with a single 'bright memory' (often Eureka! moments of mastery), they noticed that these sat on top of many less flamboyant conversations with the children about **what, how and why**. Underpinning these conversations was a respect for each child as an individual, so this is where the Theory of Change model started (fig A.9).

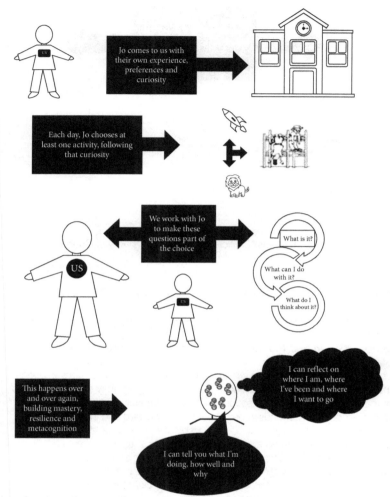

FIGURE A.11 Sandview theory of change.

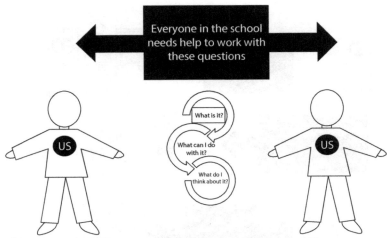

FIGURE A.12 Staff needs addition to Sandview's Theory of Change.

TABLE A.12 *Summary of project map and journey continued (1)*

The map (ctd)	The journey (ctd)
Intervention to test the theory: Staff devise an intervention programme for themselves in which they track the number and content of their metacognitive conversations with older pupils. The focus is on changing culture through staff modelling, so there are no external targets, rather staff become curious about the *what, why and how well* of their conversational practice. The hypothesis is that by directing attention to this area, staff practice will become more explicit and purposeful and that this will encourage mastery orientation in the learners.	This has (perhaps predictably) extremely mixed results. Some staff find the tracking of their conversations very challenging: they feel awkward and self-conscious about their normal 'chat', awkward and inauthentic trying to be 'metacognitive' and feel less competent in their work as a result of the reflections. A very brave soul admits to this in a staff meeting. It becomes clear that staff set the bar very high for themselves and that they could benefit from the experience – and respect! – offered to the youngest children. An important addition to the theory of change is made (figure A.12) and staff commit to brief daily peer-to-peer learning conversations, with the important proviso that everyone uses natural, non-technical language.

TABLE A.13 *Summary of project map and journey continued (2)*

The map (ctd)	The journey (ctd)
Evaluation of the theory of change – questioning the explanatory power of the theory: The staff 'loop back' to their first theory-building meeting in the light of the evidence they have generated and add strength and complexity to their working model of how children understand their learning.	The staff find the case examples that they share each day of their own and the children's metacognition and mastery both compelling and supportive. They continue to watch the data to see if the resilience and resourcefulness they see in the classroom will translate into national performance data, although they cannot agree – at least not yet! – on what 'proof' of success would look like. The difficulties of explaining exactly how the theory of change works to governors and parents continue and new questions are emerging, including 'Can the model be strong and complex?'

d) Mooredge: How do different groups of learners use feedback?

At Mooredge Sixth Form College, all A-Level History students use the e-learning portal to submit their essays. The tutors in the department mark the work using a rubric derived from the mark schemes of the exam board which is intended to allow the students to see at a glance where they have met, exceeded or fallen short of specific aspects. The rubric gives them a score and there is also an open-text box for the tutor to leave formative comments. Once work has been marked, students receive an email, containing their score and inviting them to view their feedback.

The IT support team have recently published the usage reports for the e-learning portal. Student responses to the email appear to fall into four categories. Approximately 20 per cent click on the link in the email and view their feedback within twelve hours of receipt. Another 35 per cent access their feedback, either through the direct link or by logging on to the portal within seventy-two hours. Of the 45 per cent who have not accessed the feedback at this point, more than half (25 per cent of the student body) will not have read the feedback after one month.

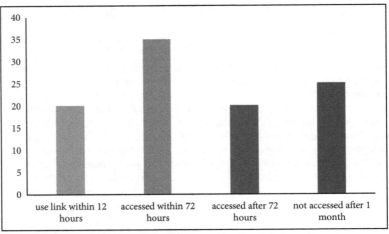

FIGURE A.13 Mooredge – baseline use of feedback in term 1.

The tutor team are quite significantly divided in their formulation of the problem. One group, led by Sam, believe that encouraging students to read the feedback through a combined 'push-pull' approach will bring the numbers up across the cohort; the other group, led by Anna, are concerned that the students not accessing the feedback might be the ones who need it most and who might be least likely to respond to a general intervention. Sam's group are working to Hypothesis A, in which the feedback system and the modes of communication are assumed to be 'good enough' and therefore the focus is on the students. In contrast, Anna's group are working to Hypothesis B, in which nothing is assumed to be 'good enough' and all aspects of the system and all actors within it are potential foci for the enquiry. This difference in positioning could have led to conflict in which one hypothesis triumphed over another or an unsatisfactory compromise in which the essence of each enquiry is diluted by the incompatible elements of the other. Fortunately, the tutor team had recently had a very successful and enjoyable development day looking at historiography, where they reconnected with their disciplinary beliefs in the importance of separate perspectives on key events.

The concurrent design evolved therefore as a purposeful division of effort: both groups use the usage reports as their shared data and then take separate but complementary research routes. The relative simplicity

Hypothesis A

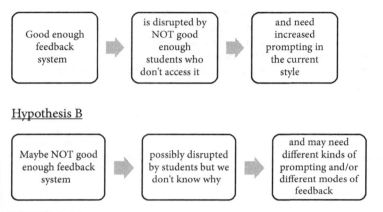

Hypothesis B

FIGURE A.14

of Hypothesis A and the proposed intervention meant that it was suited to a whole cohort design, while the complexity of Hypothesis B was better suited to a smaller group and a more iterative and fluid design.

At Mooredge the problem of students accessing their feedback was approached using two apparently competing positions (**_epistemological assumptions_**):

- an essentially behaviourist idea that the feedback system was basically fine and students needed to know that their lack of use was being monitored, so designed a broad-based intervention study to prompt better use (Route A) and

- an essentially constructivist idea that the feedback system lacked meaning and value for certain groups of students, so their decision not to access it was rational from their perspective. They designed a targeted intervention which used qualitative conversations in tutorial time to both encourage use and explore reasons for not using (Route B).

Attentive readers will have picked up on 'apparently'.

Figure A.13 reminds us of the ways in which Mooredge History students were using the feedback portal at the beginning of the enquiry: 75 per cent take a look at some point, which suggests a reasonably high level of compliance for seventeen- to eighteen-year-

TABLE A.14

Route A: Transparency and incentives(whole cohort)	Route B: Individual responses and narratives(sub-group of students who didn't/ still don't access feedback)	*Hypothesis being tested*
Week 1: Students are reminded in classes that the e-learning portal tracks their use and that staff are aware that some people wait to access the feedback or don't access it at all. The graphs are posted on the portal.		*If students were aware we were checking, they would pick up their feedback in significantly greater numbers.*
Week 2: Usage data checked and shared with students		
Week 3: All students who still haven't accessed feedback sent reminder email		*Personalised reminder will be more motivating.*
Week 4: Usage data checked and shared with students		
	Week 5: Personal tutors use regular meetings to enquire about using feedback. All students are asked whether they find the emails helpful. Students who didn't use feedback in the first set of usage data are asked what has changed. Students who are still not using the feedback are asked about this.	*We don't fully understand the reasons why students do or don't access feedback.*
Week 6: Usage data checked and shared with students		
Week 7: Staff merge the marks database with the usage database	Staff come together to analyse the conversations they have had with students.	*A1: Higher-performing students are the ones most likely to access feedback, lower-performing students the least* *A2: Students who access feedback most will show learning gains*

	B1: Students don't access feedback because they don't want to hear it B2: Students don't access feedback because they don't think it will help them
Week 8: Usage data checked and shared with students	
Week 9: Both groups come together to share their data and explore what has been learned	

olds; 20 per cent look immediately (keen? or anxious?) and 20 per cent leave it at least a few days (slightly disengaged? or fearful?). Of particular concern to all the staff are the 25 per cent who don't read the feedback.

The Route A broad-based intervention was designed to escalate awareness of the value staff placed on the feedback system, to make students aware of monitoring and to explore the link – believed to be present – between the use of feedback and performance (detailed in Table A.15). The quantitative data prioritised by this group has the potential to give a clear overall picture of several key factors: use, response to stimulus and one of the characteristics (academic performance) of student groups behaving in different ways, and so has the qualities of **transparency** and **pragmatic quality**.

TABLE A.15 *Mooredge – Exploration of the link between feedback and performance*

Route A: Transparency and incentives	Hypothesis being tested
Week 1: Students are reminded in classes that the e-learning portal tracks their use and that staff are aware that some people wait to access the feedback or don't access it at all. The graphs are posted on the portal.	*If students were aware we were checking, they would pick up their feedback in significantly greater numbers.*
Week 2: Usage data checked and shared with students	
Week 3: All students who still haven't accessed feedback sent reminder email	*Personalised reminder will be more motivating.*

Route A: Transparency and incentives	Hypothesis being tested
Week 4: Usage data checked and shared with students	
Week 6: Usage data checked and shared with students	
Week 7: Staff merge the marks database with the usage database	*A1: Higher-performing students are the ones most likely to access feedback, lower-performing students the least* *A2: Students who access feedback most will show learning gains*

Working first of all with the usage data, the researchers were able to track the change in feedback use. As figure A.15 below demonstrates, the number of 'immediate' users increases slightly but remains relatively stable throughout. After the first 'information' intervention in week 1, there is a 5 per cent decrease in the 'non-accessing' group but also in the 'within three days' group. Exhorting the students *en bloc* appeared to have mixed results.

The 'targeted email' intervention in week 3 co-occurs with an 8 per cent drop in the 'non-accessing' group, so could be considered successful in the short term. However, in week 6 there seems to be some backsliding before a dramatic shift in week 8 which sees 'non-accessing' students down to 10

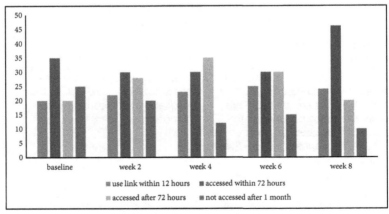

FIGURE A.15 Mooredge – feedback across the term.

per cent. The Mooredge data is a really good example of the complexity that can be revealed by having more data capture points. It would be perfectly valid to capture only at baseline and week 8 and to report that the various interventions appeared to be associated with the positive outcome; it just wouldn't be possible to ask questions about how each of the interventions potentially contributed to this phenomenon. Each researcher has to decide how much information and complexity are helpful to their enquiry. However, as in this case, where technology is capturing all the data it is possible to produce the snapshots of use relatively easily.

The other key hypothesis being explored by this group of researchers was the association between the use of feedback and grade outcomes. In figure A.16, the grade distribution for the cohort (based on mock exams the previous term) is combined with the use of feedback and reveals that the linear relationship between using feedback and doing well has some qualified support. Higher-performing students (A* and A grades) do tend to access feedback promptly. However, lower-performing students (D grade) access the feedback, although they tend to leave it for a few days before doing so. Students who don't access feedback are most likely to be scoring B or C grades.

The researchers know that the intervention as a whole has changed the behaviour (in week 8, they have no idea if this is a permanent or temporary change) of around 15 per cent of the students from no feedback to some feedback. Figure A.17 illustrates that the impact has been most

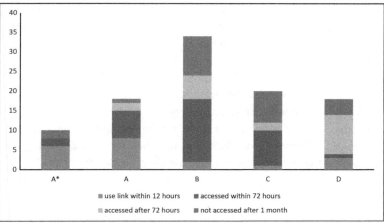

FIGURE A.16 Mooredge – Baseline association of grades with accessing feedback.

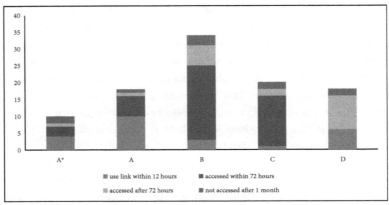

FIGURE A.17 Mooredge – Week 8: Association of grades with accessing feedback.

noticeable on the students with B and C grades, whereas higher- and lower-performing students have been much more likely to continue to avoid the feedback. Again, this could be interpreted by the researchers as a success – the largest groups of feedback avoiders have now shrunk, so that avoidance is at a similar level regardless of grade. Of course, until the next set of tests, there is no way to tell whether those students who have changed their behaviour will translate that into sustained or improved performance.

Meanwhile, the Route B researchers, believing that the reasons for students' behaviour were not adequately understood (*history of action, criticalness*), set out to find students' experiences by using regular tutorial meetings to enquire about using feedback. All students were asked whether they found the emails helpful. Students who didn't use feedback in the baseline usage data but have started to do so were asked what had changed. Students who were still not using the feedback were asked about this. In order to achieve this, the researchers quickly realised that they wanted to have a format (example in figure A.18) for collecting the information that was relatively quick and clear, so that they could make the most of busy tutorial time and still get the richness of the students' voices (*pragmatic quality* and *polyphony*).

When the researchers came together to discuss this data, they were able to begin by dividing the reasons why students had started using the feedback into two categories – intrinsic and extrinsic (Table A.15).

Number present	Emails useful	Not useful	What emails
15	7	5	3

Started using	Why?	
1	Because we were told we had to	

Still not using	Why?	
4		She doesn't like me and the comments are not fair
	Didn't know i had to	I forgot
	No response(shrug)	

FIGURE A.18 Mooredge – format for collecting information.

There was a fairly even split between intrinsic and extrinsic motivations, with some students citing both. The staff noticed that extrinsic explanations came first and speculated that students might not be as comfortable sharing their intrinsic motivations in a tutor group setting or even one-on-one with a teacher. There was also a sense that students didn't really seem highly motivated to discuss why they were now doing what they'd been told. The 'feedback avoiders' seemed to fall into two broad groups, contrasted by their willingness to communicate. The first group were characterised by avoidant responses – *'What emails?' 'Didn't know I had to.' 'Oh.. forgot, sorry'* – and accounted for more than two-thirds of that group. The remaining third were more forthright and specific in their dismissive responses: *'Don't need it, doing fine without it' 'Doesn't make sense' 'She doesn't like me and the comments are unfair'*. Again, staff speculated that the forum might have inhibited some students from sharing their views and that some of the avoidant students might have unexpressed dismissive positions.

When the two groups came together, they were able to dovetail their data and analyses: it became clear that avoidant students were the ones impacted by the personalised emails and that this intervention was a better use of resources than general emails and announcements to all students. The small number of remaining 'feedback avoiders' had quite strongly articulated views which are unlikely to shift in response to behavioural 'nudging'. The staff returned to their original ideas about

TABLE A.16 *Mooredge – Examples of intrinsic and extrinsic feedback*

Intrinsic	Extrinsic
Because I had another essay due and thought I could see what to improve	Because you said we should
I wanted to understand what I got wrong	Because we were told we had to
I wanted to compare with Jay what was said to him and to me about using sources	I thought I'd get in trouble if I didn't!

the efficacy of the feedback system and found that the overall picture was more nuanced and that the positions of the two groups had come closer together. The feedback system was being used by more students, sometimes for perceived intrinsic benefits to their learning. However, more research was needed to answer the emergent questions:

- Does using feedback improve or sustain performance?
- Are non-users right when they say feedback isn't useful?
    - If yes, how can we improve it?
    - If no, how can we convince them?
    - If yes and no, how can we have more effective learning conversations?

INDEX

effective learning 216
effect sizes (tool)
    concept 187
    evocative 191
    frequently asked questions 191
    metacognitive 191
    multiple voices 191
    pragmatic 191
    provenance 187–8
    quality criteria 190–1
    recognisability 190
    use in research 188–9
embedding, practitioner enquiry
    209–11
    brave spaces 226–8
    developing enquiry networks
      212–13
    principle of autonomy 213–16
    principle of connectivity 223–6
    principle of dialogue 219–23
    principle of disturbance 216–19
emplotment 66–7, 77
empowerment 67, 77, 265
engagement, process of 7
English as an additional language
    (EAL) 53
enquiry 9, 14, 204, 205, 227
    cycles of 10, 40, 202
    defined 7
    evidence and tools for 10
    limits 57
    nature of 49, 208
    on/off model of 11
    pathways, real-life examples of 42
    pathway using participatory
      approaches 47
    processes of 8, 23, 24
    questions 11
    real-life 14
    systematic 11
epistemic system evidence 200
Eraut, M. 3, 4
ethics 76
evidence 198, 207–8
    Achinstein's categories of 198
    forms of 199

informed policy 194
    practice agenda 75
    subjective 199–200
    types of 198
evocativeness 77, 80
exception 195–7, 209
exemplified tools, range of 81
experimental inquiry 4
exploratory qualitative approach
    58–64
exploratory quantitative approach 52–8

fallibility 194
falsifiability 31
feedback 269, 271, 275
    avoiders 72, 276, 277
    intrinsic and extrinsic 277
    vs. performance 273–6
    recoil 57
    system 68, 72, 270, 271, 273, 278
feeling of security 26–9
fitness for purpose 74, 195, 206
fixation of belief, process of 25, 28
Fixed Belief 26, 28, 30, 33
Flavell, J. H. 15
Flyvbjerg, Bent 74
focus groups 61, 256, 258–60
    diamond and cards for 62
fortune lines (tool)
    concept 82
    exemplars 83–5
    frequently asked questions 86
    metacognitive 85
    multiple voices 85
    provenance 82
    quality criteria 85–6
    recognisability 85
    use in research 82–3
free school meals (FSM) 53, 245
functional beliefs 24

generalisability 74, 207–8
Gorard, S. 40
grade summary 60
Groundwater-Smith, S. 76
Guba, E. G. 75

hard evidence 200
Hart's ladder of participation 46, 47
Hattie, J. 12, 35
Heikkinen, H. L. T. 13, 75, 79, 196, 197
High Street Primary School 21-2
Hipsburn First School 20
hypothesis 31, 34, 69-71

imposter syndrome 208
inclusivity 80, 221
individual practitioners 8, 73, 209
Initial Teacher Education (ITE) experience 217
inquiry
    belief and methods of 25
    humanist perspective on 25
    impact on 201
    methods of 26
    process of 31
    types of 198
intervention 198, 264, 275
    evaluation of 264
    to test theory 266
interview exerts 259

Kilburn, D. 213-14
Knorr-Cetina, K. 204
knowledge 3, 7, 8, 15, 193, 213
    co-constructed understanding of 8
    construction 193
    of learning 19
    of metacognition 16
    process of understanding 204
Kvernbekk, T. 195-9, 201

labour 4
Lampert, M. 2
Larsson, S. 74, 207
Lash, S. 3
leadership 209-10
learners/learning 8, 14, 15, 215, 221
    aspects of 35
    beliefs about 21
    catalytic tools for 21-2
    characteristics for 18

cohorts of 5
community 4
dispositions 15-16
effective 18, 216
experiences 261
facilitate reflection on 14-15
as focus for professional enquiry 14-16
integrated model for 17
outcome 59
personal 218
practice 5, 19
process 15, 22
productive of 219
professional 1, 6, 209-10, 216-18, 220, 221, 224, 226
real-life 210-11
self-assessment and reflection on 21
teaching and 12
theory, substantial review of 17
using feedback 68-72
Learning to Learn (L2L) enquiry project 214-15
Learning to Learn in Schools and Colleges 202
    'public face' of 203
    representation of 204
library footage 24
Lincoln, Y. S. 75
listening 221-2
literature 15-16
Little, J. W. 219
Lofthouse, R. 5
lollipop partners 20
Look Who's Talking Project 220
Lytle, S. L. 6

manageability, issues of 9
managerialism 2, 4
managerial professionalism 2, 5
managers, role of 5
mapping environments (tool)
    concept 138
    evocative 141
    exemplars 139-40